WITHDRAWN
UTSA Libraries

RENEWALS 458-4574
DATE DUE

AUG 0 6			
GAYLORD			

D1042224

THE WANING OF THE RENAISSANCE

The Yale Intellectual History of the West

General Editors:
J. W. Burrow (University of Oxford)
William J. Bouwsma (University of California, Berkeley)
Frank M. Turner (Yale University)

Executive Editor:
Robert Baldock

This series seeks to provide a chronological account of the
intellectual life and the development of ideas in
Western Europe from the early medieval period
to the present day.

Now available:

*Medieval Foundations of the Western Intellectual
Tradition, 400–1400*
by Marcia L. Colish

The Crisis of Reason: European Thought, 1848–1914
J. W. Burrow

Forthcoming:

The Intellectual Renaissance, 1400–1550 by Ronald Witt

The World of Knowledge, 1640–1720 by Peter N. Miller

Reason's Empire: The European Enlightenment, 1710–1790
by Anthony Pagden

Intellectuals in a Revolutionary Age, 1750–1860
by Frank M. Turner

The Waning
of the Renaissance

1550–1640

William J. Bouwsma

Yale University Press
New Haven and London

Library
University of Texas
at San Antonio

Copyright © 2000 by William J. Bouwsma

All rights reserved. This book may not be reproduced in whole or in part, in any form (beyond that copying permitted by Sections 107 and 108 of the U.S. Copyright Law and except by reviewers for the public press) without written permission from the publishers.

Set in Ehrhardt by Best-set Typesetter Ltd., Hong Kong
Printed in Great Britain by Redwood Books, Wiltshire

Library of Congress Catalog Card Number 00–49538

ISBN 0–300–08537–0

A catalogue record for this book is available from the British Library.

10 9 8 7 6 5 4 3 2 1

Published with assistance from the foundation established in memory of Oliver Baty Cunningham of the Class of 1917, Yale College.

Contents

Illustrations

Preface

This book was originally conceived as a survey of European high culture in the later sixteenth and earlier seventeenth centuries: I had thought of the project as an opportunity to consider together artists and thinkers who had long interested me. These notably included Montaigne and Bodin in France, Sarpi and Galileo in Italy, Hooker, Jonson, and Shakespeare in England, and Cervantes in Spain.

As I now recognize, I was at the outset, though still without quite realizing it, under the influence of Whiggish notions, absorbed in my youth, of a more or less linear conception of cultural history moving Western culture ineluctably toward the modern world. This movement was notably represented, in my mind, by these figures, who also represented the culture of the Renaissance long central to the traditional conception of progress. Under the influence of such assumptions much of high quality has been written about the origins of the Renaissance, but little or nothing about its end, the assumption still persisting that its accomplishments were fundamental to the formation of the modern world.

Under the influence of these preconceptions, I thought of my project as a study of the *climax* of the Renaissance; but it took me some time to realize, to pursue this figure further, that a climax is generally followed by a falling off, or at least by a counter-movement in the opposite direction. And I gradually became aware, as I studied them more closely, that the figures with whom I hoped to come to terms were not so easily classified as I had assumed: that in fact their understanding of themselves and the world was full of contradictions. Indeed, if they constituted a community, it was chiefly a community of ambivalence in which the characteristic Renaissance sense of creative freedom was constantly shadowed by doubt and anxiety. And gradually I recognized that there were two sides to the culture of what I had thought of as "the later Renaissance."

The conception of the Renaissance as the origin of the modern world has been generally associated with Jacob Burckhardt, but, often celebratory, it usually ignores Burckhardt's loathing for the modern world. I became increasingly convinced that the ambivalence I was beginning to sense in my various protagonists suggested that the stage of the Renaissance with which I was now grappling was, to use the expression of another great work of cultural history, almost as much the *waning* of the Renaissance as its climax.

This accounts for the two-fold structure of the present work. The book begins with an introductory chapter that aims to describe some of the general features of early modern European culture, so often, anachronistically, fragmented into a congeries of separate national histories. I then turn to a description of the features of that culture that seem to me still to express the tendencies we associate with the traditional Renaissance. The book begins with an analysis of the underlying assumptions about human being that seem to me still to have shaped Renaissance culture, and then goes on to various strands in that culture following from this that reach a climax in the later sixteenth and earlier seventeenth centuries.

Meanwhile, however, contrary tendencies were also at work which suggest that all was not well in this aspect of the European mentality. I do not, of course, reject the relevance of social and political troubles for the increasing uneasiness I discern in this period, but enough has been written by others on these matters; and I have come to believe that cultural history has its own autonomous, if not altogether independent, dynamic. In a middle section of the book I describe what might be interpreted as warning signals in the period that can be discerned even among Europe's less troubled peoples, which cannot be explained except in cultural terms: a novel concern with personal identity, shifts in the interests of major thinkers, a decline in confidence about the future, the heightening of anxiety.

For the atmosphere in which thinkers and artists operated was changing, and the final section of the book is concerned to identify developments pointing to what now seems to me the end of the Renaissance culture of freedom and creativity, though it must always be kept in mind that ends (and beginnings) in such matters are rarely definitive. And having devoted many years to the study of Renaissance culture—in which, as this book should make clear, I have always included the religious currents that shaped both the Protestant and Catholic Reformations fundamental to so much else in the deeper attitudes of the period—it now strikes me as remarkable that historians of early modern Europe have paid so little attention to the problem of the *end* of the Renaissance. The subliminal legacy of Burck-hardt has been so powerful that this question seems almost never to have arisen; wherever we locate the transition to the modern world, we are still inclined to assume that it had its origins in the Renaissance, and that there-fore the Renaissance must still be with us. The closest we have come to revising our notions about such matters has been recently to relocate the beginnings of the modern world in the eighteenth century, although most historians now, probably wisely, no longer trouble themselves with such complex questions.

I have in this connection, however, been unable to avoid altogether two general issues. One may already have been noticed by readers of this preface: that I tend to refer to the kind of study represented by this work as "cul-tural" rather than "intellectual" history. The explanation for this substitu-tion is that the term "intellectual" is not historically neutral. Indeed, it begs a large question basic to studies of this kind, for it presupposes the exis-tence of a faculty, perhaps an organ vaguely identified with the brain, that is itself a "high" thing, as the head is considered, by some obscure design implicit in our creation or biology, the highest part of the body. This organ, the *intellect*, is sometimes thought to make possible human concern with "higher things." But this notion is itself, of course, no more than a cultural artifact, a legacy from the Greeks to which we subliminally cling, even though it is singularly discordant with the otherwise dominant culture of the modern world. It is also, as a label, unduly restrictive, since it suggests a particular value attaching to abstract thought, to "ideas," to the produc-tions of those human beings whom we describe as "intellectuals," a group with which historians have usually had little difficulty in identifying them-selves. Only recently have they displayed much interest in the presumably "lower" aspects of the self, as in the—not unrelated—"lower" levels of society. But we need now to recognize that "thought" takes a multitude of forms, that it operates at various social levels, and that it generally expresses complex impulses emerging out of holistic and infinitely complex selves, unconscious as well as conscious. What can now be subsumed under the rubric of intellectual—or cultural—history, it is now clear, is vastly more complex than the Greeks, or even René Descartes, might have supposed. The term "cultural history" also has the advantage over "intellectual history" of its generality and even its ambiguity.

This does not mean that my own work is innocent of general views, though I like to believe that they have come out of, rather than shaped, my study of cultural phenomena. At the risk of exposing my naiveté by venturing into realms beyond my competence as a historian, I have come to believe that the underlying dynamic of cultural change is anxiety, which comes in two forms. Cultural systems, as I have learned from Mary Douglas and Clifford Geertz, are ultimately mechanisms for sorting out and thus giving form and meaning to the crude and variegated phenomena that impinge on human consciousness, but also on other levels of the self as well. They do so by the creation of categories and boundaries, and by making distinctions between what is relevant and what is irrelevant to human existence, between the useful and the useless, the safe and the dangerous, and by doing so, make the universe more comfortable and less provocative of anxiety.

But the indefinite multiplication of categories, distinctions, and boundaries, however necessary to human existence at one stage, is ultimately suffocating, very much in the ways so vividly described in Johann Huizinga's *Waning of the Middle Ages*. The result is a reaction toward cultural liberation, as in the Renaissance. This is why Huizinga's vision is misunderstood when it is interpreted as antithetical to Burckhardt's; on the contrary, it explains many of the phenomena we associate with the Burckhardtian Renaissance. But the creativity made possible by liberation from habitual and stultifying modes of cultural expression is itself only temporarily satisfying; the dissolution of old boundaries, old categories, old certainties, in the short run liberating, is in the long run destructive and frightening. The result is a movement in the opposite direction, toward a culture whose increasing articulation, however, is finally so stifling—again in the long run—that it eventually sets in motion a new reaction toward freedom.

The present book, then, discusses one of the major turning points in the history of European culture, one sufficiently recent to have been studied with some care. In the later Renaissance, the impulses toward liberation seem to have become unendurable, and thus to have set in motion a reaction in the opposite direction. The all-too-human tendency to simplify and stereotype other human beings is often applied to the interpretation of historical personages, to represent them as simplified products of processes we can understand, and there may be figures who can properly be interpreted—more or less—in this way. But the period covered by this book does not favor such a lack of ambiguity, and those who might be interpreted with such certainty are not often of much interest to historians. One of my discoveries in attempting to come to terms with the great thinkers and artists of this period is that almost none was simple in this way, that almost all were torn between quite contrary impulses. Thus my major impression of nearly all the figures this book treats is one of complexity and inner contradiction; that almost none was transparent is perhaps a key to the distinction of the age's cultural achievement. This explains why, having treated them in the first section of the book as representatives of the climax of the Renaissance, understood in a fairly traditional sense, I discuss the same individuals as representative of the problems, doubts, and retreats generated by the risks and challenges of Renaissance freedom.

CHAPTER ONE

The Cultural Community of Europe

Histories of particular European states are of limited use for intellectual and cultural history, which requires larger horizons, especially before the nineteenth century. Although the unity of Latin Christendom had been shattered by the Protestant Reformation and the various entities within Europe were increasingly aware of their differences, a sense of unity, still based on community in religion and culture, persisted. Richard Hooker, in his *Laws of Ecclesiastical Polity*, nicely balanced the tensions that persisted between unity and difference in Europe. He was dealing specifically with religion, but his remarks are equally applicable to cultural life. "As the main body of the sea being one, yet within divers precincts hath divers names," he wrote, "so the Catholic Church is in like sort divided into a number of distinct Societies, every of which is termed a Church within it self."

Differences among the Peoples of Europe

By the sixteenth century the various European peoples were increasingly conscious of national identities and differences. Cultivated Italians, though Italy was politically still only a geographical expression, considered themselves linguistically and culturally a nation, and were so regarded abroad. Italy was in this sense more of an entity than Germany or the Netherlands. But even in Germany political fragmentation and vulnerability to papal exploitation had produced resentments that stimulated a sense of national identity eventually contributing to the Protestant Reformation.

Elsewhere the consciousness of national identity nourished prejudice against other peoples, often expressed in negative stereotypes. These were strongest at the popular level but sometimes repeated by the more cultivated. The Flemish cosmographer Gerard Mercator, in his *Atlas* of 1585, described his German neighbors as "simple and furious blockheads," "sumptuous and brazen-faced gluttons," "distrustful slovens," and "quarrelsome dissemblers, double-hearted, and opinionative." His own Belgians, on the other hand, were "good horsemen, tender, teachable, and delicate." The *Crudities* (1611) of Thomas Coryate, who wandered through Europe mostly on foot, described the streets of Paris as the "dirtiest and so the most stinking of all that I saw in my life."

Italy was commonly resented, in Germany for money supposedly drained away by the demands of the papacy, and everywhere for the high level of its material culture and the lightness and immorality which its amenities supposedly encouraged. This kind of anti-Italianism found particular expression in England, where an anonymous pamphlet that advertised itself as "a Discoverie of the great subtiltie and wonderful wisdome of the Italians, whereby they beare sway over the most part of Christendome, and cunninglie behave themselves to fetch the Quintescence out of the peoples purses." Even the cosmopolitan Sir Philip Sidney described Italians in a letter to his brother as more guilty of "counterfeit learning . . . than in any place I do know, for from a tapster upwards they are all discoursers [chatterers]." The supposed wickedness of Niccolò Machiavelli made him into "Old Nick" and a potent symbol of Italian corruption. At the same time English scholars were trying to catch up with Italy. Roger Ascham in his *Scholemaster* (1568) boasted of the progress of England from its early "rudeness" to a proficiency in learning equal to that of Italy.

Anti-Italian sentiment had unusually deep roots in France. The notion that French civilization owed everything to the Romans was contested by a rival belief that it came from the more vigorous and freedom-loving Germanic invaders of France. It was also nourished by the medieval conception of a divinely ordained westward movement of learning, first from Athens to Rome and then from Rome to Paris. The lawyer-historian Étienne Pasquier emphasized the geographical separation of France from Italy. "God," he wrote, "wished to divide us by a high thrust of mountains, so he separated us in all things, in manners, in laws, character, humors."

There was also a positive side to this increasingly articulate nationalism. Jacques-Auguste de Thou opened his *History of His Own Time* (1604) with a patriotic declaration:

It is a maxim that I have received through hereditary tradition . . . that, after what I owe to God, nothing should be more dear and sacred to me than the love and respect owed to my *patrie*, and that I should cause all other considerations to yield to this. I have brought this sentiment into the administration of affairs, being persuaded, according to the thoughts of the ancients, that the *patrie* is a second divinity, that its laws come from God, and that those who violate them, with whatever specious pretext of religion they may cover themselves, are sacrilegious and parricidal.[1]

Similar sentiments had inspired Pasquier in 1560 to begin his *Recherches de France*, a multi-volume study of the medieval origins of French institutions intended to minimize the debt of France to Rome and Italy.

Meanwhile Spain was developing a sense of national destiny based on the completion in 1492 of its centuries-long crusade to expel the Muslims and on Spanish expansion overseas. The presence in Spain of ethnic minorities also stimulated a special concern for purity of blood. By the latter part of the six-teenth century these impulses had produced a sense of difference from the rest of Europe and a Catholicism unusually sensitive to heresy. Philip II forbade his subjects to travel abroad or attend most foreign universities, and exercised an uncommonly tight control over the publication and importation of books. The result was to strengthen an unusual rigidity in Spanish society and, along with a concern for religious orthodoxy, bring about a stagnation in science and learning. But this did not entirely inhibit Spain from cultural contact with other areas, notably with Catholic central Europe and the Habsburg court in Vienna and Prague. Spanish possessions in Italy and the Netherlands led to cultural appropriations, notably in the arts. Spanish influence was also felt elsewhere. The Habsburg emperor Rudolph II (1576–1612), who had spent much of his adolescence in Spain, continued to dress like a Spaniard, and liked to speak Spanish.

The Cultural Unity of Europe and the Republic of Letters

But intellectual and cultural movements stubbornly refuse to respect polit-ical boundaries, and much in such matters was common to all the peoples of Western Europe. Anti-foreign prejudice was criticized by Jean Bodin, who, though he traveled chiefly in books, derided the English for thinking of themselves as stronger than the French; the Italians for condemning "the cunning of the Greeks"; and, briefly mixing ancient and modern examples, the Jews and Egyptians for thinking "the Greeks fickle, as the Italians did the French, and the French the Germans." Bodin also paid tribute, if somewhat sardonically, to the progress of German learning. "As their bodies develop great size," he wrote, "so do their books. Martin [Luther] wrote more and Erasmus wrote more than anyone can read in the course of a long lifetime." A growing sense of the cultural community of Europe appears in a poem of Samuel Daniel, written to accompany the translation of Montaigne's *Essays* into English (1603), itself a notable example of European cosmopolitanism:

> It being the proportion of a happy pen
> Not to be invassall'd to one monarchie,
> But dwell with all the better world of men
> Whose spirits all are of one communitie,
> Whom neither oceans, desarts, rockes nor sands
> Can keep from the 'intertraffique of the minde.[2]

Continuing Primacy of Italy

Nevertheless, Italy was still the source, as Jacob Burckhardt would put it, of "the breath of life for all the more instructed minds of Europe." In spite of Protestant prejudices, in the sixteenth century, Italy remained a favorite stop on the Grand Tour that completed the education of upper-class Europeans. Italian literature circulated everywhere. The poet Ariosto was a model for Spenser and Cervantes, and Italian stories and plays inspired native theater elsewhere. Italian universities attracted students from abroad, notably in the sciences; and painters and composers came to Italy to learn the latest artistic styles. Rubens in his youth had, as he put it, to "see Italy and to view at first hand the most celebrated works of art, ancient and modern, and to form his art after these models." Montaigne was heavily indebted to Italian humanism, and in his maturity he made an extended trip to Italy, carefully recording his adventures and observations. He brooded over the ruins of ancient Rome, and the Roman authorities honored him with citizenship.

But the cultural preeminence of Italy was now waning, as Erasmus had noted earlier in the century. This was partly the result of the French invasion in 1494 and the prolonged warfare that followed between the French and Spanish armies, which demonstrated the powerlessness of fragmented Italy to deal politically with the new national monarchies. Power in Europe was being transferred to the western seaboard, its passage accelerated by the voyages of discovery, which favored the Atlantic powers. There was also a growing Protestant reaction to the long cultural predominance of Catholic

Italy. After the middle of the sixteenth century European leadership was shifting westward, from Italy to France and—especially in theology—to the freer atmosphere of the Netherlands. Before the end of the century political and legal thinkers, even in Italy, increasingly admired French society and institutions.

Development of the Vernaculars

Meanwhile vernacular languages were replacing Latin even in scholarly publishing as the growth of literacy among the laity increased the demand for books in native tongues. The use of the vernacular for serious purposes had begun in Italy, where the Tuscan dialect was well on the way to becoming a national language. The eminence of Dante and Petrarch in poetry and of Castiglione and Guicciardini in prose promoted the prestige of Italian, though Latin long remained the preferred language of scholarship. By the middle of the century the use of the vernacular was spreading. Sperone Speroni's *Dialogue on Languages* (1542) justified it by noting the various functions of language. By suggesting the relativity of languages to the circumstances of their origins and their different uses, he directly challenged the traditional view of Latin as the universal language appropriate to all times and places. At about the same time Joachim du Bellay argued in his *Defense and Renown of the French Language* (1549) for the value of variety among languages. He also predicted a literature in French that would rival that of antiquity. In England, the schoolmaster Richard Mulcaster boasted, "I do not think that anie language, be it whatsoever, is better able to utter all arguments, wither with more pith, or greater planesse, than our English tung is." At the same time English was being enriched by new words, from Latin, but also from other languages. Latin itself was increasingly seen as a "dead" language, an adjective first applied to it in 1570. The result was something like a "Galilean revolution" in language, as disruptive of traditional values as the revolution in cosmology.

The development of the vernaculars received encouragement from other quarters. National governments required records of law and other public documents to be written in their vernaculars rather than dog Latin. French became the official language of the courts and of all public documents in France. In English courts the vernacular was promoted over Latin and the law French used even in England since the time of William the Conqueror by the jurist Edward Coke, who believed in the expressive value of English for every purpose. "Our English language," he wrote, "is as copious and significant, and as able to express anything in as few words, as any other native language that is spoken at this day."

The Reformations, Catholic as well as Protestant, also promoted the use of the languages of the people. Protestants rejected the Latin liturgy and promoted vernacular translations of the Bible. Meanwhile preaching on both sides implied that the most sublime knowledge was communicable in the vernacular. As one of Bodin's discussants argued in his *Colloquium of the Seven Sages*, "Nothing is more ridiculous than for priests to use a foreign language which the unlearned do not understand." The expressive power of English was enhanced by the new King James translation of the Bible (1611), as German had been by Luther's vernacular translation. The Catholic reformers Pierre de Bérulle and François de Sales wrote in French for laymen; and the letters of French Jesuits, even those addressed to the generals of the order, were mostly in the vernacular. A French Jesuit proposed to counter the attractions of Protestant psalm-singing in the vernacular by encouraging Catholics to do likewise, in translations by the poet Ronsard. "The French love singing very much," he argued, "and with this weakness the devil has won over a whole world of them." Meanwhile the missionary enthusiast Guillaume Postel called for religious books in the various languages of prospective converts.

Latin was even being displaced in scholarly communication. In Italy, teaching in philosophy, medicine, and law was increasingly in the vernacular: Galileo wrote about cosmology in Italian, as he explained, so that everybody could read his work: Italian was "capable of dealing with and explaining the concepts of every field of study." Paolo Sarpi used Italian to explain highly technical legal and institutional procedures to lay rulers in his *Treatise on Benefices*. Peter Ramus broke new ground by publishing philosophical work in French; and Montaigne's *Essays* demonstrated that French could express serious thought. The publication of learned studies in English had become so well established that Robert Burton, unable to find a publisher willing to print his *Anatomy of Melancholy* in Latin, was compelled, to his distress, to bring it out in English.

The vernaculars were increasingly used for serious literature. Ronsard, the leading figure in a group of French vernacular poets known as the Pléiade, aimed to produce a vernacular poetry equal to that of antiquity. In England, humanist schoolmasters like Roger Ascham, teacher of the future Queen Elizabeth, and Richard Mulcaster, who taught the poet Spenser, were praising English. Sidney developed vernacular poetry and composed a long vernacular novel, *Arcadia*. Spenser's *Faerie Queene* was the first great epic poem in English, and English theater exposed large numbers to the expressive power of the language.

Vernacular literature was also developing elsewhere. Dutch had its champions, and Dirck Coornhert published works of religious and political controversy in Dutch. In Spain, Cervantes put a defense of the vernacular in the mouth of Don Quixote:

> Great Homer did not write in Latin, because he was a Greek, nor Virgil in Greek, because he was a Latin. In fact all the ancients wrote in the tongues they sucked with their mother's milk, and did not go out to seek strange ones to express the greatness of their conceptions. And, that being so, this custom should rightfully be extended to all nations, and the German poet must not be despised for writing in his own language, nor the Castilian, nor the Basque, for writing in his.[3]

But the triumph of the vernacular was not yet complete. Latin continued to be used in scholarship destined for an international readership. Of the six thousand books in the Bodleian Library at Oxford in 1605, only thirty-six were in English. In the schools Latin continued to be emphasized.

Unity: The Republic of Letters

But the linguistic differentiation of Europe should not obscure its cultural unity, now dramatized by contact with new peoples in America and Asia, whose exotic ways underlined the similarities between the peoples of Europe. The common elements even in most variants of European Christianity should not be forgotten. Neither Protestantism nor Catholicism was monolithic; both, rather like American political parties, tended to represent political and institutional rather than "religious" choices. What they shared was more profound than most contemporaries realized: for example, basic Augustinian assumptions about the human personality. Their affinities also help to explain the continuing popularity on both sides of the religious divide of such works as Thomas à Kempis's *Imitation of Christ*. This fundamental community helps to explain the ease of movement for intellectuals between professions of faith: for example, Isaac Casaubon, a Protestant, pensioned and employed by the newly Catholic Henri IV of France, died an Anglican and was buried in Westminster Abbey; Justus Lipsius and François Baudouin, Calvinists, converted to Catholicism. Meanwhile French Catholics were nourished by Spanish, Italian, and

Flemish spirituality; and Calvinism allied French, Swiss, Germans, Scots English, and other northern and central Europeans. In addition, like-minded scholars on each side recognized their affinities, corresponded, and read each others' books. One such community of interest included the Calvinist Casaubon, the Lutheran Gerhard Voss (Vossius), the Arminian Hugo Grotius, the Anglican William Bedwell, the Catholic Paolo Sarpi, and various Gallican lawyers who emphasized the autonomy of the French school of law.

Travel Abroad

Travel, widely esteemed for its educational value, often introduced Europeans of the upper classes to other like-minded persons. Italy was a major destination for travelers, among them Montaigne, who believed that "mixing with men is wonderfully useful, and visiting foreign countries to bring back knowledge of the characters and ways of those nations, and to rub and polish our brains by contact with those of others." There was, in his view, "no better school for forming one's life than to set before it constantly the diversity of other lives, ideas, and customs." A character in Sidney's *Arcadia* remarked that he had gone abroad "that by comparison of many things [he] might ripen [his] judgment." Sidney had done this himself. When he was eighteen he had accompanied a diplomatic mission to Paris and there made many friends; the French king made him a baron and gentleman of the royal bedchamber. From France he proceeded to Germany and then spent the best part of a year in Padua and Venice. He also attended the Frankfurt book fair and later traveled to Florence, Prague, and Cracow. "Hard sure it is to know England," he remarked, "without you know it by comparing it with others." He spoke French well, and he also learned from French and Spanish nobles "the true points of honor." Later he was in touch with scholarly circles in the Netherlands and Prague. A young Netherlander, Pieter Hooft, began a three-year tour of Europe in 1598, visiting Paris, Venice, Florence, Rome, and Naples and returning by way of Germany.

There were many reasons to travel. Burton recommended it as a remedy for melancholy. French nobles went abroad to seek military experience or employment after the end of the French civil wars, or as political or religious exiles. Religious refugees found a haven abroad: French Protestants in London and Geneva, free-thinking Italians everywhere. Giordano Bruno was variously in Geneva, Paris, London, Wittenberg, and Prague. In England he lectured at Oxford, later boasting of how well he had done debating with its theologians. He dedicated his *Expulsion of the Triumphant Beast* to Sidney in England; in France he dedicated another work to Henri III. International diplomacy required travel by ambassadors, who brought their retinues with them. The Spanish domination of Italy attracted many Spaniards, especially to the papal court in this age of the Catholic Reformation. Among them was the Jesuit political writer Juan de Mariana, already a student of Italian political thought. Envoys from the papacy, Venice, Spain, France, England and Russia resided at the Habsburg court in Vienna.

Francis Bacon, who as a youth spent years on the continent, advised travelers to call on "eminent persons in all kinds, which are of great name abroad, that [they] may be able to tell how the life agreeth with the fame." One of those to whom travelers paid homage was the geographer Ortelius, who kept an autograph album of his visitors and correspondents; it includes signatories from England, France, Spain, Portugal, Italy, and Germany. The papacy itself was relatively hospitable to Protestant visitors, perhaps in the hope of converting them.

Published accounts of foreign travel further stimulated interest in foreign parts. At least three such accounts appeared in England between 1611 and 1617: Coryate's *Crudities*; the *Relation of a Journey* by George Sandys, which provided much information about the Near East; and the *Itinerary* of Fynes Moryson, which described European life and manners and gave general advice to would-be travelers. Among other adventures Moryson included a visit in Rome to Cardinal Bellarmine, for which he posed as a Frenchman to avoid identification as a heretic.

The internationalism of European culture was also facilitated by the presence of foreign communities in major cities. These included merchants, diplomats, and artists with international reputations. Composers and musicians were in special demand. The performances of John Bull, organist in the royal chapel of Elizabeth and James I, were highly regarded in France and Germany; he spent his last years as organist in the cathedral of Notre Dame in Antwerp. Northern painters regularly completed their training in Italy. Artists and scholars from many parts of Europe were attracted by the patronage of the Habsburg court in Prague. Political exiles, among them Florentine republicans escaping the despotism of the Medici, brought Italian books and ideas to Paris.

Universities

The cultural unity of Europe was also promoted by its universities. These still taught mostly in Latin; and they were often, as they had been for centuries, international communities of scholars and students. Over six thousand Germans, most of them, to the distress of the papacy, Protestants, took degrees at the University of Padua between 1550 and 1600. Englishmen studied medicine there, including William Harvey, discoverer of the circulation of the blood. So did increasing numbers of Greek and Jewish students. Many Czechs attended universities in France, England, Spain, and the Netherlands. English Protestants studied in Swiss and German universities, English Catholics in Rome and Belgium.

Much of the intellectual activity of the period still centered on universities. Although the University of Paris languished during the civil wars, in Europe generally university enrollments were burgeoning. In England, the student bodies of Oxford and Cambridge grew rapidly, partly because of the need for well-educated clergy to defend the Protestantism of the Church of England, partly to take advantage of job possibilities in the expanding state bureaucracy. Law was thus an unusually popular field of study at the Inns of Court in London, as it was for similar reasons in Spain. Among older universities that of Padua remained important, its intellectual freedom protected by Venetian rule. The poet Tasso studied philosophy there with Sperone Speroni and rhetoric with Carlo Sigonio; Galileo was converted to Copernicanism at Padua. Charles University in Prague, under the tolerant patronage of Rudolf II, was friendly to the new science as well as to the arts. The University of Louvain had the most prestigious theological faculty in Catholic Europe; Lipsius left Calvinist Leiden for Louvain in 1592 after his conversion to Catholicism.

New universities in the Protestant Netherlands developed rapidly. The University of Leiden, founded in 1575, was soon the largest in Europe; open to innovation, it developed practical studies such as engineering and new subjects such as Near Eastern languages and geography. Its faculty included two of the greatest scholars in Europe, Lipsius before his conversion, editor and champion of Tacitus, and the textual critic J.J. Scaliger. German universities declined after the Reformation but revived in the later sixteenth century; among the most respected was the Calvinist University of Herborn. In Italy, the prestige of the new Collegio Romano, established by the Jesuits, was growing; excelling in theology, classical and biblical studies, and mathematics, it attracted students from every part of Europe. But in spite of this expansion and the vitality of some universities, all was not well.

Then as now, older universities were resistant to change and had largely ignored the innovations of the Renaissance; their curricula and methods remained largely scholastic and Aristotelian, and they tended to perceive themselves as guardians of orthodoxy, whether the orthodoxy of the churches or of governments.

They had other problems as well. In Catholic countries, especially Spain and the French capital of Paris, they were often in turmoil over Jesuit efforts to penetrate their ranks, especially in faculties of theology. The University of Louvain tried to organize a coalition of Catholic universities to resist the Jesuits. The prestige of Catholic universities also suffered from the transfer to Rome of their traditional role in defining doctrinal orthodoxy. Everywhere universities were also threatened by the encroachment of secular governments. Both Paris and Louvain were compelled by financial distress to admit to their faculties professors designated by the crown; and German universities, which had once attracted many foreign students, became increasingly provincial because of pressure from governments to train local clergy, schoolteachers, and bureaucrats. Rulers also sometimes forbade their subjects to attend universities outside their states.

Older university men like Burton complained of the decline of learning, which he attributed to the expansion of student bodies by the admission of less-qualified students. "For what do we expect can happen," he asked plaintively, "when every day, pell mell, poor sons of Alma Mater, sprung from the soil, mannikins of no rank whatever, are eagerly admitted to degrees?" There was therefore much discussion in England of university reform, but with little result owing to basic disagreements. Puritans, who controlled colleges at both Oxford and Cambridge, objected to scholastic training because, they argued, it left graduates ignorant of Scripture; but Hooker thought that learning would perish under a Puritan regime. For others, reform meant the recovery of humanistic learning.

Learned Societies and Academies

Dissatisfaction with the universities helps to explain the emergence of circles of men with common intellectual or esthetic interests outside the universities. An early example, in the last decades of the sixteenth century, was an informal group, meeting regularly in Venice, that included a number of local patricians, Paolo Sarpi, Galileo during his stay at Padua, and foreign visitors who interested them. Its discussions ranged over scientific, literary, and philosophical questions, and were characterized by one participant as highly democratic and "aiming at understanding the truth." Giordano Bruno, passing through Venice, attended during the period of his greatest interest in French thought; at his heresy trial in 1592, the Inquisition showed some interest in this group, which was also reading Bacon's *Essays*.

Other groups of learned Italians were coming together in more formally organized academies. Most of these had broad interests but some had a particular emphasis. In Rome, the Accademia dei Lincei, established in 1603 to discuss mathematics and experimental science, was of particular importance. Interested in the encyclopedic organization of knowledge, it assembled an important library notable for its inclusion of scientific works; Galileo was admitted to the membership in 1611. Bringing together engineers, military men, prelates, and courtiers, it took all knowledge for its province. As its constitution stated, "The Lincean Academy desires as its members philosophers who are eager for real knowledge and will give themselves to the study of nature, especially mathematics; at the same time it will not neglect the ornaments of elegant literature and philosophy, which, like graceful garments, adorn the whole body of science." In Florence, the Accademia della Crusca published in 1612 the first dictionary of any vernacular language, the product of two decades of work.

The interests of the Accademia degli Incogniti, established in Venice in 1630, were very different. Including most of the intellectuals of Venice, its meetings were staged as debates. With its motto *Ignoto Deo* (to the unknown God), it aimed to question everything and was sometimes accused of a dangerous freedom of thought. It was particularly important for the origins of opera; members of the academy established the most successful opera theater in Venice.

Meanwhile similar organizations were appearing in other countries. In Spain, they sprang up in Madrid, Seville, and Valencia. They were organized in Paris after 1620; the most important met at the home of the brothers Pierre and Jacques Dupuy, whose "Académie Putéane" included philosophers, scholars, and scientists, and met daily. Its most distinguished member was Pierre Gassendi, a devout priest who was also an early atomist, a publicist of the new science, and a fierce anti-Aristotelian. Academies devoted to raising standards in the arts were being formed in northern Europe.

Correspondence Networks

Universities and academies brought together learned men of diverse origins who kept in touch with each other; and students, after leaving university, did so through international correspondence networks, often in Latin. Travelers also followed Bacon's advice that a traveler should not "leave the countries where he hath travelled altogether behind him; but maintain a correspondence by letters with those of his acquaintance which are of most worth." Letters exchanged news, opinion, and advice, taking somewhat the place of modern newspapers. In addition, courier services were organized by universities. Books and other items were also exchanged; the English historian William Camden sent part of his history of the reign of Queen Elizabeth (1615) to the French historian Jacques-Auguste de Thou, and Sarpi sent melon and cauliflower seeds to a correspondent in France.

Some scholars carried on an enormous correspondence. Between seven and eight thousand letters to and from Grotius have survived. Sarpi wrote often to French and Dutch Protestant scholars as well as to Gallican lawyers and to scientists in the circle of the Dupuy brothers. Hugo Blosius, court librarian in Vienna, drew central Europeans of many kinds into an epistolary community. An interconfessional correspondence network including Spanish, Dutch, English, Swiss, and French scholars discussed biblical scholarship and Near Eastern philology.

Some scholars circulated or published their letters, for letter-writing was still considered a serious branch of literature in a tradition going back to Cicero. Petrarch and Erasmus both polished and published their letters. Lipsius published his letters to some seven hundred correspondents after preparing them with appropriate attention to his public image.

Thus, whether through acquaintance at universities, membership in academies, tourism, books, or correspondence, European thinkers and artists constituted an international Republic of Letters. Within this larger community were sub-groups based on common interests: occult, scholarly, scientific, legal, historical, religious, esthetic, even utopian. Such communities provided social and spiritual support for cultural activity at a time when bourgeois republics, once major patrons of Renaissance culture, were disappearing in Italy, and universities everywhere were declining.

Patronage

The patronage by aristocrats and princely courts of artists and intellectuals, whose works had little public market, was essential for their support. Galileo moved in 1610 from the university circles of Pisa and Padua, in which he had developed his ideas, to the court of Cosimo II, Grand Duke of Tuscany, and was supported handsomely; in return, his fame testified to the greatness of his patron. The architects, painters, and poets patronized by rulers created for them an iconography of power that had practical as well as symbolic value.

International competition among would-be patrons for distinguished artists also facilitated cultural exchange. The emperor Rudolph II was a great collector of artists as well as art, which he purchased all over Europe. A contemporary described him as "the greatest art patron in the world at the present time." The eccentric painter Giuseppe Arcimboldo directed entertainments at Rudolf's court, which was also frequented by the scientists Johann Kepler and Tycho Brahe, a German and a Dane respectively, as well as by the English astrologer John Dee, previously in the service of Queen Elizabeth. The culture of the Spanish court was almost as cosmopolitan. Philip II (1556–98) was the greatest art patron of his time; among the painters he employed were both the Italian Titian and the Flemish Rubens. At the same time printers in the Spanish Netherlands distributed Spanish scholarship throughout Europe. Nor did Philip ignore Spanish artists. Particularly interested in architecture, he built the Escorial, a great palace designed by Juan de Herrera to demonstrate the greatness of Spain. It included a royal residence filled with art of the period, a convent, a church, and a mausoleum for the royal family.

Other courts of Europe were following the same path. In France, poetry was taken into the service of the crown under the well-educated queen mother, Catherine de' Medici. Royal pensions, gifts, and honors rewarded the group of French poets known as the Pléiade, of whom Ronsard is now best known. Good classicists, they aspired at once to make French the equal of Italian as a literary language and to glorify the French monarchy; they praised the religion of the state and celebrated its policies and its victories.

The English court under the Tudors had been relatively untouched by the culture of the continent, but with the early Stuarts this began to change. Court masques, in which Ben Jonson collaborated with the architect Inigo Jones, glorified James I (1603–25) as the center of the universe who transformed winter into spring, reduced wilderness to order, made the earth fruitful, and restored the golden age. Charles I (1625–49), whose queen was French, was also surrounded by courtiers with cultural interests developed abroad.

The papacy and the cardinals residing in Rome constituted another center of courtly patronage. Cardinal Giovanni Ciampoli was an early patron of Galileo, and during the earlier seventeenth century several popes began the transformation of Rome into a city of great architecture that dramatized the power of the church. Urban VIII, himself a classical scholar, employed in this task the great architect and sculptor Giovanni Bernini, who designed among other monuments the colonnade in front of St. Peter's that proclaims the glorious mission of Rome to embrace the world.

Printing

In his celebration of German culture, the fifteenth-century humanist Conrad Celtis had included the invention of printing, which by the sixteenth century had spread everywhere, preserving and disseminating the products of cultural activity and contributing to the cultural unity of Europe. Presses in Venice, Basel, Antwerp, Lyons, Prague, and other places produced books for a European market, publicizing them at regional and international book fairs, especially that of Frankfurt, which put out catalogues of new titles. The preparation of patristic and classical texts for publication also brought groups of scholars together from various countries.

As literacy grew, book publication became increasingly profitable, and the number of books in print rapidly rose. Between the introduction of the printing press in the mid-fifteenth century and the end of the sixteenth, some 28,000 works appeared; in France alone close to a thousand titles were being published every year. Print runs varied but could be as many as five thousand copies. As better texts appeared, philological scholarship rapidly advanced and ancient writings were translated into the various vernaculars, further diffusing classical culture. Thus Montaigne, though knowing little Greek, was able through the translation by Jacques Amyot (1559) to read Plutarch, one of his favorite authors; without such translation, he wrote, "we ignoramuses would have been lost . . . thanks to it we now dare to speak and write; from it the ladies give lessons to the schoolmasters; it is our breviary." Texts were also translated from one vernacular to another. Thomas North translated Amyot's French version of Plutarch's *Lives* into English. The availability in French of the popular German literature of roguery, in English of French romances, and in German of numerous Spanish works, as well as an adaptation of Rabelais in German by Johann Fischart (1575), suggests an even broader audience. Cervantes could read a wide range of Italian authors, some in Spanish translation; his own *Don Quixote* was popular in England and elsewhere. Both Shakespeare and Francis Bacon had read Montaigne's *Essays* in the translation by John Florio, who also published an Italian–English dictionary in 1598. Twenty per cent of the works published during the reign of Queen Elizabeth were translations;

comparable proportions seem likely elsewhere. In London itself John Wolf specialized in printing books in Italian, including those of Machiavelli. Conversely, William Bedell, as English ambassador to Venice, supplied books by English writers to Sarpi. The works of Italian humanists were generally available north of the Alps, and Italian works on the arts influenced artistic practice elsewhere, notably in France and England. The *Six Books of the Commonwealth* (1576) of Jean Bodin was widely read in its Italian translation.

The availability of books in vernacular languages also led to the assimilation of words and phrases from one language into others. Purists were troubled by this, but it had obvious advantages. Richard Mulcaster believed that it enriched English, such borrowing being the "*prerogative* and libertie" of every language.

Religious books made up the largest category of publications everywhere. Among Protestants the books most in demand were vernacular Bibles: by 1640 some 630,000 English Bibles and 400,000 New Testaments had been printed. As an English bishop observed, charges of heresy against the English church could easily be disproved because "nowadays the Holy Scripture is abroad, the writings of the apostles and the prophets are in print, whereby all truth and Catholic doctrine may be proved, and all heresy may be disproved and confuted." On the other hand, as John Foxe pointed out in his *Book of Martyrs* (1563), "The Pope, that great Antichrist of Rome, could never have been suppressed . . . except this most excellent science of printing had been maintained." But printing was also an instrument of the Catholic Reformation. Printed papal bulls and other ecclesiastical pronouncements helped to centralize the Roman church. Among the scholarly productions of this period were massive editions of the church fathers, as well as works of contemporary devotional writers. The *Introduction to the Devout Life* (1608) by François de Sales went through five French editions in the author's own lifetime and was translated into other vernacular languages.

Centralizing national governments also found printing useful. Standard lawbooks and collections of statutes could now be made widely available to local judges. Royal edicts and official opinion could be easily circulated, even—since books and pamphlets were cheap—among the lower classes. The printing press helped to make public opinion a factor in politics.

There were other, more general, consequences. Instruction manuals and descriptions of distant places for travelers reduced the element of chance in human affairs. Even more profound, though harder to assess, was the experience of readers now confronted with numbered pages, consistent punctuation, running heads, indexes, the regularity of the spatial organization of pages, and other devices that promoted a sense of order. Books also helped to stabilize and standardize the vernacular languages. Such developments shaped expectations and habits of mind that eventually extended beyond readers to a larger public. In addition, books made available vast amounts of new data, making memory less necessary; readers could look up things they had forgotten, past wisdom could be fixed and preserved from generation to generation. As Bacon observed:

> the images of men's wits and knowledges remain in books, exempted from the wrong of time, and capable of perpetual renovation. Neither are they fitly to be called images, because they generate still, and cast their seeds in the minds of others, provoking and causing infinite actions and opinions in succeeding ages: so that, if the invention of a ship was thought so noble . . . how much more are letters to be magnified, which, as ships, pass through the vast seas of time, and make ages so distant to participate of the wisdom, illuminations, and inventions, the one of the other.

In addition, as Bacon also knew, books could record and disseminate new knowledge, and the awareness of this helped nourish the idea of progress.[4]

Since books were vastly less expensive than the manuscripts they replaced, many more persons could now afford private libraries. University libraries were also growing rapidly; at Oxford, the Bodleian, endowed in 1602 by Sir Thomas Bodley, received copies of all books printed in England. Cheaper books circulated among a more popular audience. The advantages of print over oral communication were often celebrated, as by Samuel Purchas:

> By speech we utter our minds once, at the present, as present occasions move (and perhaps unadvisably transport us): but by writing Man seems immortall, conferreth and consulteth with the Patriarchs, Prophets, Apostles, Fathers, Philosophers, Historians, and learnes the wisdom of the Sages which have been in all times before him; yea by the translations or learning the Languages, in all Places and Regions of the World: and lastly, by his own writings surviveth himself, remaines (litera scripta manet) thorow all ages a Teacher and Counsellor to the last of men: yea hereby God holds conference with men, and in his sacred Scripture, as at first in the Tables of Stone, speakes to all.[5]

The printing press figured regularly in the claims of Europeans to superiority over the rest of the world. Guillaume Postel called it "the lance and sword" of the impending triumph of Christ.

Reading and Authorship

The availability of books raised questions about reading. Bacon recognized the problem of selectivity. "Some books," he advised, "are to be tasted, others to be swallowed, and some few to be chewed and digested; that is, some books are to be read only in parts; others to be read, but not curiously; and some few to be read wholly, and with diligence and attention." Like many modern critics, Montaigne saw the possibility of diverse readings of the same text, which raised questions about the authority commonly attributed to such texts as the Bible, Homer, and Plato. This led him to an unusually active conception of reading. "An able reader," he noted, "often discovers in other men's writings perfections beyond those that the author put in or perceived, and lends them richer meanings and aspects." Sarpi doubted that readers could ever understand with certainty the exact intention of an author. Grotius pointed out that the meaning of a text and even of a word depends on the cultural practice of its time, and this implied that the interpretation of texts required a knowledge of history. Humanists had long recognized this, but in their dogmatic quarrels scholars tended to forget it.

The widespread circulation of their works also stimulated some writers to a novel consciousness of themselves as *authors*. A traditional view of authorship as a leisure-time activity for gentlemen had led some fashionable writers to deny a seriousness in their writing that might suggest a need, not consistent with gentle birth, to earn a living. Montaigne knew men who were ashamed to confess that this might be the case. Venetian aristocrats who wrote opera librettos were sometimes reluctant to admit that it was anything but a gentlemanly recreation. But Ben Jonson audaciously published his own works in 1616, thus helping to establish the respectability of authorship; and Cervantes gloried, if somewhat obliquely, in the popularity of *Don Quixote*, publishing it in two parts, and in the second celebrating the popularity of the first with a testimonial to its wholesomeness:

> Children finger it, young people read it; grown men know it by heart, and old men praise it . . . there is not a gentleman's antechamber in which you will not find a Don Quixote. When one lays it down, another

picks it up; some rush at it; others beg for it. In fact this story is the most delightful and least harmful entertainment ever seen to this day, for nowhere in it is to be found anything even resembling an indelicate expression or an uncatholic thought.[6]

The popularity of such works everywhere was a further tribute to the internationalism of European culture.

CHAPTER TWO

The Liberation of the Self

Medieval culture had inherited from classical antiquity a model of order patterned on the cosmos. Since the cosmos had been created by God, its order was the archetype of all order, order *per se*. The cosmos was perceived as an organized and finite whole, consisting of two parts. Above were the heavens, below was the earth. The heavenly bodies, themselves perfect and therefore immutable, were seen as arranged in a hierarchy and were believed to move in perfect circles; linear movement would have signified their "need" to change place and implied some imperfection. Beyond their orbits were the stars, and beyond them the empyrean, the abode of God himself.

Below the heavenly bodies, but also at the center of their various circular orbits, was the site of imperfection and change in the universe. This part of God's creation included the visibly changing moon and the earth, where other kinds of change occurred. At the very center of the earth, and thus farthest from God, was hell. The shape of this universe might thus be described as an inverted cone.

The whole arrangement had both physical and spiritual significance. It was also in some respects paradoxical: earth was the lowest and most degraded place in the universe, but at the same time its center and the focus of all the spiritual influences and energies of the universe, not only because God's grace was peculiarly focussed on its inhabitants, but also because the heavenly bodies were not inanimate but believed to influence events on earth; only the human will was entirely free of their intervention. A high degree of determinism was thus built into the system.

The system also had the advantage of being easily intelligible to human beings because it was finite, but also because the various heavenly bodies were like signposts, marking the way through its vast spaces, making it picturable to human beings. The order of this universe, as God's own conception of order, was taken to be the model for all order on earth. It stipulated the primacy of the whole over its parts, a requirement especially significant for government, both spiritual and secular; and it was also taken to prescribe hierarchy in all human relationships. The scheme also had implications, as we will see, for ethics and knowledge. Finally, since it presupposed a fixed and ideal order in all things, it was crucial for perceptions of time and change.

The traditional conception of the self, in accordance with this cosmology, assigned to reason—often identified with the soul as the highest part in man—a position analogous to that of God in the cosmos. Below it, arranged in a hierarchy, were the several supposedly discrete faculties of the self: the will, the passions, and lowest of all the body. The will in a properly ordered personality was thought to function as the obedient servant of reason, relaying its commands to those lower and—because of original sin— often refractory layers of the self, the passions and the relatively contemptible body. But this traditional conception of the human personality, ultimately a reflection of the Greek element in European culture, had already been contested in the earlier Renaissance, a development connected with the return to biblical roots that was a major element in Renaissance culture. This conception was increasingly under attack during the later Renaissance, but by the same token it had stimulated a reaction toward the renewal of the old hierarchy of the self.

Two intellectual and spiritual movements had, since the fourteenth century, attacked the traditional conception of the self. One was the radical doubt central to nominalism, which by the fifteenth century was dominant within scholasticism. For nominalists, human beings could only know what was accessible to the senses; beyond this, there was only the higher knowledge revealed in Scripture and grasped by faith. The other was Augustinianism, with its roots in the rhetorical tradition rather than in philosophical rationalism, which, at least since the time of Petrarch, had nourished Renaissance humanism. For Augustine and his Renaissance followers, the crucial areas of human being were the affections and the will, both seen as dependent not on reason but on the quality of the heart. This facet in the thought of the many-sided Augustine was especially prominent in his *Confessions*, a work not highly valued before the Renaissance. This aspect of Augustinianism contributed to the disintegration of hierarchical conceptions in all domains of thought, to the high regard for rhetoric in the Renaissance, to a growing biblicism that shaped both the Protestant and Catholic Reformations, to an emphasis on time, change, and history, and to a growing concern with action and social responsibility, not always highly esteemed in traditional culture. Just as Aristotle had been the great ancient hovering over medieval intellectual life (and continued still to be venerated by many), Augustine shaped, at least indirectly, much of what followed until well into the seventeenth century.

In its impact on the understanding of the self, Augustinianism pointed to the directness and individuality of its relation to God. Behind this development was a gradual shift from the authority of Aristotle to that of the Bible, the result of cultural discomforts long gathering. The traditional conception of the self as a hierarchy of discrete faculties remains powerful even now, and it persisted in important circles through the period of the Renaissance. It did so partly because the traditional faculties were long perceived as scientific fact rather than cultural artifact. We nevertheless encounter in Renaissance thought hints of a very different conception of the self: doubts of the value and power of reason and a blurring of the boundaries between the several supposedly distinguishable faculties arranged in order below it, language implying a view of the self as a mysterious and undifferentiated unity, its quality a reflection of another faculty previously little recognized, "the heart."

By the later sixteenth century we find many references to the heart and a new conception of the self in much religious discourse, both Catholic and Protestant. Calvin, slightly earlier, was already agonizing over the place of the heart in a traditional hierarchy he still felt bound to accept, and the Lutheran mystic Johann Arndt, in his *True Christianity* (1606), located original sin, repentance, and faith all in the heart. François de Sales saw the heart as "the source of all our actions," and Pascal would famously insist that "the heart has its reasons that reason knows not of." For Richard Hooker, the heart was at once the source of godliness and the essential organ of thought. "My whole endevor is to resolve the conscience," he declared in the preface to his *Laws of Ecclesiastical Polity*, "and to shewe as neere as I can what in this controversie *the hart is to thinke*, if it will follow the light of sound and sincere judgement."

But concern with the heart was not confined to the overtly devout. For Richard Burton, in his *Anatomy of Melancholy* (1621), the heart was not only "the *Sun* of our body, the King and sole commander of it," but also "the seat and organ of all passions and affections." The new importance attached to the heart was in the background of William Harvey's discovery of the circulation of the blood. Harvey argued that the heart of an animal "is the basis of its life, its chief member, the sun of its *microcosm*; on the heart all its activity depends, from the heart all its liveliness and strength arise." The heart was increasingly recognized to be essential to life itself: it is our *core*, as its Latin and French etymologies tell us, its quality suffusing the whole of the self, giving life at once to the mind, the will, the passions, and the body. Harvey's discovery was not merely of physiological interest; it reflected a deeper cultural shift.

The new, non-hierarchical model of human being to which it pointed redefined the relations between the mind or soul, previously identified with the highest levels of the self, and the body. Montaigne struggled with this problem, coming out, with some help from Aristotle, in favor of the unity of soul and body, though unable quite to abandon the old hierarchy:

> The body has a great part in our being, it holds a high rank in it. Those who want to split up our two principal parts and sequester them from each other are wrong. On the contrary we must couple and join them together again. We must order the soul not to draw aside and enter-tain itself apart, not to scorn and abandon the body (nor can it do so except by some counterfeit monkey trick), but to rally to the body, embrace it, cherish it, assist it, control it, advise it, set it right and bring it back when it goes astray; in short to marry it and be a husband to it, so that their actions may not appear different and contrary, but harmonious and uniform.[1]

Burton was of much the same opinion. "As the body works upon the mind," he insisted, "the mind most effectually works upon the body," though he made the point somewhat negatively, finding it "hard to decide which of these two do more harm to the other." In Spain, St. John of the Cross shifted from a Platonic sense of the antagonism of body and soul to belief in their inseparability.

The unity of soul and body also pointed to a unified and ultimately mys-terious self. Montaigne thought of human nature as a composite of "secret parts which cannot be guessed, mute factors that do not show, sometimes unknown to their possessor himself, which are brought forth and aroused by unexpected occasions." Far from being depressed by this insight, he took satisfaction in its interesting possibilities, which, as he saw, suggested the individuality and uniqueness of every human being.

Others shared his view, though not always with such equanimity. As Donne exclaimed, "Poor intricated soul! Riddling, perplexed, labyrinthine Soul!" Sidney thought human judgment "so uncertain that the same person can be at once most famous and most infamous, and neither justly." The Venetian rabbi Simone Luzzatto developed his sense of complexity into an attack on ethnic stereotypes. "If it is so difficult to define the internal

motions of a single person," he asked, "how much more difficult to determine those of an entire nation?" It is hardly surprising that the word
"psychology" (in Latin, *psychologia*) was a coinage of this period.

Thinkers also recognized the changeability of the self. Montaigne, studying himself, observed constant changes, so that he could not portray "being"
but only "passing." Human beings, for him, were inconsistent, contradictory, unpredictable: "we do not believe what we believe, and we cannot rid
ourselves of what we condemn." We are "all patchwork, so shapeless and
diverse in composition that each bit, each moment plays its own game.
And there is as much difference between us and ourselves as between us
and others." It was impossible to generalize about human being:

> A spirited mind never stops within itself; it is always aspiring and going
> beyond its strength; it has impulses beyond its powers of achievement.
> If it does not advance and press forward and stand at bay and clash, it
> is only half alive. Its pursuits are boundless and without form; its food
> is wonder, the chase, ambiguity."[2]

"The human understanding," for Bacon, "is unquiet; it cannot stop or rest,
and still presses onward, but in vain. Therefore it is that we cannot conceive of any end or limit to the world, but always as of necessity it occurs
to us that there is something beyond." Pascal would bring this line of
thought to a climax: "Our nature consists in motion; complete rest is death."
Hobbes, in summing up, recognized how this differed from traditional
wisdom:

> The felicity of this life, consisteth not in the repose of a mind satis-
> fied. For there is no such *Finis ultimus* (utmost ayme) nor *Summum
> Bonum* (greatest good) as is spoken of in the Books of the old Morall
> Philosophers. Nor can a man any more live, whose Desires are at an
> end, than he, whose Senses and Imaginations are at a stand. Felicity is
> a continuall progresse of the desire, from one object to another; the
> attaining of the former, being still but the way to the latter. The cause
> whereof is, That the object of man's desire, is not to enjoy once onely,
> and for one instant of time; but to assure for ever, the way of his future
> desire.[3]

This vision of human existence as incessant movement suggests something like Mikhail Bakhtin's portrayal of human existence as unfinalizable

dialogue. This period saw the origins of that constantly tentative and shifting genre of self-expression, the essay.

Some thinkers, if not Montaigne, insisted on a goal for the movement of the mind. Here Hooker and his Puritan opponents were in agreement. For Hooker, we should never be content with earthly existence but always aspire to "that which exeedeth the reach of sense": we seek something we do not know, yet desire "doth so incite [us] that all other knowne delightes and pleasures are layd aside. . . . so that nature even in this life doth plainly claime and call for a more divine perfection." The Puritans made this goal-oriented vision less mysterious and more militant, conceiving of life as an unending struggle, externally with ungodliness, internally with sin. Bacon identified the goal as an apocalyptic progress through science.

This dynamic conception of the self also dethroned reason. The self had no sovereign; it had, instead, a center, the heart. The heart was subtler than reason; it did not so much command as influence every aspect of the personality. Indeed, the will, the passions, and the body, though still figuring in discussion of the self, were hardly more than conceptually discrete. The self was finally a unity, its quality wholly dependent on the heart.

Reason, so long glorified, was now in some quarters suspect. Montaigne was an articulate critic both of the cognitive and the ethical claims attributed to it. Nothing, he declared, was "so clear and easy as to be clear enough to her; the easy and the hard are one to her; all subjects alike, and nature in general, disavow her jurisdiction and mediation." He doubted the capacity of reason to discern order in the universe and of knowledge to produce wisdom, happiness, or virtue. He saw learning—although it clearly gave him great satisfaction—as an impediment to action. Bacon described the intellect as "an uneven-mirror" that "mixes up its own nature with the nature of things." Hobbes noted the tendency of even "the ablest, most attentive, and most practised men" to deceive themselves with reason.

Nor, Montaigne argued, could reason control other levels of the self. It could do little more than rationalize desires originating in its various areas. As "an instrument of lead and of wax," it was "stretchable, pliable, and adaptable to all biases and all measures." The will was not the obedient servant of reason but rebellious and disorderly, no more "amenable than our other parts" to its decisions. Does the will, he asked, "always will what we will? Doesn't it often will what we forbid it to will, and that to our evident disadvantage?" He noted his inability to control his penis, his facial expressions, the beating of his heart, his bowels. Nor could reason itself be controlled; instinct, as in animals, was a better guide. Don Quixote, too, doubted the power of reason to control the self: "primary impulses," he argued, "are not within man's power to check." Sarpi was particularly acute in seeing how supposedly rational judgments, at least those of Venice's enemies, were shaped by motives hidden even from themselves.

Indeed, the very conception of "reason" was often now problematic. An egregious example of its ambiguity was Guillaume Postel, the missionary enthusiast, for whom it could mean, at various times, all knowledge not based on Scripture, knowledge based on sense experience, mathematical demonstration, knowledge derived from private mystical experience, and even all truth, including that known only from Scripture. For Hooker, man "by reason attaineth unto the knowledge of [both] thinges that are and are not sensible," but it could also signify "common sense." Reason had thus become little more than a word to conjure with. Claimed by all sides in a factious climate, it had lost much of its old dignity.

If any among the traditional faculties of the self were now stronger than others, they were the will and the passions. Will, no longer guided toward virtue either by reason or toward wickedness by passion, was increasingly seen as autonomous. Bodin called the will the "mistress of human activity." For St. John of the Cross, it was central to prayer, more important than the mind. Hooker stressed its role in faith: "That the minde . . . maie abide in the light of faith, there must abide in the will as constant a resolution to have no fellowship at all with the vanities and workes of darkeness." For François de Sales, the will had been installed by God as monarch in the personality; and "the will alone, as if drawing gently at the breast," was the site of religious experience.

The degree of the will's freedom was debated. Neo-Stoic moralists insisted on its absolute power to control the self; the Jesuits and the inhabitants of Campanella's City of the Sun also argued for its freedom. Hooker's Calvinist theology did not prevent his allowing some freedom to the will. Descartes, for whom even rationality originated in an act of will, argued that nothing "truly pertains" to man but "the free disposition of his will." Burton, like many others, was ambivalent.

Seen as dependent on the quality of the heart rather than as independent or as emanating from the "lowest" parts of the self, the passions could now be regarded as resources for life rather than threats to virtue. Books discussed them, like Thomas Wright's *Passions of the Mind in General* (1601). Works on rhetoric naturally took a special interest in the subject, and its importance was reflected in the popularity of lyric poetry, mostly inspired by erotic passion. Montaigne envisaged the soul itself as a bundle of passions. For the Venetian Paolo Paruta, passion was prior to intellect, and reason could at most only regulate it.

Traditional condemnation of the passions receded. Hooker attacked want of feeling, and Burton rejected Stoicism because the passions were "natural, and not to be resisted." Montaigne condemned the Stoic view of pity as "a vicious passion," and was skeptical of the impassivity attributed to the younger Cato, Socrates, and Lucretius. "For all his wisdom," he insisted, "the [Stoic] sage is still a man: what is there more vulnerable, more wretched, and more null? Wisdom does not overcome our natural limitations." Bérulle opposed Stoicism on the same ground. Hobbes went further; for him fear and desire, those bugbears of Stoicism, were essential to thought, which was the child and servant of desire. The feelings were central to the spirituality of the age, as the sermons of Donne and a host of Puritan divines attest. This was often the case with Catholics too. The Jesuit Louis Coudret was pleased that many "wept during [his] sermon as a result of the divine message penetrating their hearts." "Let us speak the language of the heart, bathed in sweetness and love," wrote St. John of the Cross.

The positive view of will and the passions was paralleled by respect for the body, traditionally viewed with distrust as rebellious to reason and enslaved to passion. Montaigne denounced "that inhuman wisdom" that would make us enemies of the body, and defended its "natural pleasures" as gifts of God. Burton paid tribute to the "admirable art and harmony" of its composition and was opposed to such mortifications of the flesh as fasting; he also defended as "good and lawful things honest disports, pleasures and recreations . . . feasts, mirth, musick, hawking, hunting, singing, dancing," all created by God for human use. There may also be a hint of respect for the body in Jesuit opposition to the inclusion of *castrati* in the choir of the Sistine Chapel in Rome. The representation of male genitalia in Renaissance nudes, and more specifically the sexuality of the infant Jesus, also suggests some departure from traditional distrust of sex, long considered only a function of the body.

The senses had often been distrusted because of their location in the body, and because they were variable and bound to earthly things. They now grew in esteem. This was especially true of sight and hearing. With the support of Aristotle, who had disputed Plato's notion of appearances as only deceptions, sight had already become, in common opinion, the noblest of the senses, though still perhaps the most dangerous. Hooker described sight as "the liveliest and the most apprehensive sense of all other" and as basic to memory, "farre more easie and durable than the memorie of speech can be." Montaigne thought it the pleasantest of the senses. That it could be used to dramatize power was evident at court, where being seen was crucial to the courtier, just as a ruler was expected to dazzle beholders.

But sight was the primary sense for a deeper reason: because light, which can be perceived only by the eye, was identified with knowledge, long commonly understood as "enlightenment." Bacon made the most of the conception. Having noted that the first work of creation was "the light of sense"—the last being "the light of reason"—he proclaimed the aim of the great project described in his *Novum Organum* as "the kindling of light in the darkness of philosophy." He concluded his description of the project with a prayer: "Therefore do thou, O Father, who gavest the visible light as the first fruits of creation, and didst breathe into the face of man the intellectual light as the crown and consummation thereof, guard and protect this work, which coming from thy goodness returneth to thy glory.[4] It is no coincidence that optics was a major concern of scientists in the period, which saw the development of both the telescope and the microscope. Pascal marveled at their revelation of both the largest and smallest things in nature.

At the same time the imagination, which had previously received little attention, was being celebrated. But appreciation of it had some way to go. Traditionally and etymologically, it was the faculty of "imaging," considered dangerous unless tied by memory to the real world God had created; liberated from such constraints, imagination seemed a blasphemous effort to rival the Creator. It still had this significance for the late scholastic scientist Pedro Fonseca. For others, imagination was dangerous. Even the enlightened physician Johann Weyer blamed witchcraft on a deluded imagination. In the dedication of his massive work *On the Deceptions of Demons* (1583), he argued that "witches can harm no one through the most malicious will or the ugliest exorcism, that rather their imagination . . . makes them only fancy that they have caused all sorts of evil." But eventually, as clarity and distinctness became guarantors of truth, visual metaphors—images—would be central to philosophy. For Descartes, imagination would be indispensable to cognition.

Meanwhile the liberation of the senses and the imagination stimulated the flowering of the visual arts, painting and perspective, cartography, mystical visions, and literature. Shakespeare's Prospero used it in *The Tempest* to change and enslave others; and while its power was clear in *A Midsummer Night's Dream*, its uses were ambiguous:

The lunatic, the lover and the poet
Are of imagination all compact.

But Shakespeare put it to his own uses in the choruses of *Henry V*, which call on the audience to "imagine" scenes or events offstage. Montaigne discovered in retirement the pleasures of imagination.

The satisfactions of hearing, as the achievements of this period in music attest, were also celebrated, stimulated too by Protestant emphasis on hearing the Word. It was thought to have an advantage over sight, which was confined to surfaces, whereas sound could penetrate to the depths of things and reach the heart. Meanwhile the new science had demonstrated that the eye, according to which the sun goes around the earth, gave no sufficient access to the truth of things. The ear was also more important than the eye for theater; audiences went, as it was commonly put, to *hear* rather than to *see* a play. Jonson (though Sidney and Spenser still insisted on the primacy of the eye) ranked hearing above seeing; and discussions in the Venetian Accademia degli Incogniti, so important, as already noted, for the origins of opera, tended to agree. Early Florentine musicologists studied ancient musical texts and developed a new theoretical understanding of music; and from Florence the musical art spread rapidly. Burton knew as well as Shakespeare that music was a specific for melancholy, and Monteverdi deliberately aimed to move the passions. Music was also being combined with dance, the auditory with the visual, in ballet and court masques. It was also prized by religious groups; though less positively regarded for worship by Calvinists, it was of major importance for Catholics, Lutherans, and Anglicans. Hooker praised music as "a thing which delighteth all ages and beseemeth all states, a thinge as seasonable in griefe as in joy." He also thought it a powerful element in the moral life, for good or ill, because of its "admirable facilitie" to

> expresse and represent the minde more inwardlie then any other sensible meane the verie standinge rising and fallinge, the verie stepes and inflections everie way, the turnes and varieties of all passions whereunto the mind is subject; yea so to imitate them, that whether it resemble unto us the same state wherein our mindes alreadie are or a cleane contrarie, wee are not more contentedlie by the one confirmed then changed and led away to the other. In harmonie the verie image and character even of vertue and vice is perceivde, the minde delighted

with theire resemblances and brought by havinge them often iterated into a love of the thinges themselves.

But "for which cause," he added darkly, "there is nothinge more contagious and pestilent then some kindes of harmonie." The warning was necessary because of its effect "even in that verie parte of man which is most divine."[5]

These cultural achievements went hand in hand with the development of a conception of *human* creativity. This was shocking because, in the traditional view, the only true creator is God; human art was limited to the imitation of nature, God's creation. But now, as in Sidney's *Apologie for Poetry* (1580), we encounter views, aided by Platonism, close to the notion of full human creativity. Sidney argued that divine inspiration aided the poet to *transcend* nature:

> Only the Poet, disdayning to be tied to any such subjection [to nature], lifted up with the vigor of his owne inuention, dooth growe in effect another nature, in making things either better than Nature bringeth forth, or, quite a newe, formes such as neuer were in Nature. . . . so as hee goeth hand in hand with Nature, not inclosed within the narrow warrant of her guifts, but freely ranging onely within the Zodiack of his owne wit. Nature neuer set forth the earth in so rich tapistry as diuers Poets haue done, neither with plesant riuers, fruitful trees, sweet smelling flowers, nor whatsoeuer els may make the too much loued earth more louely. Her world is brasen, the Poets only deliuer a golden.[6]

The mimetic conception of art was broadening out.

The possibility of human creativity was also suggested by the creation story in the first chapter of Genesis; the creation of human beings in God's image implied that they, like God, could perhaps also create, possibly even *ex nihilo*. The painter Federigo Zuccaro employed the conception in his *Idea of Painters, Sculptors, and Architects* (1607):

> Because of His goodness and to show in a small replica the excellence of His divine art, [God] having created man in His image and likeness with respect to the soul, endowing it with an immaterial, incorruptible substance and the powers of thinking and willing, with which man could rise above and command all the other creatures of the World except the Angel and be almost a second God, He wished to grant him

the ability to form in himself an inner intellectual design; so that by means of it he could know all the creatures and could form in himself a new world . . . so that with this Design, almost imitating God and vying with Nature, he could produce an infinite number of artificial things resembling natural ones, and by means of painting and sculpture make new Paradises visible on earth.[7]

Francesco Patrizi described the poet as "a maker of the marvelous in verse . . . of the marvelous in language." Julius Caesar Scaliger maintained that poetry "fashions images more beautiful than the reality of those things which are, as well as images of things which are not. . . . [It does not seem], as in the case of other arts, to narrate things like an actor, but like another God to produce the things themselves." "There are two creators," Tasso proclaimed, "God and the poet." The French poet Agrippa d'Aubigné declared that he had stolen his own powers of invention, like Prometheus, from God. Montaigne neatly turned the tables on philosophy by suggesting that philosophy itself, which had traditionally claimed to mirror nature, was no more than a human artifact, its conceptions "created by each man's imaginative genius, not by the power of his knowledge." Philosophy, he concluded, "is but sophisticated poetry." This, of course, was hardly to deny its value.

While Zuccaro hinted that human creativity might be capable of undoing the fall, other writers saw in it more clearly human possibilities. The poet Giambattista Marino aimed to give pleasure by his capacity to astonish the reader with extravagant descriptions. "Let him who cannot amaze work the stables," he suggested. Meanwhile Vincenzo Galilei, father of the scientist, wanted to divorce music from theology and metaphysics, linking it to rhetoric as a purely human art, a notion important for the first experiments with opera at the Medici court.

For Sidney, poetry could delight but it was also an assertion of human freedom, since the poet ranges "only within the zodiac of his own wit." Other artists were also attracted by the freedom implicit in human creativity. Giovanni Battista Guarini, noting the analogy of poetry with oratory, pleaded for the liberation of literature from fixed rules. Cervantes advocated freedom in literature from the rules of the ancients, arguing that "Time changes everything and betters Art." Poetic creation was d'Aubigné's way of asserting himself against the rigidities of Calvinism.

Thus a sense was growing of the originality and individuality of human artifacts. If the best art is simply the most successful imitation of nature, it might be argued that works of art would ideally be identical. But the changing conception of human being now suggested that works of art, as human creations, might be as various as human beings themselves. Thus an even broader corollary of the individuality of human beings was the variety of everything in existence. Here, perhaps, nominalism made some contribution to esthetics. Nothing, any longer, could be seen as a particular expression of an eternal idea or archetype.

The uses of imagination were not, however, confined to the arts. Hooker assigned it a major role in Christian spirituality. "The minde," he remarked, "while wee are in this present life, whether it contemplate, meditate, deliberate, or howsoever exercise it selfe, worketh nothinge without continuall recourse unto imagination the onlie storehowse of witt and peculiar chaire of memorie." But imagination also enforced the significance of ritual gestures such as signing the cross, an act by which that mysterious unity, the self, participates fully in worship:

> Seeing that our weakenes while wee are in this present world doth neede towardes spirituall duties the helpe even of corporall furtherances, and that by reason of naturall intercorse betwene the highest and the lowest powers of mans minde in all actions, his phancie or imagination, carryinge in it that speciall note of rememberance than which there is nothinge more forcible, where either too weake or too stronge a conceipt of infamie and disgrace might do great harme, standeth allwaies readie to putt forth a kind of necessarie helpinge hand, wee are in that respect to acknowlidg the good and profitable use of this ceremonie.[8]

Here the imagination is the bond of unity among the previously discrete higher and lower faculties of the personality, and worship itself depends on the new conception of the self.

This more positive view of imagination, as a highly individual activity of the self, was accompanied by a growing inwardness that, as already noted, helps to explain the new popularity of Augustine's *Confessions*, the influence of which has been discerned in the willingness of Montaigne, Descartes, and Pascal to write in the first person. Reading, and what Burton called "the incurable itch to write" in "this scribbling age," also contributed to awareness of the individual self. Humanists since Petrarch had studied the classics as reflections of distinctive personalities; Petrarch had been concerned with the individuality of his own style; and Montaigne now carried to an extreme this tendency to individuation. For Montaigne, the goal of writing was self-understanding and self-acceptance; for others, it would be self-perfection or individual responsibility for what had traditionally been considered a function of community. Calvinist spirituality regularly began with a review of the self, and Foxe's martyrs had made their own desperate and individual choices. Sarpi emphasized personal responsibility in religious matters; only after strenuous efforts to make his own decisions, he argued, could the individual shift responsibility to superior authority. Private judgment thus took precedence over obedience. Anglicans, though the Book of Common Prayer was intended to promote community, insisted that the "unlearned" should personally understand its prayers. Such tendencies were carried over into secular thought. For Descartes, intellectual activity, though leading to universal truths, had in the first instance to be private and individual.

Various elements in the liberation of human being were gathered together in the characteristically Renaissance conception of man's creation in God's image and likeness, a common theme of Renaissance humanism and one notably shared by the Society of Jesus. Freedom of the will was an important element in this and was often seen as enduring after the fall. It was thought to be expressed both in human creativity and in service to others, for which Christ supplied the perfect model. The learned physician Laurent Joubert included the human body among the traces of the divine image, arguing on this ground for its proper care. The influence of the conception has also been discerned in the glorification of secular rulers, as in the paintings of Rubens. Kepler regarded his scientific work as a way of expressing God's image, and Galileo, a man of more than one culture, came close to it in his *Dialogue Concerning the Two Chief World Systems*, in which one of the participants lists those "marvelous inventions men have discovered" that had long figured in humanist discussions of the divine image: painting, music, architecture, navigation, and literature.

Nor was this idea always gender-specific. The new conception of the self, the supposed inferiority of women having been closely connected to their association with the body, was potentially important for their promotion to equality with men. Some Renaissance feminists, among them Guillaume Postel, argued for the dignity of women on the ground that they too possessed such "male" characteristics as reason. Luis de Leon, confessor to St. Teresa, insisted that women too had been created in God's image. He honored her as a saint, although he thought God's working so conspicuously through a woman paradoxical, and Teresa herself maintained a traditional humility about her sex. Nevertheless, the positive treatment of women in the fiction of Sidney, who had been surrounded since his birth by educated women, suggested new possibilities for feminine dignity.

The conception of human being described in this chapter had major consequences for most aspects of the culture of the period. It was connected—both as stimulus and consequence—to the period's historicism, its scientific discoveries, its social and political arrangements, and, perhaps most obviously, its political and religious attitudes. The dethronement of reason also reshaped what it could mean for human beings to "know" something, the subject of the next chapter.

CHAPTER THREE

The Liberation of Knowing

Traditionally, reason, as the highest human faculty, had been the primary instrument of knowledge, useful for every kind of truth except for the religious truths revealed in the Bible. These last had a higher source and were not fully accessible to reason, although reason was often considered valuable for expounding the meaning of Scripture; and the writings of classical antiquity were profoundly respected for the natural reason they were thought to incorporate. But confidence in knowledge obtained in this way had been seriously undermined by the Renaissance dethronement of reason. The result was a general crisis of knowing that came to a head in the period of this study and that encouraged a search for more reliable kinds of knowledge.

Books remained a major vehicle of knowledge, preserving and transmitting it as in the past, their importance increased by the Catholic and Protestant Reformations, which had called for reform by returning to the origins of Christianity as recorded in Scripture and in the writings of the ancient church fathers. This reinforced a persistent and growing dependence on books. "To be at leisure without books is another Hell, & to be buried alive," wrote Burton. Even his knowledge of sexual attraction, one element in his melancholy, came from books.

But books were now being read somewhat differently. Medieval thinkers, though inclined to see the various schools of ancient philosophy as representing successive stages in the development of a coherent body of wisdom, had recognized disagreements among them and employed reason to determine which was correct. By the later sixteenth century, scholars were able increasingly to identify conflicts among the various schools of ancient philosophy, and some humanists read the classics less as sources of timeless truth than as revelations of individual personalities and of their own times. Montaigne approached the ancients out of a "particular curiosity to know their souls and genuine opinions"; he enjoyed the gossipy "lives and fortunes" of the philosophers in Diogenes Laertius as much as—in a telling phrase—"the diversity of their doctrines and fancies." Francesco Patrizi identified ten successive schools of Aristotelianism, and Burton noted differing perceptions even of Socrates in antiquity. Thus the old idealization of the ancient world as the source of all truth was giving way to selective appreciation of the ancients based on the personal preferences of readers. Montaigne ridiculed the common practice, taught in schoolrooms (including those in which he had been a pupil), of accumulating passages from ancient texts on particular subjects in what were known as commonplace books. These, for Montaigne, were "hardly useful except for commonplace subjects," serving only "to show us off, not to guide us."

It was increasingly difficult to consider any ancient (much less a modern) author as authoritative. A reader now, for Montaigne, should "pass everything through a sieve, and lodge nothing in his head on mere authority and trust; let not Aristotle's principles be [first] principles to him, any more than those of the Stoics and Epicureans." Following this rule, he found Plutarch and Seneca to his taste but dismissed much of Cicero as windy and boring. He drew on the classics, he claimed, chiefly to express better what was already in his own mind. Under these conditions the authority of knowledge conveyed by books came under growing attack, especially from thinkers aware of the new science. In a letter to Kepler in 1610, Galileo attacked their opponents for treating the knowledge of nature as though it could be transmitted in "a book, like the *Aeneid* or the *Odyssey*." Kepler attacked the Rosicrucian Robert Fludd for relying on the ancients rather than "the natural order." Bacon thought it showed "a feeble mind to grant so much to authors."

Sometimes thinkers went further, their confidence in ancient wisdom weakened by recalling that those who represented it were not only pagans but sinners. "Women are bad, and men worse," wrote Burton, "no difference at all betwixt their and our times." Bacon took a dim view of the Greek philosophers, whom he compared to boys "prompt to prattle, who cannot generate, for their wisdom abounds in words but is barren of works." On this ground he described "the entire class" of philosophers as "Sophists," the only difference being that the Sophists of antiquity had been "wandering and mercenary, going about from town to town, putting up their wisdom for sale, and taking a price for it," while those of his own day were "more pompous and dignified, as composed of men who had fixed abodes, and who opened schools and taught their philosophy without reward." Descartes rejected ancient authority entirely, opposing to it the authority of reason itself.

There were growing doubts, indeed, about the capacity of words, the stuff of books, to mirror reality. It was increasingly common to oppose "things" to "words," as in Shakespeare's "What's in a name?" Montaigne, that master of words, professed to prefer things: "Fie on the eloquence that leaves us craving itself, not things!" Opponents in polemical exchanges regularly charged each other with using words without substance. Bodin attacked Roman lawyers for disputing "in schoolboy fashion over words and trivia." Campanella criticized Pico della Mirandola for philosophizing "more in words than in Nature." Even Burton claimed to "respect matter, not words." Language was losing its supposed correspondence to reality; as a sign it increasingly seemed conventional and arbitrary. Indeed, signification increasingly seemed arbitrary in many areas. Ignatius Loyola's famous "Rule for Thinking with the Church," which called on his followers to agree that black is white and white black if so instructed by the church, was, among other things, a rejection of language. For many Protestants, Christ was no longer truly present in the Eucharist, which had become simply a sign.

Widespread translation from one language to another also destabilized language and contributed to a growing awareness of linguistic drift. Montaigne, while recognizing its growth in expressive power, noted how language "slips out of our hands every day, and has halfway changed since I have been alive." Mulcaster saw languages as living organisms that develop, are gradually perfected, and finally decay. Claudio Tolomei provided a purely historical account of language as early as 1555. Inventions since antiquity such as mechanical timepieces, navigational devices, gunpowder, and the printing press required names, further suggesting the human and conventional character of language.

Although new words troubled conservatives, they were defended by others. "They that will haue no newe woordes devised where there is want," wrote one, "seme not well to consider howe speach groweth, or wherefore it was devised by man: For names are not giuen unto things afore the things themselves be inuented. Therfor olde names will not serve to make new deuises knowen." A suggestive parallel is provided by the shift at about the same time from precious metal as the basis for the value of money to value determined by government fiat, i.e., arbitrarily.

Montaigne summarized the point. "The name is a sound which designates and signifies the thing," he wrote; "the name is not a part of the thing or of the substance, it is an extraneous piece attached to the thing and outside of it." Unlike some of his contemporaries, he was little troubled by this; like Rabelais, he exploited the vagaries of language—its failure to mirror reality—to open up possibilities of paradox, irony, and humor. On the other hand he was aware of inconveniences in this development, blaming it for "most of the occasions for the troubles of the world." Galileo took the problem very seriously; he reprimanded a critic of his views on sunspots on the ground that "names and attributes must be accommodated to the essence of things, and not the essence to the names, since things come first." Bacon saw words as "but the images of matter," so that "to fall in love with them is all one as to fall in love with a picture." For the essayist Sir William Cornwallis, words were "but clothes; matters substance." It was increasingly clear not only that truths can be conveyed in any language, but also that truth is itself largely a function of language. Hobbes would conclude that understanding is "nothing else, but conception caused by Speech." This pointed to the modern recognition that human beings create meaning through language.

It is hardly surprising that the scholastic mode of demonstration, so completely dependent on language, was under attack. Galileo represented his opponents as men who "retire into their studies and glance through an index and a table of contents to see whether Aristotle has said anything about them; and, being assured of the true sense of the text, consider that nothing else can be known." Bacon criticized logic as "not nearly subtle enough to deal with nature; and in attempting what it cannot master, [it] has done more to establish and perpetuate error than to show the way to truth."

The loosening of language from things had major consequences. It implied that one expressive language is as good as another, a belief that played some role in the gradual substitution for Latin of the vernaculars. But most importantly it contributed to a growing skepticism that found ancient authority in the *Outlines of Pyrrhonism* of Sextus Empiricus, first published for a Renaissance audience in 1562. It was also favored by the developing awareness, driven by the increasingly intensive scrutiny of ancient texts, of disagreements among ancient philosophy. Augustine's view of classical philosophy as a "city of discord" now took on new authority. To this were added the religious controversies of the period, in which opposing sides were often less likely to win others over than to induce doubts about all truth claims. Protestants and Catholics, as Stephen Greenblatt put it, "demonstrated brilliantly how each other's religion—the very anchor of reality for millions of souls—was a cunning theatrical illusion, a demonic fantasy, a piece of poetry." The dogmatism of each side generated skepticism on the other.

Meanwhile nominalist reservations about the value of reason were sup-plemented by the concern of humanist schoolmasters to improve both the minds and expressive skills of their pupils by staging debates (in Latin) on both sides of stock questions. Montaigne showed the results of such train-ing in many of his essays. "There is much to be said," he wrote, "on all matters, both for and against," and "there is no reason that does not have its opposite." Bacon could also argue, in the jargon of schools, *in utramque partem* (on both sides).

Nevertheless, it should be emphasized that the skepticism developed under these conditions was not necessarily inconsistent with Christian belief; indeed, it strengthened a perennial tendency to base Christianity on faith rather than reason: faith in the promises of Scripture for Protestants, in the teachings of the church for Catholics. Ecclesiastical authority on both sides often encouraged the rejection of reason. For Montaigne, the basis of skepticism was honesty and humility in the presence of a faith that "pre-sents man naked and empty, acknowledging his natural weakness, fit to receive from above some outside power; stripped of human knowledge, and all the more apt to lodge divine knowledge in himself, annihilating his judgment to make more room for faith."

Montaigne's *Essays*, immediately popular everywhere, were understood to be making a strong case for skepticism. Planted in him by his education, this tendency in his thought was strengthened by his detestation of the dog-matism accompanying the religious wars; because of them, he complained, "we are not allowed *not* to know what we do not know." "Is it not better," he asked, "to remain in suspense than to entangle yourself in the many errors that the human fancy has produced? Is it not better to suspend your conviction than to get mixed up in these seditious divisions?" For him, the insurmountable limitations of the human condition and "the consciousness of our ignorance and weakness" severely restrict what can be known. He thought skepticism the only plausible philosophy for "a living, thinking, rea-soning man," not least because it permits the enjoyment of "all natural plea-sures and comforts," the employment and use of all "bodily and spiritual faculties in regular and upright fashion." Skepticism was well accommo-dated to the new, more holistic conception of human being.

Montaigne was notably skeptical of the new science; but he had no more confidence in the old. And though professing loyalty to Catholicism, he also doubted reports of miracles; he did not believe in witchcraft; he challenged the notion of an immutable law of nature; he denied the possibility of objective knowledge of anything. In all these matters he professed to follow Augustine.

A more coherent exposition of Montaigne's skepticism was provided by Pierre Charron's *On Wisdom* (1601). Charron was a devout priest who attacked scholastic theology for its reliance on rational demonstration and championed fideism against atheism. "Let us accept the 'very learned ignorance' of Nicholas of Cusa," he wrote: "let us say with Dionysius the Areopagite and Augustine: *melius scitur nesciendo*. This admission of ignorance is the finest of religious acts." There was now, he observed, "no opinion held by all or current in all places, none that is not debated and disputed, that has not another quite contrary to it held and maintained." A more systematic defense of skepticism was provided by Francisco Sanchez, a professor at Toulouse and author of *Quod nihil scitur* (1581), which argued against Aristotle that words can provide no knowledge of things. Bodin, in a work he prudently chose not to publish, argued that the more one wishes to know and the more carefully one inspects minute details, the more one realizes that one does not know.

Skepticism can be discerned in many places. There are hints of it in major scientists, occasionally overwhelmed by the difficulties of their work. Kepler admitted that God had expressed himself "not directly, clearly, limpedly," but in a way that compels human inquirers to enter "labyrinths of meaning." Galileo, hardly an extremist, denounced "the vain presumption of understanding everything" as the equivalent of "never understanding anything," and cited Socrates, "who knew how little he knew," as a model. Sarpi doubted the ability of the human mind to penetrate to anything beyond the surfaces of things, and was especially dubious about the possibility of understanding human affairs. Italy was widely known as a hotbed of skepticism.

England also harbored skeptics. Puritans often doubted everything but Scripture; William Perkins insisted on the limits of all knowledge. Although Bacon was more confident about sense perception than about reason, he emphasized the limits of all knowledge, seeing the mind as an untrustworthy mirror. Sidney's friend Fulke Greville made the point strongly. "What then," he asked rhetorically, "are all these humane Arts, and lights, But seas of errors?" Burton believed that "God in his providence, to check our presumptuous inquisition, wraps up all things in uncertainty." Marlowe's Faustus, his learning useless, bound himself to the devil, and Shakespeare's protagonists are often full of doubts: lovers, lunatics and poets, in their "shaping fantasies," he suggested, apprehend "more than cool reason."

From skepticism it was a short step to relativism, which owed much to the new astronomy but was ultimately rooted in Augustine's reservations

about classical culture. It was also implicit in the subjectivity and historicism of Renaissance humanism. Problems that arose in translating works
originating in one culture into the language of another and the growing
sense of authorial identity—reflected in dedications of books claiming that
whatever truths they contained were not universal but unique inventions of
the author—only aggravated the tendency further.

Montaigne, himself a lawyer, although doubting everything else, had no
doubts about the workings of his own mind and concluded that truth was
relative to his own conception of it and that it might even vary from moment
to moment. The most common error in the world, he suggested, was the
universalization of one's own perceptions of reality. "It seems to each man,"
he wrote, "that the ruling pattern of nature is in him; to this he refers all
other forms as to a touchstone. The ways that do not square with his are
counterfeit and artificial. What brutish stupidity!" He noted the variety of
opinion—and therefore its relativity—among other things on manners,
wealth, and ideas of feminine beauty. He also insisted on the relativity of
the notion of "civilization":

> Each man calls barbarism whatever is not his own practice; for indeed
> it seems we have no other test of truth and reason than the example
> and pattern of the opinions and customs of the country we live in.
> *There* is always the perfect religion, the perfect government, the perfect
> and accomplished manners in all things. [Opinion alone] gives value
> to things. . . . Purchase gives value to the diamond, and difficulty to
> virtue, and pain to piety, and harshness to medicine.

All of this, he observed, complicated but also pointed to the importance of
self-knowledge, individual and collective, in human relations.

Humanistic legal scholarship in France during this period was
demonstrating the relativity of Roman law, earlier believed to reflect eternal
principles of justice, to the particular needs of ancient Rome, thereby
casting doubt on its applicability to contemporary Europe. François
Hotman's *Anti-Tribonian* (1567) argued that every polity is unique, "often
changing according to the seasons, and the mutation of the manners and
condition of a people." Hotman concluded that French law should reflect
the particularities of France. Étienne Pasquier's *Recherches de la France* also
emphasized the diversity among bodies of law resulting from the "diversity
of manners that arises in people according to the diversity of regions and
environment." One of the protagonists in Bodin's *Colloquium* argued for the
relativity of custom, giving as an example the role of dance in worship. Sarpi

emphasized in his *History of the Council of Trent* the relativity of laws and institutions to local conditions, noting even that morality varies according to the needs of societies. Burton suggested that "our writings, are as so many dishes, our readers guests, our books like beauty, that which one admires, the other rejects; so are we approved as men's fancies are inclined." Even Hooker, ever practical, noted that laws must be adapted to particular circumstances. Hamlet would assert that "there's nothing either good or bad, but thinking makes it so," and similar tendencies have been noted in the Spanish dramatist Lope de Vega. These tendencies reached a climax in Hobbes's argument that good and evil are defined by societies in whatever way suits them.

Relativism also led to attacks on systematic philosophy. Like Augustine, Montaigne pointed to the disputations among philosophers as evidence of their "meanness of spirit" and the uselessness of their subject; they merely "exchanged one word for another often more unknown." Sarpi held that the proper function of philosophy was to destroy the delusion that concepts must correspond to realities. "A thing conceived," he wrote, "does not necessarily exist."

These objections were serious enough; even more so was Montaigne's charge of the irrelevance of philosophy to life. Like Hamlet, he thought Stoicism useless for comfort. Its weakness was especially apparent in its dualism. "Philosophy is very childish," he charged, "when she gets up on her hind legs and preaches to us that it is a barbarous alliance to marry the divine with the earthly, the reasonable with the unreasonable, the severe with the indulgent, the honorable with the dishonorable," or again "that sensual pleasure is a brutish thing unworthy of being enjoyed by a wise man; that the only pleasure he derives from the enjoyment of a beautiful young wife is the pleasure in his consciousness of doing the right thing, like putting on his boots for a useful ride." Sarpi agreed that philosophy could only lead to false conceptions of life.

The whole philosophical tradition was included in this indictment, but Montaigne particularly abhorred scholasticism, which relied heavily on logic, and which he considered useless and pedantic. Learning, he insisted, should serve the active life. Bacon condemned it on similar grounds; dealing with "the first principles of things and the highest generalities of nature," it could do "little for the welfare of mankind; whereas utility and the means of working result entirely from things intermediate." Montaigne, who deplored—though he also loved and collected—useless knowledge, noted that all the wisdom of the ancients could not make them happy, or his own contemporaries virtuous. "A hundred students have already caught syphilis," he charged, "before they came to Aristotle's lesson on temperance." "It is a strange fact," he mused again, "that things have come to such a pass in our century that philosophy, even with people of understanding, should be an empty and fantastic name, a thing of no use and no value, both in common opinion and in fact."

Scholasticism was particularly attacked for its servile Aristotelianism. The Accademia dei Lincei was notably hostile to the latter; Prince Federico Cesi, its founder, proposed "to fight Aristotelianism all the way." Galileo attacked "Peripatetics who go about philosophizing without any desire to learn the truth," and found it remarkable "that we attempt to learn from Aristotle that which he neither knew nor could find out." Pedro Ibanez, the spiritual advisor of St. Teresa, thought scholastic theology destructive of spiritual things. Burton agreed. "How man doth it puzzle!" he exclaimed: "what fruitless questions about the Trinity, Resurrection, Election, Predestination, Reprobation, Hell-Fire, &c!" Bacon dismissed scholastic science as "fantastical and ill defined."

The attack was sometimes extended to all formal philosophy. Sarpi thought a systematic approach to any author, even Aristotle, Plato, Aquinas, or Scotus, "pedantic, neither serving knowledge or improving the mind, but rather making for subtlety, ostentation, and stubborn pertinacity." Aristotle himself drew special attack as a symbol of rigidity and the closed mind. The University of Padua, though it had its Aristotelians, was a bastion of anti-Aristotelianism. Major French thinkers attacked his influence in religion. Montaigne thought him "the prince of dogmatists," so obscure as to represent skepticism "in an affirmative form." Galileo believed him "more intent on arriving at a goal previously established in his mind than on going wherever his steps directly lead him." One of Galileo's admirers condemned Aristotle's work as "a litigious piece of writing which, after two thousand years of interpretation, is still not understood even by those philosophers who have sworn to believe what it dictates." Bacon considered him the supreme instance of human pride and attacked his concern with words to the exclusion of things. Galileo ridiculed his disciples as "humble slaves" nourished from infancy to believe that to philosophize consists only in making

> a comprehensive survey of Aristotle, that from divers passages they may quickly collect and throw together a great number of solutions to any proposed problem . . . as if this great book of the universe had been written to be read by nobody but Aristotle, and his eyes had been destined to see for all posterity.[1]

Another critic loathed the Aristotelians because "the discovery of a falsity in a book revered by them does not seem less of a sacrilege than burning down a temple." To Bacon, Aristotelian scientists,

> knowing little history either of nature or time, did out of no great quantity of matter and infinite agitation of wit spin out those laborious webs of learning which are extant in their books. For the wit and mind of man, if it work upon matter, which is the contemplation of the creatures of God, worketh according to the stuff, and is limited thereby, but if it work upon itself, as the spider worketh his web, then it is endless, and brings forth indeed cobwebs of learning, admirable for the fineness of thread and work, but of no substance or profit. . . . Instead of a fruitful womb for the use and benefit of man's life, they end in monstrous altercations and barking questions.[2]

Hobbes asked, "When men write whole volumes of such stuffe, are they not Mad or intend to make others so?"

Others opposed Aristotelianism because it failed to take human existence seriously. For Burton, "School Divinity" was "a labyrinth of inextricable questions, unprofitable contentions, incredible folly." This being so, he lamented, "what shall become of humanity?" Others were dismayed by Aristotle's paganism, especially because of his belief in the eternity of the universe, which contradicted the biblical doctrine of creation; the inhabitants of Campanella's City of the Sun opposed him for this reason. His chaplain, William Rawley, quoted Bacon as saying that Aristotle's philosophy was "only strong for disputations and contentions, but barren of the production of works for the benefit of the life of man." Bacon was especially opposed to Aristotle's subordination of man to nature; for him, nature existed for man.

Many thinkers not only rejected Aristotelianism but now doubted the possibility of any methodical or systematic knowledge; and this had major consequences, central among them a kind of practical nominalism. Bacon attacked all systems of thought in his indictment of the idols of the Market Place and of the Theater, by which he meant philosophical systems. "In my judgment," he wrote, "all the received systems are but so many stage plays, representing worlds of their own creation after an unreal and scenic fashion." He praised Protestantism for having eschewed systems like those that "in great variety flourished among the Greeks"; and, himself a lawyer, he opposed any but a chronological arrangement of laws. Montaigne, as already noted another lawyer, held much the same view. He admitted, as a matter of faith, that, given God's infinite wisdom, all existence must be "good and ordinary and regular"; but "we do not see its arrangement and relationship." Human knowledge is limited to "detached pieces." These might be arranged and harmonized by art, but he doubted the ability even of art to impose order on nature, which to human eyes is "complex, minute, and accidental." This was why Montaigne could only write essays, taking "the first subject chance offers." Pascal too denied that nature had an intelligible order; its truths were all "independent of one another," and only "our art" could bring them together. "But this," he concluded, "is not natural. Each keeps its own place." Sarpi, who resisted system at every level—in science, in politics, in religion, in law, in philosophy—made the point more generally: membership in a category, he observed, is not a quality inherent in anything; each thing is simply what it is. This explained why particular problems were soluble but disputations about the general and universal were meaningless. Order, in this perspective, was no more than a human construct. The histories written in this period, including Sarpi's, illustrate in their particularity the age's nominalist mind-set. Paolo Paruta, too, not only discerned no general patterns in history but rejected the feasibility of imitating ancient models, pointing in this way to a new kind of historicism based on the uniqueness of each event, each moment.

Thus thinkers of this period, no longer able to rely on the wisdom of the ancients, less confident of reason, and disoriented by linguistic change, were desperately concerned to find other, more dependable ways of knowing. Montaigne's *Que sais-je?* (What do I know?) was a troubled rather than a rhetorical question, and it drove him to look within himself for an answer; Puritans found certainties in Scripture. The judicious Hooker emphasized varieties in knowing: revelation for mysteries beyond the reach of reason, the senses for the needs of this life, but reason still on more obscure matters. "The truth is," he declared, though not without a hint of doubt, "that the mind of man desireth evermore to knowe the truth according to the most infallible certainety which the nature of thinges can yield."

Montaigne was unusual in his pessimism about human knowledge of any kind; but others still sought it, though now in various places. Hooker, for whom all knowledge was precious, insisted that to reject the possibility of knowledge "were to injurie even God himselfe, who being that light which none can approch unto, hath sent out these lights whereof we are capable, even as so many sparks resembling the bright fountain from which they rise." Galileo looked beyond the "eccentrics, deferents, equants, epicycles, and the like" of the "mathematical astronomers" for "real, actual, and distinct things" and "the true constitution of the universe." Bacon, although "the state of knowledge" was neither "prosperous nor greatly advancing," was convinced "that a way must be opened for the human understanding entirely different from any hitherto known," in order not just "to guess and divine, but to discover and know."

Even the yearning for certainty could now seem dangerous. Burton denounced it as the cause of the fall in Eden, still a source of torment, and found it especially reprehensible in theologians. Hobbes thought it responsible for the disposition of men both "to believe lyes, and tell them." Driven by necessity, the legal profession was beginning to discriminate among degrees of certainty. And the yearning for certainty was an important element in the legitimation of curiosity, traditionally condemned as a sin and evidence of insufficient faith. Montaigne, for whom the whole world was "a school of inquiry," considered it a major task of education to instill "an honest curiosity to inquire into all things, whatever is unusual." "A spirited mind," he wrote, doubtless meaning his own, "never stops within itself. Its pursuits are boundless and without form; its food is wonder." Guillaume Du Bartas and Maurice Scève praised curiosity in their poetry. Curiosity was behind the growing numbers of collections of (literally) wonder-full objects from around the world. Books describing wonders, such as Pliny's *Natural History*, went through many editions. The surgeon Ambroise Paré published a book of *Monsters and Marvels* (1573), which described, with illustrations, monstrous births. Curiosity also figured positively among the shepherds of Arcadia idealized by Guarini. Campanella thought the Chinese inferior to Europeans because they lacked it: they seemed not men but like worms born inside a cheese, "who reckon nothing more nor better in the world beyond their own cheese from which they are nourished, sustained, hidden, or as worms born in man's stomach who know nothing of man, nor his mind, cocooned away, not wanting to be disturbed." "Stick your head out beyond your cheese," he exhorted them.[3] Burton was delighted with his knowledge, even of "the secretes of the Heavens and of Nature, and the order of the universe," which give "greater happiness and pleasure than any mortal can think or expect to obtain." Hobbes, in a passage exploiting the old equation of knowledge with sexual intimacy, identified that "Lust of the mind" which gives a "delight in the continuall and indefatigable generation of Knowledge" as a major difference between men and animals; this, he believed not only led to belief in God but "exceedeth the short vehemence of any carnall Pleasure."

But no satisfactory foundation for certainty yet proposed had achieved general acceptance. One result of its absence was the making of lists of only vaguely comparable items, such as Montaigne often composed. Another was the writing of "essays" and other works consisting of essentially unrelated miscellanies, reflections without context. The *Mémoires-Généraux* of the French lawyer Pierre de l'Estoile suggest an undiscriminating compulsion to record anything and everything. For many, the problem of ordering knowledge had become insoluble.

The problem, nevertheless, was taken seriously. Montaigne appealed to habit and custom, which he interpreted as sources of practical knowledge for ordinary people, more effective in real life than the self-conscious knowledge of intellectuals. His chief criterion of truth was utilitarian: the true was the useful. "If a man were wise," he argued, "he would set the true price of each thing according as it was most useful and appropriate for his life." He maintained that reason was a mockery unless it aimed at contentment. "The sum of its labors," he concluded, "must tend to make us live well and at our ease." Conversely, he professed to despise "useless" speculation; it was "the bane of our condition that often what appears to our imagination as most true does not appear as most useful for life." The most useless disciplines, he thought, because largely speculative, were "astrology, law, dialectic, and geometry." Here he claimed to be on the side of Cicero and Socrates; actually he was closer to Petrarch and Erasmus. Hooker was not far from this position, arguing that "the generall and perpetuall voyce of men is as the sentence of God him selfe. For that which all men have at all times learned, nature her selfe must needes have taught; and God being the author of nature, her voyce is but his instrument."

Arguments from utility figured prominently in political and religious discourse. To justify various secular arrangements Hooker appealed to their practical value rather than to cosmic order or even Scripture; on this basis he argued for the distinctive dress and superior wealth of those whose authority was necessary for social order. For Sarpi, the primary use of the mind was practical; Galileo, whose interests were often as much technological as theoretical, emphasized the utility of mathematics in architecture, painting, and military engineering. For Bacon, truth and utility were one; science was not "an opinion to be held, but a work to be done." He proposed to mobilize learning, like a general, for use, and called on humankind "to join in consultation for the common good." Even Hooker, however much he respected "reason," was less concerned to define it than to describe what it could do. Hobbes, as in so much else, would bring the utilitarian approach to reason to a climax. "The Light of humane minds is Perspicuous Words," he wrote. "Reason is the *pace*; Encrease of *Science* the Way; and the Benefit of man-kind the *end*." With this concern for the practicality of knowledge humanist emphasis on the active life was reaching its peak. Montaigne characteristically made the point in personal terms. "If I study," he wrote, "I seek only the learning that treats of the knowledge of myself, and instructs me how to die well and to live well." He relished the old story of the stargazer who stumbled over an obstacle in his path. Learning, as Bacon wrote, "if it be severed from charity and not referred to the good of men and mankind, it hath rather a sounding and unworthy glory, than a meriting and substantial virtue." It was "a true account of the gift of reason" that it should "contribute to the benefit and use of men." Such practical reason would produce a sense of proportion about oneself, reduction of the fear of death through acquaintance with mortality, the imprint of goodness and the general enlargement of the mind. The Venetian circle around Sarpi, which was reading Bacon, believed strongly in the practical uses of scholarship. In France, scholarly lawyers like Pasquier and Pithou searched for evidence of the rights of the crown and the autonomy of the Gallican church. Rome was a center for scholarship useful to support papal claims. Protestants were making similar use of scholarship. The Calvinists François Baudouin—later converted to Catholicism—and Isaac Casaubon studied the ancient church as a model for present-day reform. Most Puritans in both old and New England believed strongly in learning as an adjunct to theology.

More surprising was a growing tendency to argue for Christianity, in the manner of Machiavelli, on the ground of its utility in this world rather than its truth. Hooker sometimes did this. "The verie worldlie peace and prosperitie," he argued, "the secular happiness, the temporall and naturall good estate both of all men and of all dominions hangeth chieflie upon religion." Montaigne too noted the practical and political value of piety, a point that may have been important in his own life. "It is easy to discern," he observed, "that some sects have rather followed truth, others utility, whereby the latter have gained credit." To be sure, he believed in the truth as well as the utility of Christianity, but he might have learned from Augustine that such arguments were dangerous.

Other thinkers were searching for ways of knowing consistent with the new conception of human being, in which so much more than reason was involved. Among these was knowledge through material things, obtained by the senses, that could take into consideration impressions of the world that might be surrounded with affect, as with the reports of André Thevet concerning the New World. Thevet's truth-claims were based on his having *seen* the amazingly "new and strange things" of Brazil, which, as he wrote of the stars over the southern hemisphere, he "never would have come to know even after listening for ten years to a doctor laboring over an astrolabe or a globe." Such empiricism would play a major role in the scientific thought of the age.

These attitudes pointed to a growing interest in ordinary experience, ordinary people, and the details of daily life, which was facilitated by the fact that such matters could now be expressed in ordinary language. This interest too had large implications for what it meant to know. Protestants in large numbers insisted on the priesthood of all believers, i.e., of ordinary people; and Hooker emphasized the ethical significance of "the daylie affairs of this life." Many Catholics, following François de Sales, rejected the spiritual elitism implicit in withdrawal from the world, choosing to live their faith in ordinary life.

Even physics, long preoccupied with loftier matters, tended increasingly to deal with objects observable in everyday life, and the origins of modern technology have been traced to growing interest in the practical arts. Tasso praised the practical order kept by a mother in the household. Jonson, for all his classicism, celebrated the ordinary in detail:

> Room, room, make room for the bouncing belly,
> First father of sauce, and deviser of jelly,
> Prime master of arts, and the giver of wit,
> That found out the excellent engine, the spit,
> The plow, and the flail, the mill, and the hopper,
> The hutch, and the bolter, the furnace, and copper,
> The oven, the bavin, the mawkin, the peel,
> The hearth, and the range, the dog, and the wheel.[4]

Dutch painters were giving an unusual glow to scenes of daily life; and in literature the novel, a genre largely devoted to ordinary life, was now emerging.

Montaigne demonstrated the possibility of expressing serious thought in the language of ordinary people in his essays, in which, as he claimed, any topic, even a fly, might be "equally fertile" for his purposes. Claiming to be himself "one of the common sort," he elaborated on the disadvantages of greatness. In his *Essays*, he wrote, he had "set forth a humble and inglorious life." But this was no insignificant subject, because "you can tie up all moral philosophy with a common and private life just as well as with a life of richer stuff." Thus he admired Socrates, not—as had generally been the case previously—as a source of heavenly wisdom but as a model for earthly life; the mouth of Socrates, he pointed out, was "full of nothing but carters, joiners, cobblers, and masons" and of "inductions and similes drawn from the commonest and best-known actions of men." Montaigne idealized the lives of ordinary people; "a hundred artisans, a hundred plowmen, [are] wiser and happier" than university rectors. He loved travel because it exposed him to novelty. It was no accident that his final essay concluded with an attack on the extraordinary.

Montaigne was not alone in his taste for variety. Paruta celebrated the variety among people. Bodin noted it among animals, climates, ways of life, and cities. Burton thought it therapeutic to experience the variety of places and fashions. Marguerite of Navarre loved variety in flowers: "The more diversified our bouquet, the handsomer it will be." The *Icon animarum* of the French-born Scotsman John Barclay, popular in both France and England, was an extended discussion of the variety of things. The variety of books now available delighted Sir Philip Sidney. Hooker praised the diversity of creation, particularly in the polities and ceremonies in Christendom. The rich collected rare and precious objects that reflected the variety in the world.

This taste encouraged a tendency to mix materials from different cultures and systems of thought. Such eclecticism had long been characteristic of Renaissance humanism; rhetoricians regularly combined, for purposes of persuasion, a fundamental skepticism with Stoic, Aristotelian, and Platonic material. Stoicism and Neoplatonism were both popular partly because of their eclecticism. This did not mean, however, that the intellectual products of the age were generally no more than a hodgepodge of disparate ideas; the better authors usually sought to make their own whatever they appropriated. Burton wrote of his borrowings: "The matter is theirs most part, and yet mine, whence it is taken appears, yet it appears as something different from what 'tis taken from." The philosopher Omer Talon explained his own eclecticism:

If there is anything in the writings of Plato that suits and is useful to me, I accept it; if there is anything good in the gardens of Epicurus, I do not despise it; if Aristotle purveys something better, I accept it; if the merchandise of Zeno is more vendable than that of Aristotle, I abandon Aristotle to give myself to Zeno; if everything sold in the shops of the philosophers is vaine and useless, I buy nothing at all.[5]

The Reformation in England drew at once on Catholic tradition and various writings of Erasmus, Luther, Calvin, and Zwingli. The varied resources of Western culture presented themselves as a tempting feast from which, careless of the risks of indigestion, one could choose whatever looked appetizing.

The presence of heterogeneous materials pointing in quite different directions strengthened a tendency to paradox already central to Erasmus's praise of folly as ultimate wisdom. Paradoxical proverbs like *festina lente* (make haste slowly) were popular. Montaigne reveled in the anomalies and paradoxes of human existence. As he remarked of his own writing, "It may be that I contradict myself, but the truth I never contradict." For all his alleged rationalism, Hooker gloried in the paradoxes of Christianity. As he proclaimed in a sermon, "The very center of Christian beliefe, the life and soul of the Gospell of Christ doth rest in this, that by ignominye, honour and glory is obtained; power vanguished by imbecillitie; and by death salvation purchased." Paradox was not merely decorative but central to English Metaphysical poetry.

Burton had been nourished by *The Praise of Folly* and identified himself, as an observer of the human scene, with Democritus, known in antiquity as the laughing philosopher. He also noted that we tend only to laugh at the folly of others, though he confessed that he was "as foolish, as mad as any one." Jonson's *Everyman in His Humor* was another anatomy of human folly. In Spain, *Don Quixote* might be described as an extended praise, in an Erasmian sense, of folly.

Knowledge was thus surrounded by a host of problems: problems intensified by the need to digest vast amounts of new knowledge, the result at once of historical and philological scholarship, of geographical discoveries, and of advances in science. These developments will be discussed in the next three chapters.

CHAPTER FOUR

The Liberation of Time

Traditional culture had recognized two kinds of time. The more significant was sacred time, which was ultimately biblical; in this conception time was linear and goal-directed. It had begun with God's creation of the world, had moved through a series of divinely directed events recorded in the Scriptures, culminated in the appearance of Jesus, and was now seen as advancing toward a climax: the end of the world, an event awaited by some with joy but by most with dread as the time of judgment. For the righteous it would culminate in eternal union with God, but ecclesiastical authority discouraged speculation about when this would occur because it was both unknowable and disturbing.

The other kind of time was secular, a legacy of classical antiquity. It was not linear but cyclical and repetitive. It reflected the regular movements of the heavenly bodies, and consisted of endless cycles in which all things mature, decay and perish, like human life itself. In this conception only the heavens were perfect and immutable, but change ruled the earth, the place of decay and corruption. Only in the short run was progress discernible here, and it would soon be reversed; hope for an earthly future was inconceivable for either individuals or societies. Unusual events might be recorded in chronological order in the form of annals, but this way of dealing with the past excluded the mysteries that had perplexed Augustine in the *Confessions* and did not encourage reflection.

History, in this perspective, could be only a record of the rise and fall of kingdoms and empires, and was chiefly of interest because the deeds of the ancients exemplified perennial virtues and vices. Machiavelli's description of the natural cycle of governments was based on this conception, and Bodin incorporated it with some changes in emphasis:

> Once the commonwealth has come into existence, if it is well ordered, it can secure itself against external enemies or internal disorders. Little

by little it grows in strength till it reaches the height of its perfection. But the uncertainty and mutability of human affairs make it impossible that this pre-eminence should last long. Great states often fall suddenly from their own weight. Some are destroyed by the violence of their enemies at the very moment when they feel themselves most secure. Others decay slowly and are brought to their ends by internal causes. As a general rule the most famous commonwealths suffer the greatest changes.[1]

Change, he concluded, "happens to all things in the ordinary course of nature." The Venetians, to be sure, whistling amidst the dark realities of modern politics, tried to believe that Venice would endure without change to the end of time, but Bodin thought this impossible.

Given these conceptions, time and change had for centuries seemed of little significance. But this had begun to alter with the emergence of towns, in which time was increasingly measured and valued for a variety of human uses, a process facilitated by the development of mechanical clocks after the twelfth century. Time was increasingly seen as a resource, open-ended and linear rather than cyclical, to be utilized, hoarded, treasured. Under these conditions middle-class families could set long-range goals for their descendants. For Montaigne, in his declining years increasingly aware of its passage, time was an inestimable good, to be prized, effectively used, and enjoyed even in old age. The Protestant rejection of special holy days was largely based on the belief that they wasted a precious, God-given resource. Much of the vitality of the new culture was based on a recognition of the value of time. Galileo directly challenged the traditional conception. In his *Dialogue*, Sagredo exclaims, "I cannot without great astonishment hear it attributed, as a prime perfection and nobility of the natural and integral bodies of the universe, that they are invariant, immutable, inalterable, etc., while on the other hand it is called a great imperfection to be alterable, generable, mutable, etc." Galileo identified change with life itself, shrewdly attributing prejudice against it to the fear of death.

Recognition of change in the heavens was closely related to a growing consciousness of change in human affairs, which nourished a novel historical perspective central to humanism. The intensive study of ancient culture by humanists had revealed not only that its supposedly perennial values had in fact changed over time, but above all that a great gulf had intervened between the supposed glories of antiquity and the present. By comparison with antiquity, their own time seemed a "dark age" of barbarism. Important, too, was the rhetorical principle of decorum, which held that discourse should be appropriate not only to its intended audience but also to its time. This pointed to the recognition that language was not a vehicle of eternal truths but reflected its time and place. Politically active groups, notably including lawyers, gradually absorbed the new historical perspective this implied. The eminent scholar-lawyer John Selden criticized on this basis England's chief justice, Sir Edward Coke, for his static view of the English constitution.

Change was not always regarded positively; it was often accompanied by apprehension and a sense of loss. Religious reformers contributed to the fear of change by emphasizing that it had brought decay to the church; this is why, for decades, reform could only mean return to the past, a circumstance reflected in the backward-looking prefix in such words as reform, renaissance, and a host of others.

But meanwhile a growing eagerness for "news" suggested that change need not always be frightening, attributed to imperfection in nature, or dismissed as the meaningless work of fortune. Interesting events were first called "news" in the sixteenth century, which also saw the earliest newspapers. News bulletins began to circulate throughout Europe. "It is always good to find out something new," wrote an early Spanish purveyor of news. Burton professed to deplore this attitude but testified to its intensity. "Men's nature," he wrote, "is still desirous of news, variety, delights; and our wandering affections are so irregular in this kind, that they must change, though it be for the worst." Indeed, he gathered news himself, every day and of every kind, describing its varieties with telling exuberance. Venice, as a center of international commerce, was considered a good place for news; Bodin located his *Colloquium* there as the best place for "easy access to anything new or worthy of note anywhere in the world by means of letters from friends." Sarpi, on the other hand, thought Paris the best source of news. "The things that happen in that most noble kingdom and in that great city," he wrote a colleague, "deserve to be received for the instruction of everybody."

Novelty was also celebrated in other ways. Bacon gave to a major work the title *Novum Organum* (New Instrument), presumably to attract readers. He applauded innovation. "Surely every medicine is an innovation," he wrote, "and he that will not apply new remedies must expect new evils; for time is the greatest innovator. . . . they that reverence too much old times, are but a scorn to the new." He thought that the "arts and sciences should be like mines, where the noise of new works and further advances is heard on every side." Galileo promoted his own discoveries partly on the ground of their "entirely unexpected and novel character." The Jesuit schools, for all their classicism, encouraged interest in novelties. An English school-master boasted that he had "no feare of noveltie."

Less orthodox figures had their own reasons to rejoice in change. Bruno remarked on his own "great desire to see new customs" that would enable him "to meet intelligent men, and to acquire, if possible, some new truth." For Campanella, the new would "always endure and must thus not be feared." Interest in geographical discoveries opened up a "new" world, a term that often suggested deficiencies in the old.

The attractions of the new knowledge did not necessarily exclude appreciation for the old. The Erasmian Juan Luis Vives, still an authority on education, had insisted on the utility of both. "Even knowledge of that which has been changed is useful," he began judiciously:

> whether you recall something of the past to guide you in what would be useful in your own case, or whether you apply something which formerly was managed in such and such a way, and so adapt the same or a similar method to your own actions, as the case may fit. *Indeed, there is nothing of the ancients so worn out by age and so decayed, that it may not in some measure be accommodated to our ways of life.* For although now we may employ a different form, the usefulness yet remains.[2]

Hooker was worried lest the past be forgotten; he wrote his *Laws of Ecclesiastical Polity* so that "posteritie may know we have not loosely through silence permitted things to passe away as in a dreame." But a tension persisted for centuries between traditional and ancient learning.

A positive response to change meanwhile stimulated a concern to make the stream of events intelligible, more friendly and useful in the present. The later Renaissance remembered, preserved, resuscitated, and re-created the past; and as this occurred, succession in time began to replace hierarchy as a means of organizing many kinds of knowledge. Histories for diverse audiences and purposes—not always strictly historical—proliferated, as Sidney reported, somewhat condescendingly:

> For the method of writing history, Bodin hath written at large; you may read him, and gather out of many words some matter. . . . [In narrative history] you have principally to note the examples of virtue of vice, with their good or evil successes, the establishment or ruins of great states, with their causes. . . . Besides this, the historian makes himself a discourser for profit, yea, a poet, sometimes, for ornament:

an orator, in making excellent orations which are to be marked, but marked with the note of rhetorical remembrances; a poet in painting forth the effects, the motions, the whisperings of the people, which though in disputation one might say were true, yet who will mark them well shall find them taste of a poetical vein, and in that kind are gallantly to be marked, for perchance though they were not so, yet it is enough they might be so.[3]

There was still, in Sidney's understanding of history, more than a trace of the moralism that had been central to its traditional uses. Bodin had reacted against this. "Although," he argued, "many think that the praise of good and the vituperation of evil are among the advantages of history, this service can be performed more truthfully and better by philosophers, whose particular function it is, than by historians." Burton took a dim view of contemporary historians, seeing them as partisan or as parasitical pedants.

But some historians were concerned to make their work more accurate, for cultivated readers were increasingly dissatisfied with unsupported assertions, bloody and romantic events, and extensive reliance on older works. William Camden, historian of Elizabeth's reign and the first English writer to use the phrase "Middle Ages," complained of the obscurity of the earliest histories of Britain, though he also recognized the difficulty of getting things right. "Who is so skilful," he asked, "as in this dark ocean of antiquity to struggle with time without splitting on the rocks?"

But Camden participated in a general advancement of historical knowledge. Bodin dared to correct ancient authority on points of fact in his *Method for the Easy Comprehension of History*: the notion of method in such matters was itself symptomatic. Progress in philology facilitated the study of antiquity, both classical and biblical; and knowledge of the Jewish and Christian past was deepened by the study of non-biblical writings and better patristic texts. Postel in France and Bedwell and Selden in England studied Arabic and other Near Eastern languages. The historical-philological work of Hugo Grotius was especially advanced; his *Annotations on the Old and New Testaments* discerned parallels between practices described in Scripture and those of pagan peoples. Previously obscure ancient texts were opened up by Isaac Casaubon.

The importance of chronology was increasingly recognized. As Bodin wrote, "Those who think they can understand histories without chronology are as much in error as those who wish to escape the windings of a labyrinth without a guide." J.J. Scaliger, another Frenchman, established modern methods in chronology in his *De emendatione temporum* (1583). These advances made it easier for scholars, following in the footsteps of Lorenzo Valla, to identify anachronisms. History was beginning to emerge as a discipline, and chairs in the subject were created at the universities of Leiden and Göttingen. Historians began to see their work, no longer subordinate to ethics or politics, as a quasi-scientific enterprise.

Some historians sought to offer learned and responsible narratives of events, and truth began to take precedence over rhetoric. History, for Bodin, was simply "the true narration of events," and he thought it impossible "to give pleasure as well as to impart the truth." Montaigne distrusted rhetorical history because it aimed at persuasion rather than truth; he also doubted the relevance of ancient experience to his own time. This did not exclude the possibility that history might be useful, but that it should be truthful was demanded on every side. As Francesco Patrizi put it in his *Ten Dialogues on History* (1560), histories provided two values, truth and utility; but the author took care to put truth first. Sarpi claimed to think nothing more important for reforming the church than a true account of its past. His opponent Baronius professed to agree; they differed only on what was true. Camden informed his readers that "the love of truth" was the "only Scope and Aim" of his history of Elizabeth; removing its truth would be "nothing else but to pluck out the Eyes of the beautifullest Creature in the World; and, in stead of wholesome Liquor, to offer a Drought of Poison to the Readers Minds." He had guaranteed its truth by inserting nothing of his own. Bodin argued not only that a good historian should "be free from all bias," but that he should "rid himself of all feeling." Don Quixote piously declared history to be "like sacred writing, for it has to be truthful; and where the truth is, in so far as it is the truth, there God is." Ben Jonson paid tribute to the achievements of truth-seeking scholars, whom he often cited:

> What fables have you vext! what truth redeem'd!
> Antiquities search'd! opinions dis-esteem'd!
> Impostures branded! and Authorities urg'd!
> What blots and errours, have you watch'd and purg'd
> Records, and Authors of! Innovations Spide!
> Sought out the Fountaines, Sources, Creekes, paths, wayes,
> And noted the beginnings and decayes![4]

Some historians now ceased to invent speeches in the ancient manner. "Unless they be the very same *verbatim* or else abbreviated," Camden declared, "I have not medled withall, much less coined them of mine own

Head." Selden followed the same principle in his studies of medieval law:
"I vent to you nothing quoted at second hand," he wrote, "but ever lov'd
the Fountain, and when I could come at it, used that Medium only, which
would not at all, or at least, deceive by Refraction." Sarpi and Baronius, to
be sure, both used sources to confirm rather than to establish their positions, but they also quoted at length from archival materials, thus emphasizing the link between argument and evidence.

Many of these figures were lawyer-historians concerned to establish the
legitimacy, against a traditional universalism promoted by both imperial and
ecclesiastical Rome, of the laws and institutions of particular states. In
France as in England, lawyers saw that both law and history were concerned
with origins, precedents, and the evaluation of evidence discoverable
through investigation. It was also increasingly recognized that knowledge
of the law was inseparable from knowledge of its history. As François
Baudouin observed in 1561, "Historical studies must be placed upon a
solid foundation of law, and jurisprudence must be joined to history."

French lawyers studied Roman, but also feudal and customary law.
Though insisting on their loyalty to Catholicism, they looked to history for
evidence of the "Gallican liberties" establishing the autonomy of the
French church in order to justify resistance to the decrees of Trent. Clovis
and Charlemagne, not the pope, they claimed, had founded the French
church. Gallican writers also argued that the papal state had originated in
the gifts of Pepin and Charlemagne, rather than in the Donation of Constantine. Jacques Leschassier's *Treatise on the Ancient and Canonical Liberty
of the Gallican Church* (1606) studied the ancient and medieval councils and
canons of the church, presenting the autonomy of the French church as a
model for the general reform of Catholicism. But the richest product of
French legal historiography, perhaps because less contentious, was the
Recherches de France of Étienne Pasquier, a compilation of sources for
French medieval history published in a series of volumes after 1560.
Pasquier's historical perspective nourished an almost organic conception of
culture and institutions:

Any man of understanding, without acquaintance with the complete
history of a people, can almost imagine its overall temper when he
studies its ancient statutes and ordinances; and by the same token can
make a sound conjecture about what its laws must have been by looking
at its manner of life. For to speak truthfully, well-ordered laws in any
country form a habitude of manners and morals among those subject

to them, which over the long run appears to be imprinted on them by the disposition of their nature.[5]

Though, as Gallicanism suggested, scholars sometimes depended on myths of their own, they were also distinguishing more and more clearly between history and myth. In his *Commentaries on Civil Law* (1557), the lawyer François Connan attacked the venerable notion of a golden age in the remote past, in which he saw only "the rule of lusts, factions, evils, seditions, plunderings, war, and an absence of equity and justice." The various founding myths attributing the origins of peoples to wandering ancients, usually refugees from Troy, also came under attack. Although historical myths always die hard, the Trojan origin of the French and English monarchies was increasingly contested. Thus, in a set of notes on Michael Drayton's poetic representations of the English past incorporating mythical material, Selden declared that much here was no more believable than Ariosto's *Orlando Furioso*, Spenser's *Faerie Queene*, or "Rabelais his strange discoveries"; he went on to attack "the whole chaos of Mythic invention." In Rome, Bellarmine, and Baronius himself (though sidestepping the issue in his Ecclesiastical *Annals*), were doubtful about the authenticity of the Donation of Constantine. But the tendency to cling to a mythical legacy about the past would remain strong in later centuries, as in our time.

Under these conditions it was increasingly difficult to accept classical testimony uncritically. Montaigne eventually denied altogether the relevance of ancient experience to the present. Prolonged familiarity with the classics could breed, if not contempt, at least disillusionment, as in the case of Burton's estimate of the sages of antiquity:

Their actions, opinions, in general, were so prodigious, absurd, ridiculous, which they broached and maintained; their books and elaborate treatises were full of dotage. Writers generally rave in their books, their lives being opposite to their words, they commended poverty to others, and were most covetous themselves, extolled love and peace, and yet persecuted one another with virulent hate and malice. They could give precepts for verse and prose, but not a man of them could moderate his affections. Their musick did shew us tearful measures, & how to rise and fall, but they could not so contain themselves as in adversity not to make a lamentable tone. They will measure ground by geometry, set down limits, divide and subdivide, but cannot prescribe what is proper for a man, or keep within compass of reason and discretion. They can square circles, but understand not the state of their own souls; describe right lines and crooked, &c, but know not what is right in this life.[6]

Jonson, classicist though he was, rejected the monopoly of truth by the ancients; and Shakespeare in his history plays, far from idealizing antiquity, read into it all the faults of Elizabethan England.

Bacon was particularly scornful of received wisdom. It was, in his view, "barren of works, full of questions; in point of enlargement slow and languid, carrying a show of perfection in the whole, but in the parts ill filled up; in selection popular and unsatisfactory even to those who propound them; and therefore fenced round and set forth with sundry artifices." The beginning of wisdom, it seemed to him, foreshadowing Descartes, was "purging and sweeping and leveling the floor" of his mind. It was necessary to make a new beginning.

Along with doubts about the wisdom of antiquity went tendencies to question even the political achievement of Rome. Bodin denied that there had been only four monarchies, held that the empire of Charlemagne had been greater than any in the past, and added to the old list of empires the more recent ones of the Arabs, Portuguese, Spaniards, and Turks. Meanwhile the survival of Venice for so many centuries, when no ancient polity had survived so long, provided another basis for questioning the superiority of antiquity.

Thus a major element in the concern to identify change was a growing historical perspective on antiquity. This had already found expression in earlier humanism with the recognition that the ancient past was not only remote but also significantly different from the present, that its lessons for the present were limited, and that, for better or for worse, a new age had dawned. Peter Ramus attached particular importance to the fall of Constantinople for sending Byzantine scholars into exile in the West, and thus in an important sense ending European continuity with antiquity. The result, for him, had been a sudden "divine light of new times and new letters." This vision, however doubtful, was the source of a new myth.

This sense of discontinuity lay behind Montaigne's rejection of applying ancient words to things of his own time. "In our century," he declared, we "unworthily assign the most glorious surnames of antiquity to whomever we think fit." Thus "divine," which may have been appropriate for Plato, or "great" for ancient rulers, was "fantastic" when applied to Aretino or modern rulers. Montaigne was suggesting here his disdain for the present, but behind this were deeper problems about understanding the past that formed another element in the skepticism of the age. How, he asked, exploiting his judicial experience, could historians presume to

> be responsible for the thoughts of persons unknown and give their conjectures as coin of the realm? Of complicated actions that happen in their presence they would refuse to give testimony if placed under oath by a judge; and they know no man so intimately that they would undertake to answer fully for his intentions.[7]

The new perspective on antiquity was brought sharply into focus by Pierre de Larivey in 1611:

> I know well that many only care for *antiquity*, which they esteem so highly that they would like to locate it in heaven and condemn all those who are not like them and are not of their opinion. Others, since ages differ from one another and today the same things are no longer used as twenty years ago, believe that modern comedies should not be like those of sixteen hundred years ago or more, our lives not being like theirs. They say that in Greece or Rome people used another language, another way of life, other customs, other laws, and—which matters more—a religion entirely contrary to our Catholic Christianity.[8]

Political history still made up the bulk of historical writing; even the work of Baronius was essentially a political and institutional history of the church. Camden insisted that "affairs of war and policy" were the proper subjects of history. This was why Giovanni Botero and others still praised history for the education of princes. But political history was now less concerned with the virtues and defects of individuals than with the development of states, with politics rather than ethics. Bodin thought political experience necessary to evaluate the past. The change from rulers to states also found expression in a growing shift from universal history to the histories of particular polities, a change that made Sir Walter Ralegh's *History of the World* (1614) seem rather old-fashioned. The republican Gianmichele Bruto, like Machiavelli before him, stuck to Florence, whose history he depicted as a tragic decline into despotism and a warning to other republics. Bacon's *History of the Reign of Henry VII* stressed the value of history for statecraft as exhibited in a particular case.

The major center for general reflection about history was Padua, where the central figure was Francesco Patrizi, author of a series of dialogues *On*

History (1560). Defining history as the narrative of past actions, Patrizi emphasized, like Machiavelli, attention to change and practical utility, contrasting history in this respect with philosophy. As he has the future doge of Venice, Leonardo Donà, observe, philosophy depends on universals and teaches by reason, history on particulars and by experience. Patrizi also emphasized the value of skepticism in dealing with sources, noting that testimony about the past is always shaped by a point of view.

But the most substantial product of Venetian-Paduan historiography was Paolo Sarpi's *History of the Council of Trent*, first published—because of its anti-papal bias—in London in 1619. Sarpi's view of the past was notable for its rejection of the myth of the primitive church as a changeless model for all time, although his work was shaped by a myth of his own that cast the papacy since antiquity in a malevolent role. Instead of looking to "fortune" to explain events otherwise mysterious, like Machiavelli, Sarpi saw history as a continuously unfolding process that had to be explained by evidence and in terms of the possibilities of this world. He recognized the difficulties in historical explanation but nevertheless insisted that "something can be said"; thus he described the corruption he discerned in the church as a gradual result of changing conditions, and Protestantism—contrary to the orthodoxies of Catholics and Protestants alike—not as the result of the malevolence or the genius of Luther, but of "causes more potent and recondite."

But history, for all its growing precision and sophistication, still retained a connection with rhetoric, especially because of the supposed educational value of history. Bodin thought that its universal accessibility made history ideal for pedagogy: it "needs the assistance of no tool, not even of letters, since by hearing alone, passed on from one to another, it may be given to posterity." Ralegh condemned contemporary statesmen for their ignorance of history, which was now exercising "all the wits of the world." The connection of history with rhetoric was also reflected in a continuing preoccupation with its formal qualities, to which a new genre of *artes historicae* gave much attention, though chiefly repeating ancient commonplaces. The concern with form had at least two advantages: it assigned to the historian an active and creative role in the composition of history, and it helped to make the past relevant to contemporaries. Much of Patrizi's discussion was essentially rhetorical, and Sarpi emphasized the historian's duty to select and shape his narrative. His *Council of Trent*, itself a masterpiece of forensic rhetoric, might be described as an extended set of rhetorical dialogues.

Meanwhile an increasing awareness of time and change brought growing numbers of readers to histories of every kind. Translations were widely available to those who lacked a classical education or foreign languages; in England, not only the major classical historians had been translated but also the histories of Machiavelli, Guicciardini, Sarpi, Commynes, and Bodin. Ralegh's *History of the World*, though formidably long, learned, and expensive, was widely read. The *History of His Own Time* of Jacques-Auguste de Thou (1604–08), though on the Index, was popular even in Rome. Sarpi's *Council of Trent* went through four Latin editions within a decade and was translated into German, French, English, and Italian. Bodin recognized the popularity of history by undertaking to guide its readers. One must understand, he wrote, "the use of each [history] and in what order and manner each ought to be read," and always read analytically in order to see "the cohesion of the whole and the parts in mutual harmony."

Much of the popularity of history reflected a growing national consciousness, as in the case of Camden's history of Elizabeth. The poet Pierre de Ronsard celebrated the French past in his *Franciade*, composed at the request of the king. As poetry, this illustrated Burton's view of histories as providing diversion: "Who is he," Burton asked,

> that is now wholly overcome with idleness, or otherwise involved in a labyrinth of worldly cares, troubles, and discontents, that will not be much lightened in his mind by reading of some enticing story, true or feigned, where (as in a glass) he shall observe what our forefathers have done, the beginnings, ruins, falls, periods of common-wealths, private men's actions displayed to the life, &tc.[9]

For Bacon, historians (along with poets) were "the best doctors" in the knowledge of human affairs, painting forth "with great life, how affections are kindled and incited, and how pacified and restrained . . . how they work, how they vary . . . how they are enwrapped, one within another . . . how to set affection against affection, and to master one by another, even as we use to hunt beast with beast." For Paruta, history revealed the complex and contradictory quality of experience, developed sophistication about the world, and, by facilitating comparison, stimulated self-knowledge. Montaigne described history as "everybody's business." Historians, he wrote, "are pleasant and easy; and at the same time man in general, the knowledge of whom I seek, appears in them more alive and entire than in any other place—the diversity and truth of his inner qualities in the mass and in detail, the variety of the ways he is put together, and the accidents that threaten him." History, in short, tells the truth about the human condition, no longer understood as an element in a systematic and coherent world-picture but in all its temporality, variety, and unpredictability. Its growing readership tells us something, therefore, about the general mentality of the age.

Its ability to reflect what was now widely perceived as the real world of human affairs also helps to explain the eagerness to exploit history by a variety of special interests. Not only Sarpi but Protestants too exploited history to discredit the papal church. Foxe's *Book of Martyrs* (1563) dealt with its subject within a larger conception of history, in which all those who had been treated as heretics by the papacy constituted a hidden church that had kept the true faith alive since antiquity. It also depicted the emperor Constantine, son of an English mother and ruler over the church in his time, as a predecessor of Queen Elizabeth. The *Magdeburg Centuries* (Basel, 1559–74), prepared under the direction of the Lutheran Matthias Flacius Illyricus, depicted the papacy as the tool of Antichrist over the centuries. It provoked, in response, both the *Ecclesiastical Annals* of Baronius (1588–1607) and Bellarmine's more theologically oriented *Controversies of the Christian Faith* (1586–93). During the same period various anti-papal groups within the Catholic fold were also turning to history to demonstrate the deep roots of their claims to autonomy. The interested motives behind such work did not prevent it from making real advances in historical understanding.

Many of the anti-papal historical writings discerned in the history of the church an alternation between periods of corruption and reform, unity and division, grandeur and decay, which retained something of the ancient cyclical conception of history. But, as Pasquier's work suggests, this was increasingly mingled with a vision of the past that points to the relativity of peoples, customs, and institutions to the peculiarities of time and place. Hooker reveals this historicism in his willingness to adapt "the lawes of Christ" to "such particularities as have the nature of thinges changeable according to the difference of times, places, persons, and other the like circumstances."

By the same token it was increasingly difficult for serious historians to see the hand of God in events. Montaigne, with heavy irony, doubted whether, because of the uncertainties of history, it befitted "a theologian, a philosopher, and such people of exquisite and exact conscience and prudence" to write histories; and Bodin criticized the universal history of Melanchthon for its preoccupation with "religion and piety" and attacked the traditional notion of the four monarchies that had long provided a framework for universal history. Hooker ridiculed the apocalyptic interpretation of Scripture by Puritans, and Shakespeare was providing human explanations for events in English history. Giacomo Aconcio's *On Method* (1558), though professing belief in providence, immediately set it aside in favor of examples of human prudence "in our private and public actions both in peace and war." Church history, even Christian beliefs, could now be treated as products of time and place rather than as timeless and universal. This was a profoundly troubling notion. Selden's *History of Tythes* (1618) displeased James I because it historicized an institution he considered changeless. Meanwhile other scholars were seeking the rational meanings they assumed to underlie pagan mythologies, though their explanations were sometimes as unlikely as the myths themselves.

Human beings were thus increasingly depicted as the makers of their own history. Here Hooker is of special interest, if only because his piety can hardly be doubted. He avoided the nostalgia that led many of his contemporaries to idealize the past, and he recognized the rule of change in earthly affairs. From this he concluded that laws, customs, and institutions must constantly be adjusted to differences in time and place. To adapt this view to Christian faith, he distinguished between an invisible church, which was immune to change, and a visible church, whose history, like other things of this world, was a matter of common experience, continuous with the past, to be sure, but, like a living organism, constantly adapting to change. Such views also supported humanist awareness of the discontinuity between the ancient and medieval past.

These developments in the understanding of the past reflected a growth in knowledge of many kinds that, imaginatively projected into the future, prepared the way for the emergence of the idea of progress. The point could be made modestly, as by the Puritan Robert Bolton, who cited the nice trope, already current in the Middle Ages, of contemporaries as dwarves sitting on the shoulders of giants and therefore able to see farther. Other thinkers emphasized particular advances. Montaigne recognized progress in learning through a process of trial and error. Bodin was even bolder, pointing to the growing knowledge both of nature and of new worlds across the seas, and to the printing press, which alone could "easily vie with all the discoveries of the ancients." Bacon believed that the moderns had surpassed the Greeks. He applauded "the increase and progress of systems and sciences," and advanced the paradoxical notion that the modern age was older and thus wiser than antiquity. Similar attitudes toward antiquity were developing among composers of music, aided perhaps by their ignorance of music in antiquity.

The notion of the superior knowledge of their own time was also developing among those less formally educated. Bernard Palissy, a surveyor and potter, declared in his *Most Worthy Discourses* (1580):

> Through practice I prove that the theories of many philosophers, even the most ancient and famous ones, are erroneous in many points. Anyone can ascertain this for himself by taking the trouble to visit my workshop. . . . I assure you, dear reader, that you will learn more about natural history from the facts contained in this book than you would learn in fifty years devoted to the study of the theories of the ancient philosophers.[10]

The spread of such views among the populace was probably at least as significant as the development of an idea of progress among the learned.

Galileo and Montaigne both anticipated Milton's belief that knowledge would continue to grow through freedom of debate. "Philosophy itself," Galileo declared in the person of Salviati, "cannot but benefit from our disputes, for if our conceptions prove true, new achievements will be made; if false, their rebuttal will further confirm the original doctrines." "No," he concluded, "save your concern for certain philosophers; come to their aid and defend them. As to science itself, it can only improve." Thus the ingredients were being assembled for new conceptions of time and history that challenged traditional notions both of eternal recurrence and of decline from an original perfection.

CHAPTER FIVE

The Liberation of Space

As we have seen in earlier chapters, the old conceptual modes that had ordered European thought were crumbling and giving way to new modes of understanding. Similar changes were at work too in the perception of space; the boundaries that had made it intelligible and relatively comfortable were also disappearing. This was going on in two areas. Most of the earth was being opened up and contact was being made with new and unfamiliar peoples and cultures. And at much the same time the traditional understanding of the earth's place in a finite and intelligible universe was challenged by a revolutionary and awesome new cosmology.

These new dimensions of space, earthly and cosmic, were often connected in the minds of contemporaries. Both explored what had previously been unknown, ignored boundaries previously surrounded with numinous awe, and vastly expanded the horizons of knowledge. Toralba, perhaps the wisest among Bodin's "seven sages," compared the investigation of "nature and its hidden causes" with voyaging to distant lands. Galileo thought "news" from Mexico analogous to "reports from the moon." And Burton, puzzled by disputes about cosmology, suggested that they were as difficult to understand as the discovery of America; in both cases, he reflected, God "reveals and conceals to whom and when he will." Bacon combined both kinds of discovery in his vision of a future decreed by providence. "The passing through or perambulation of the globe of the earth and air," he argued, together "increase or multiply the sciences" and so "were destined to occur in the same age and century." Bruno compared himself to Columbus; he had, in a different sphere, shown how

to ascend to the sky, compass the circumference of the stars, and leave . . . the convex surface of the firmament. [He had] freed the human mind and the knowledge shut up in the strait prison of the turbulent air, penetrated the sky, wandered among the stars, passed beyond the borders of the world, effaced the imaginary walls of the eighth, ninth, tenth, spheres.[1]

New Worlds

Among the "news" that fascinated Europeans, the discoveries of new worlds and peoples figured prominently. The peculiar expansiveness of Europe had been expressed earlier in the crusades, which popes still hoped to revive; this mentality had also been displayed in the late medieval missions to Asia. But the decisive phase of European expansion began with the fifteenth-century Portuguese expeditions down the African coast and eventually to India, followed by those of Columbus and others to what was commonly regarded as "the new world," a pregnant phrase especially for what it implied regarding Europe. The excitement generated by novel contacts with the non-European world was expressed in an oration by Loy Le Roy in 1559 celebrating the discovery "even of things unknown to the ancients—new seas, new lands, new species of men, new constellations."

The impulses behind the discoveries were mixed. Economic motives were clearly at work, but these were usually combined with others, political, religious, and cultural. The expedition to Brazil described by Jean de Léry drew support from both the French crown and Calvinist Geneva "to prepare a place for all those [French Protestants] who might wish to retire there to escape persecution . . . and even to bring the savages to the knowledge of their salvation." The Jesuits went all over the world as missionaries, notably to China, where they found much to admire. The erstwhile Jesuit Postel, excited by the new contacts of Europeans with peoples around the world, agitated for their conversion. The religious motive sometimes merged with that of a "civilizing" mission for Europe.

Travelers' accounts of the outside world were eagerly read by Europeans. The best of the new travel literature was collected in several volumes of *Navigations and Voyages* by the Venetian Gian Battista Ramusio, and in England by Richard Hakluyt and Samuel Purchas. There was also a steady market for atlases that could represent visually areas previously unknown, such as the *Theatrum orbis terrarum* (Antwerp, 1570) of Abraham Ortelius and Gerard Mercator's *Atlas* (Louvain, 1585–95). Maps circulated knowledge of areas previously unknown and gave Europe a sense of its own spatial identity in a larger world.

With this came a more general self-consciousness, one element in which was the sense that the non-European peoples had been discovered and the world conceptually united by the initiative of Europeans. Burton imagined himself surveying the whole earth from above, like a bird. The discoveries may have marked the beginning of European imperialism, but they also expressed a dynamic apparent in other aspects of European culture. As a result a wave of new products, new knowledge, and new words swept over Europe, stimulating openness, wonder, excitement, and imagination. For Bacon, "By the voyages and travels of these later times, so much more of nature has been discovered than was known at any former period" that he anticipated further discoveries and eventually mastery over all nature.

Curiosity, both cause and consequence of the discoveries and previously considered dangerous to the soul, was increasingly seen as a virtue. Hooker noted "the wounderful delight men have, some to visit forrein countries, to discover nations not heard of in former ages, we all to know affaires and dealings of other people, yea to be in a league of amitie with them." A Portuguese near-contemporary, Mendes Pinto, who published an account of his travels in Asia in 1614, described a fellow adventurer in China approvingly as "by nature a very curious person" so that "he decided to throw all caution to the wind." He was himself filled with amazement at the "wonders" of China: its huge cities, its administrative organization, its agricultural wealth, its temples and palaces. Europeans wanted to know what the natives of America looked like and were willing to pay for the information. John White's drawings of Indians, first published in 1590, went through seventeen editions in most European languages in the next thirty years; a number of American Indians were also brought back to France and exhibited to the curious. Private collections of exotic objects were a further tribute to curiosity. Montaigne still had some reservations about curiosity, except in himself. Curiosity reopened questions once considered settled. One was the cause of darker skins among exotic peoples, whether, as traditionally believed, because of Ham's sin against Noah, or by exposure to the sun in southern climates. Another was the origin of peoples in the New World. Léry, though admitting he might be wrong, thought they descended from Ham; Postel, from Japheth, the forefather of the peoples of Europe, though he was vague about his passage to the New World; Bruno, doubting that Adam and Eve had originated the whole human race, insisted on some altogether separate origin.

Travel literature often included legendary material and repeated such misunderstandings and distortions as had pervaded earlier accounts of the non-European world. But some European observers described as accurately as possible what they had seen. Léry took such care to observe the Indians of Brazil that he still seemed to see them before his eyes. But, he went on, "their gestures and expressions are so completely different from ours" that it was difficult "to represent them well by writing or by pictures." They inhabited a place where

> everything—the way of life of its inhabitants, the form of the animals, what the earth produces—is so unlike what we have in Europe, Asia, and Africa, that it may very well be called a "New World" with respect to us. . . . I have seen things as fantastic and prodigious as any of those—once thought incredible—that Pliny and others mention.[2]

In Mexico, although sufficiently horrified by their paganism to destroy their sacred books, the Franciscans eventually studied the languages of the natives, learned as much as they could about their customs and religion, and tried to educate the Spanish authorities about them. Matteo Ricci observed sophisticated China in much the same spirit during his thirty years of residence, travel, and association with Chinese intellectuals. He learned Chinese and studied Chinese customs, laws, and literature. Thus he could claim far more authority for his account of "this alien world" than earlier writers. The ideal of the objective observer, however deceptive it may have been, was also developing, another major consequence of contact with alien peoples.

Nevertheless, the New World was still of far less interest to most Europeans than the Near East, to whose antiquity they traced their own cultural origins. Postel's *République des Turcs* (1560) was something like a bestseller, as was the *Itinerary of Constantinople and Asia* (1581) by the imperial ambassador to Suleiman the Magnificent, Ogier de Busbecq. Nevertheless, the traditional sense that Christendom was altogether special was beginning to decline. Bodin saw Europeans as originating in a general movement and intermingling of peoples, all of whom, he wrote, "for a long time have been fused in repeated waves of migration" caused largely by variations in climate. At the same time the circumnavigation of the earth meant that the whole earth could now be represented by a globe that could be held in one's hands. So a young man, on receiving the gift of a globe from his father, remarked, "Before seeing it, I had not realized how small the world is": a reaction that would soon be intensified by the new cosmology. Another potential blow to the self-image of Europe was implicit in the eschatological hopes of some religious groups who looked forward, though sometimes fearfully, to the onset of a new age.

Meanwhile the reactions of Europeans, however seriously they tried to understand exotic peoples, were inevitably shaped by their familiar modes of thought. Léry called the vengefulness of his Indians "a fine example of the corrupt nature of man," pronounced the bats of America less dangerous than birds described by Ovid, and was reminded of Psalm 104 on God's hand in nature by the beauty and bounty of Brazil. The Spanish historian Francisco Lopez de Gomara modeled his account of Cortez's conquest of Mexico on Herodotus, and even the Indian convert Bernardino de Sahagun represented Aztec oratory as the "rhetoric, moral philosophy, and theology of the Mexican people." For Purchas (who had certainly never been there), the virgins who served in the temples of Mexico had "Abbesses," did "penance," and "rose at midnight to the Idols mattins." The Mexicans also had "High Priests or Popes" and "cloysters or Monasteries" "which they called Religious," for young men, whose "crowns were shaven, as the friars in these parts." The geographer Nathanael Carpenter compared the American Indians, who were "not yet reduced to civility," to the ancient Germans described by Tacitus.

Ricci often treated the Chinese in European terms. For him, a "chancellor" administered examinations in "philosophy" to candidates for bureaucratic positions, in an educational system that graduated "bachelors," "licentiates," and "doctors." He compared the eloquence of Chinese scholars to that of Isocrates. Mendes Pinto compared Chinese judges to Capuchins because of their austerity and incorruptibility, and identified a bronze monster as a "Lucifer." This sort of thinking could also be reversed: a Jesuit of the time tried to understand the spiritual needs of uneducated Italians by comparing them with the natives of America.

Some Europeans were concerned to protect native peoples against European rapacity; Mendes Pinto condemned the cruelty and hypocrisy of the Portuguese in East Asia. But the Indians of America aroused particular compassion. Jesuit theologians followed such earlier champions of the Indians as Francisco de Vitoria and Bartolomé de Las Casas in opposing their enslavement, which had been justified on the grounds that, lacking Christianity, they were "slaves by nature." For Bellarmine, "all men were equally created in God's image, with a mind and reason," and from this he concluded that Europeans had no rights over native peoples. Francisco de Suarez argued that the law of nature was written "in the minds and in the hearts even of the infidels." Montaigne attacked the greed and cruelty of the conquerors of Mexico and Peru, denouncing the destruction of "certain nations of the Indies" as "a monstrous and unheard of case." Burton pitied the enslaved Indian miners, who had been reduced to "the extremity of human misery." Sahagun collected and translated many texts in order to preserve native culture.

Some Europeans professed to discern seeds of Christian belief in native cultures. Several of the sages in Bodin's *Colloquium* cited reports of conceptions of purgatory, virgin birth, and bodily resurrection among the American Indians. Asian religions also fascinated Europeans. Pinto saw intimations of Christianity in Chinese assistance to shipwrecked Europeans, concern for the poor, prayers of thanksgiving and for the souls of the dead, and the opposition of a good god to a wicked world. Ricci contrasted the monotheism of China with the polytheism of early Europeans, which had made them "monsters of vice"; he also discerned in Chinese culture hints of the Trinity and a belief in rewards and punishments after death. He admired the Mandarin ethic, as "quite in conformity with the light of conscience and with Christian truth." By 1624 Jesuit missionaries were also studying Tibetan Buddhism, in which they discerned hints of the Virgin Mary and other Catholic saints. An Italian Jesuit in India was so impressed by Hinduism that he built a church on the model of a Hindu temple, purified himself with ritual baths before mass, and gave to his "converts" a tiny cross attached to Hindu insignia.

Dissatisfaction with European ways was one source of favorable accounts of exotic cultures. China, with its rich material civilization and ripe culture, invited special admiration. Ricci reported that the Chinese monarchy strictly disciplined its magistracy and always avoided nepotism. In China, too, moral philosophy rather than mathematics or medicine was the most honored study. In short, the Chinese exemplified ideals important but unrealized in Europe and thus might qualify for salvation through obedience to natural law. In China, too, private persons were not allowed to carry arms, and "fighting and violence among the people" were practically unknown, "save what might be concluded by hair pulling and scratching." There too philosophers, not military leaders, their minds "ennobled by the study of letters," decided questions of war and peace. As a result, China was notably peaceful. Pinto admired Chinese technology and thought China the wealthiest country in the world.

Such reports were widely circulated in Europe. Burton was impressed by reports that in China there was "not a beggar or an idle person to be seen." Montaigne thought China "a kingdom whose government and arts, without dealings with any knowledge of ours," surpassed Europe in many ways; its history taught him "how much ampler and more varied the world is than either the ancients or we ourselves understand." The Japanese were already being praised for their politeness, and for the poise and intellectual quickness of their children. The non-European world was becoming a mirror in which to examine the blemishes of Europe.

Favorable accounts of the natives of the Americas also reflected such European conceptions as that of the vigor and purity of primitive peoples, a notion that had its beginnings in Tacitus's account of the ancient Germans. Burton made the connection explicit. Peter Martyr had early associated the Indians with the golden age, and other Europeans concluded, from their non-European origins, that they had been untouched by original sin. Ronsard was not alone in associating their unembarrassed nudity with unfallen innocence. Montaigne also emphasized their innocence, hinted at the perfection of their language by comparing it to Greek, and professed concern lest they be corrupted by exposure to Europe. An English account described the kind reception of two English visitors by the Indians of North Carolina, a people "gentle, loving, and faithful, void of all guile and treason, after the manner of the Golden Age." The place itself produced "all things in abundance as in the first creation, without toil or labor." Ralegh treated Guiana in much the same way. Léry praised his Indians for their youthful bodies and unusual longevity, concluding that they must "truly drink at the fountain of youth" and praising their egalitarianism and respect for elders, their gratitude, gregariousness, and pacifism.

The discoveries had many results for European culture. They had a major impact on the literary imagination. The account of an English shipwreck off the coast of Bermuda inspired Shakespeare's *Tempest*, and Tasso's horizons were broadened to border a world that now included "the land of the Goths, Norway, Sweden and Iceland," as well as "the East Indies and the new found lands in the vast ocean beyond the Pillars of Hercules."

The notion of a "new" world set off, in other minds, meta-historical speculation. The classical scholar Lipsius wondered whether its discovery implied the senescence of the old world, drawing on the tradition of the transit of civilization from east to west:

Once the East flourished: *Assyria*, *Egypt* and *Iewrie* excelled in warre and peace. That glorie was transferred into *Europe*, which now (like a diseased bodie) seemeth vnto me to be shaken, and to haue a feeling of her great confusion nigh at hand. Yea, and that which is more (and neuer ynough) to bee maruelled at, this world hauing now bene inhabited these fiue thousand and fiue hundred yeares, is at length come to his dotage. And that we may now approoue againe the fables of *Anaxarchus* in old time hissed at, behold now there ariseth els wher new people, & a new world: o the law of NECESSITY, wonderfull, and not to be comprehended: All things run into this fatall whirlepool of ebbing and flowing: And some things in this world are long lasting, but not euerlasting.[3]

Montaigne thought that the young and primitive new world, already "not at all behind us in natural brightness of mind and pertinence," would rise as Europe declined, unless—a troubling possibility—"contagion" from Europe should corrupt it. Postel was more optimistic: he thought the discoveries foreshadowed the rejuvenation of Christianity and the old world. For Bacon, they were a source of hope for human knowledge. "By the distant voyages and travels which have become frequent in our times," he wrote, "many things in nature have been laid open and discovered which may let in new light upon philosophy."

This pointed to the contribution of the discoveries to a decline in the authority of antiquity. The Jesuit historian Jose de Acosta, having learned from Aristotle to expect increasing heat below the equator but finding increasing cold, could only "laugh at Aristotle's *Meteorology* and his philosophy." Léry was deeply impressed by the practical experience of a sea pilot. "Not that I condemn or wish in any way to disparage the sciences acquired and learned in schools and by the study of books," he concluded, "but I must ask that you not so settle on a mere opinion, whosesoever it may be, that you cite mere reason against the experience of a thing."

Another result was to intensify tendencies to eclecticism and relativism. A large European literature was rapidly made available describing the variety in the world among religions, legal systems, and customs in such matters, for example, as marriage and burial of the dead. Samuel Purchas's *Pilgrimage* (1613) and Robert Brerewood's *Enquiries Touching the Diversity of Languages and Religions in the Cheife Parts of the World* (1614) surveyed the religions of the world. Ricci, who praised Confucius, described only such "manners and customs" in China as differed from those in Europe because they would "reveal something new." Mendes Pinto artfully placed side by side, without comment, the religious exhortations of the leaders of Christian and Muslim troops before battle, to the advantage of the latter. Léry observed the amazement of the Indians at seeing European women clothed, and was surprised by the harmony among wives in polygamous households. That Indian women softened roots and millet in their mouths to make them edible for others was, he decided, no more disgusting than treading grapes to make wine: "the one custom is as good as the other."

Burton, having noted the variety of diets around the world, concluded that "custom is all in all."

The discovery of variety in religions was especially unsettling. As one of Bodin's discussants remarked:

> With such a large number of religions before us, perhaps it is possible that none of these is the true religion; on the other hand, it is not possible that more than one of these is true. Since the priests of all religions disagree among themselves so violently, it is safer to admit all religions than to choose one from many, which may, perhaps, be false, or to exclude one, which may be the truest of all.[4]

Montaigne also showed how radically the new knowledge could weaken the self-confidence of Europe:

> Of this very image of the world which glides along while we live on it, how puny and limited is the knowledge of even the most curious. Not only of particular events which fortune often renders exemplary and weighty, but of the state of great governments and nations, there escapes us a hundred times more than comes to our knowledge. We exclaim at the invention of our artillery, of our printing; other men in another corner of the world, in China, enjoyed these a thousand years earlier. If we saw as much of the world as we do not see, we would perceive, it is likely, a perpetual multiplication and vicissitude of forms.[5]

Europe was acquiring a new, potentially humbler, perspective on itself and its place in the world.

The discoveries also aggravated some of the less amiable qualities of Europe; its self-centeredness, its internal jealousies and competitiveness, its preoccupation with power and control. That Europeans had "discovered" the New World, and in addition had brought with them the one true religion, printed Bibles, and firearms, were all exploited to justify conquest. A new triumphalism figured on the title-page of the atlas of Ortelius, which showed "Europa" enthroned over the world.

Imperialism and exploitation soon triumphed over the openness and benign interest in native Americans of Léry and Montaigne and the humanitarian concern of Bartolomé de Las Casas, whose *Destruction of the Indies* (1552) had vigorously attacked Spanish exploitation. At first often viewed as innocent children of nature, the Indians were now represented as devil-worshippers. Spanish claims to domination were based on an interpretation of the "just war" to include, as the Jesuit historian Jose de Acosta argued, war "in accordance with the desire of Providence." The claims of France and Britain were based on the equally self-serving assumption that the lands of America were vacant, since their populations consisted largely of tribes without fixed habitation. Additional claims for England were advanced on the ground that the Indians were of Welsh descent, or that King Arthur had long ago assembled an overseas empire. The hard-headed Dutch, who had gone to the East Indies after 1590, following the route they had learned from Spain and Portugal, seem to have been less concerned to make their imperialism respectable. Grotius, who thought seriously about the Dutch empire, was chiefly interested in the value of the Indies for prosperity at home. The attitude of the Dutch East India Company to natives was expressed by Jan Pieterszoon Coen, Governor-General of the East Indies after 1617, who replied to a critic, "May not a man in Europe do what he likes with his cattle? Even so does the master here do with his men, for these with all that belongs to them are as much the property of the masters as are brute beasts in the Netherlands." In justifying his ruthlessness, Coen claimed that "the teaching of nature and what has been done by all peoples from age to age has always been sufficient for me." In Spain, Juan de Sepulveda justified the exploitation of the Indians on the ground that, lacking Christian faith, they were "slaves by nature" whose subjugation was necessary for their conversion.

The Liberation of the Cosmos

Meanwhile perspectives were also expanding to include the spaces surrounding the earth, with equally exhilarating but even more disturbing results. The traditional understanding of the cosmos (in Latin *mundus, caelum,* or *universum*) had made it relatively friendly. A composite of Christian theology and the metaphysics of Aristotle, like much else in pre-modern culture, it saw the universe as a finite and orderly unity. Within this unity, it distinguished between the heavens above and the earth below. The heavens were perfect and immutable, their only movement circular; linear motion would have meant change of place and implied imperfection. Only the earth, along with the obviously variable moon, was imperfect and subject to change. Its location, however, was equivocal. Within the cosmos as a whole, the earth, the abode of fallen mankind, was the place of imperfection. Hell was located at the earth's center, the farthest point in the universe from God.

But in another sense the earth was central to the system, its location implying the special significance of human beings. The heavenly bodies might be pictured as the divine audience in a cosmic amphitheater, their attention focussed on the drama of salvation taking place on the stage below. They were thought, not being quite inanimate, to transmit spiritual influences from heaven to earth. Thus astrology was generally accepted as a legitimate branch of science, although it was not thought to compromise freedom of the will. But its influence on non-human nature, notably on crops and the weather, was unquestioned. The major principle of organization in this system was the combination of hierarchy with qualitative distinctions; its "up" and "down" had absolute rather than relative significance. What was higher was superior in authority and power to what was below.

But for all its clarity, and to some degree because of its clarity, this comprehensive structure had become increasingly unstable. It was undermined both by cultural developments and by scientific observations that seemed to contradict its theoretical order. It also reflected its pagan origins, and from a Christian point of view its defects were increasingly awkward. Whereas the Scriptures emphasized the absolute difference between God and his creation, this cosmology blurred the difference by making the heavenly bodies, themselves quasi-divine, mediators between God and earth. For religious reasons, indeed, some aspects of Aristotelian science had already been declared heretical in the thirteenth century. Even before the growing biblicism of Renaissance humanism, nominalism had recognized this problem and sought to neutralize it by distinguishing between God's absolute power, which was infinite, and the "ordained" or limited power by which he had chosen to exercise it. Even more fundamentally, the nominalist limitation of natural knowledge to particular sense-data worked against all system-building. Nominalism pointed toward a biblical religion of faith and feeling.

Other problems with the old cosmology were posed by systematic observation of the heavens that subverted the neatness of the traditional scheme and undermined its larger implications. Many students of "nature" in the later sixteenth century, although compelled by their Christian assumptions to abandon Aristotle on the eternity of the universe, still clung to the old system in other ways because it was still thought to support Christian belief—a few passages from the Bible could be cited in its favor—and because Aristotelian science had not been superseded as a system; but perhaps mostly because old ideas rarely disappear quickly. However, other natural philosophers largely abandoned Aristotle, especially in the scientific circles of Paris and even in Rome. Bacon accused the Aristotelians of trivializing science. What was needed was, in Thomas Kuhn's phrase, a "paradigm shift."

Such a shift had been proposed by Copernicus in *On the Revolutions of the Heavenly Bodies* (1543). His work, which was presented after his death as only a "hypothesis," displaced the earth from the center of the planetary system, replacing it with the sun. But the full significance of Copernicus's innovation depended both on better observations and, even more important, on mathematics. The observations were largely made, though he was not a Copernican, by the Dane Tycho Brahe, who watched the heavens more systematically than anybody before him; his observations made the old cosmology increasingly untenable. But although Brahe had envied the ancients for having learned mathematics "in infancy without trouble," the application of mathematics to astronomy was most fruitfully made by Galileo Galilei, a professor at the universities of Pisa and Padua before being invited to the court of the Grand Duke of his native Florence.

Mathematics was acceptable even to conservatives because it was rooted in antiquity and associated with the venerable names of Pythagoras and Plato. By the later sixteenth century it was making important advances, stimulated by practical as well as scientific interests. The Dutchman Simon Stevin invented the decimal system, and the Scot John Napier developed logarithms, algebra, analytic geometry, and calculus.

Another conception, originating in antiquity and now stimulating scientific circles, was atomism. It was held in high esteem by some in part because of its identification with the earliest Greeks. Though dimly regarded by ecclesiastical authority because of its association with the "atheism" of Lucretius and the heresies of Bruno and Campanella, atomism had been encouraged by the publication in 1563 of Lucretius's *Of the Nature of Things*, which depicted the universe as an infinite space populated by innumerable worlds. It now stimulated such sober thinkers as Sarpi and Galileo in Italy, Bacon and Hobbes in England, and the Paris circle of Pierre Gassendi.

As these impulses from antiquity suggest, the notion of an opposition between Renaissance humanism and scientific advance is largely mistaken. Major figures in the scientific movement were skilled rhetoricians and loved the classics. The influence of humanism probably contributed to the desire for a more "elegant" conception of the heavens to replace the unwieldy Aristotelian cosmos, now full of asymmetries and contradictions that stimulated the desire for a new kind of science. William Gilbert, who studied the magnet, hoped to eliminate the "confusion" in traditional science. Galileo praised truth for its beauty.

The alliance of humanism and science is evident in other ways. Like earlier humanists, advocates of the new science rejected the jargon-filled Latin of scholastic science. Galileo, as a writer, mobilized impressive rhetorical skills; he was witty, sarcastic, and capable of making his opponents seem petty and stupid. Sometimes he quoted poetry. He compared the surface of the moon as revealed by the telescope to "the tail of a peacock sprinkled with azure eyes, [which also] resembles those glass vases which have been plunged while still hot into cold water and have thus acquired a crackled and wavy surface." He used the metaphor of an organ to describe sunspots, expressing the hope that his telescope would be

> of admirable service in tuning for me some reed in this great discordant organ of our philosophy—an instrument on which I think I see many organists wearing themselves out trying vainly to get the whole thing into perfect harmony. Vainly, because they leave (or rather preserve) three or four of the principal reeds in discord, making it quite impossible for the others to respond in perfect tune.[6]

He chose the open dialogue form so often used by humanists for his *Two Chief World Systems* because, he explained, it meant "not being restricted to the rigorous observance of mathematical laws" and allowed "for digressions, which are sometimes no less interesting than the principal argument." The alliance between rhetoric and humanism would last at least until Hobbes, himself no mean rhetorician.

Galileo's affinities with humanism are also apparent at a deeper level in his attitude to change. Like many humanists he was acutely conscious of his own place in history; he hoped to be celebrated by statues, columns, and "imperishable literary monuments" for venturing beyond the earth into heaven itself. And far from lamenting change, he was pleased to discover it in the heavens, shrewdly attributing its rejection by contemporaries to their fear of death; for Galileo, change was a condition of life. "It seems to me unreasonable," he wrote, "to call that 'corruption' which produces a chicken from an egg. Besides, if 'corruption' and 'generation' are discovered in the moon, why deny them to the sky?"

His rhetorical skills as well as his mathematics were put into the service of the new vision of the cosmos. "With absolute necessity," Galileo declared, "we shall conclude, in agreement with the theories of the

Pythagoreans and of Copernicus," that the planets revolve around the sun. This meant not only that the earth was itself a "heavenly" body, but also—this was of crucial importance—that the traditional distinction between heaven and earth was untenable. Galileo sharpened the point by his observation of sunspots with his telescope. While other observers tried to explain them away, for Galileo they further demonstrated the uniformity of a universe governed throughout by unchanging physical laws.

Even more was involved. Because the telescope gave access to much that could not be seen by the naked eye, the "horizon of reality" was no longer identical with "the horizon of visibility." The telescope, for Galileo, raised the hope "that in time things will be seen which we cannot even imagine at present." The indefinite expansion of the cosmos enabled humanity, as Hans Blumenberg has remarked, to step "into an already existing freedom." And what the telescope had done for large and distant objects the microscope, developed a few decades later, would accomplish for the subvisible universe.

From this point on there seemed to be no limits, imposed by any authority, to human discovery. "In my opinion no one," Galileo wrote, "should close the road to free philosophizing about mundane and physical things, as if everything had already been discovered and revealed with certainty." Indeed, perhaps following Augustine (and like ourselves), Galileo speculated on the possibility of other, still unknown, worlds in space. To deny this possibility would be to deny the omnipotence of God. Some thinkers now celebrated the impending completion of all human knowledge, as in a letter to Marin Mersenne from the Dutch mathematician Isaac Beeckman regarding the forthcoming publication of Mersenne's ambitiously titled *Harmonie universelle*. With the completion of this work, Beeckman surmised, Mersenne would "surely have robbed all of us of all occasion to think anything further about philosophical matters."

The new science was also allied with humanism in its tendency to leave the spiritual and metaphysical realm to theologians and philosophers in favor of the world of ordinary experience. Kepler, almost as important as Galileo in working out the implications of Copernicanism, insisted that the earth is our true home, not to be abandoned in favor of allegedly "higher" realms:

It is apparent that it is not proper for man, the inhabitant of this universe and its destined observer, to live in it as though in a sealed room. In that case he would never have succeeded in contemplating the heavenly bodies, which are so remote. On the contrary, by the annual revolution of the earth, his home, he is whirled about and transported in this most ample edifice so that he can examine and with the greatest accuracy measure the individual members of the house [of the universe]. . . . Moreover in the interest of the contemplation for which man was created, adorned, and equipped with eyes, he could not remain at rest in the center. On the contrary, he must make an annual journey in this boat, our earth, to perform his observations.[7]

Francis Bacon, who thought much about the social significance of science, emphasized its utility. He reassured his servant, a man who "loved this world." by telling him that *"the World was made for man, and not man for the World."* The human race, for him, might not be at the center of the universe but was nevertheless central to it:

if man were taken away from the world, the rest would seem to be all astray, without aim or purpose . . . leading to nothing. For the whole world works together in the service of man; and there is nothing from which he does not derive use and fruit . . . insomuch that all things seem to be going about man's business and not their own.[8]

Human beings, he wrote, had been created by God not only to be "delighted in beholding the variety of things and vicissitude of times, but raised also to find out and discern the ordinances and decrees, which throughout all those changes are infallibly observed."

And in spite of their humanism, some scientific thinkers were breaking radically with the past by rejecting the written word, at least as a source for knowledge of nature. Kepler disdained the scientific authority of the church fathers, pointing out the errors made even by "holy Augustine." The truth, for him, was even holier. Montaigne criticized people who admit "none but printed evidence, who do not believe men unless they are in a book, or truth unless it is of a competent age. We dignify our stupidities when we put them in print." Hobbes took much the same position. "Words," he declared, "are wise men's counters, they do but reckon by them: but they are the money of fooles, that value them by the authority of an *Aristotle*, a *Cicero*, or a *Thomas*, or any other Doctor whatsoever, if but a man."

But though detested by conservatives, there was little in the new cosmology that preempted the nineteenth-century "conflict" between religion and science. Bacon, to be sure, sounded an apocalyptic note suggestive of sectarian Christianity. Humanity, he predicted, would be restored through the progress of knowledge to its original perfection:

Therefore it is not the pleasure of curiosity nor the quiet of resolution, nor the raising of the spirit nor victory of wit, nor faculty of
speech, nor lucre of profession, nor ambition of honor or fame, nor
inablement of business, that are the true ends of knowledge; some
of these being more worthy than other, though all inferior and degenerate: but it is a restitution and reinvesting (in great part) of man
to the sovereignty and power . . . which he had in his first state of
creation.[9]

But the new cosmology did not seem, to its major proponents, to endan-
ger Christianity. For Galileo, his discoveries were entirely consistent with
Catholic orthodoxy, which did not require any particular conception of the
physical universe; one of his motives, he claimed, had been to preserve the
Roman Church from error. It made more sense to Kepler to locate divine
influence at the center rather than on the periphery of the solar system. For
him the universe of the new science was more awesome than the old. Bacon
thought that scientific knowledge would aid faith. "If the matter be truly
considered," he wrote, "natural philosophy is, after the word of God, at
once the surest medicine against superstition and the most approved
nourishment for faith, and therefore rightly given to religion as her most
faithful handmaid, since the one displays the will of God, the other his
power."

Indeed, many theologians thought Copernicanism consistent with
Catholic orthodoxy. In 1611 a day was set aside to honor Galileo at the
Jesuit College in Rome. Bérulle saw his own spirituality as analogous to
the new science, "for Jesus is the sun that is immovable in his greatness and
that moves all other things." Mersenne defended Galileo and insisted that
science and the church should be allies in support of truth.

The new cosmology was made suspect, however, by enthusiasts who
spelled out what seemed to the church to be heterodox implications. Bruno
proclaimed as a certainty the infinity of the universe, about which Galileo
had been cautious. This truth, Bruno declared, by enabling mankind "to
discover the infinite effect of the infinite cause, the true and living sign of
infinite vigor," only enhanced the "excellent glory and majesty of God." He
also speculated that this infinite space might be populated by an infinity of
worlds like our own. Campanella, too, speculated on these matters; Bodin
thought it beyond doubt that "there are infinite stars."

But the new science was disturbing above all because it broke the long-
established connections of science with theology and metaphysics. As
R. Hooykaas puts it, Galileo had destroyed "the numinous holy character

of nature." He had erased the old difference between heaven and earth, and the heavens accordingly could no longer provide the model for human order. Science, now thoroughly secularized, could pursue truth anywhere. This could be frightening.

But the new science also extended to nature the troubling relativism released in ethics by the geographical discoveries. Galileo recognized that an infinite universe might have "as many centers and as many lower and higher places as there are world-bodies, and orbs that turn around different points." Sarpi realized that any observation must be relative to the position of the observer. "The earth," he pointed out, "would look to a man on the moon as the moon looks to us on earth." Particularly disturbing was the loss, once the earth was no longer central, of the privileged situation of human beings in a universe increasingly seen as infinite. An infinite universe had no comforting boundaries or intelligible order. Even the ground under one's feet was no longer a source of security; Hamlet, in Francis Fergusson's words, was "not even sure which way is up." John Donne's lament that "new philosophy calls all in doubt" reflected not merely skepticism but despair in the presence of the unintelligible. It is hardly surprising that some reputable scientists, not all of them Jesuits, resisted the new cosmology.

It was especially difficult to believe that an infinite universe had been created to serve finite human purposes. Galileo had himself seen this, although he still argued that God had created the universe chiefly *propter nos*. Purpose, indeed, was largely absent from the new science, which tended to replace final with efficient causes. This achievement carried a high price, and it inevitably encountered strong resistance. Galileo proposed to limit the Scriptures to showing simply "how to go to heaven, not how heaven goes."

He was not alone. Fulke Greville, poet, patron of learning, and favorite of Queen Elizabeth, made much the same point. "Forsake not Nature, nor misunderstand her," he wrote: "her mysteries are read without faith's eyesight." Meanwhile Bacon was dividing all knowledge into three completely separate kingdoms: the kingdoms of God and of politics, revealed by Scripture, and the kingdom of nature known through human sense and reason.

For thoughtful persons, therefore, the new cosmology simply confused further an already disordered universe. Burton, although at first sufficiently impressed by Galileo's telescope to wonder what he might see through it himself, finally decided that astronomy was only a set of "absurd and brainstruck questions, intricacies, froth of human wit, and excrements of curiosity," a lunatic folly in which the world was "tossed in a blanket" by contending astronomers. He could only conclude that the heavens were the most disorderly part of the universe, but in any case that "what is above us does not concern us." Montaigne was skeptical about the possibility of any knowledge on such matters; one theory would always give way to another. Campanella criticized both the new and traditional astronomy as mere mathematical abstractions, like "play money instead of gold." Bodin was non-committal.

Protestant and Catholic authorities were alike in their hostility to the new science. The Archbishop of Pisa argued dogmatically "that, since all created things are made for the service of man, it clearly follows as a necessary consequence that the earth could not move like the stars." But the most formidable opponent of the new science was Cardinal Bellarmine. Bellarmine had initially thought it acceptable simply as a hypothesis to "save the appearances"; and Jesuit scientists had at first encouraged Galileo. But eventually Bellarmine had seen the gravity of the new ideas. They would, he charged, antagonize "all theologians and scholastic philosophers [a group to which he notably belonged], injure the faith, and contradict the Scriptures." He cited against Galileo the psalm describing the sun as "exulting like a strong man in running its course." Everybody, he observed, "experiences clearly that the earth stands still, and that the eye is not deceived when it judges the sun to move, just as one is not deceived when judging that the moon and the stars move." He was joined by others in attacking Galileo, especially after the publication of his *Dialogue Concerning the Two Chief World Systems* (1632). In 1616 the Inquisition formally condemned Galileo's views as "foolish and absurd" and forbade him to "hold, teach, or defend" them. After he defied this prohibition in 1632 by publishing his *Dialogue*, he was summoned to Rome, tried, condemned, and forced to recant. Many Protestants, although lacking the apparatus for formal condemnation, were for similar reasons hostile to the new science.

The distress of believers in the face of these novelties was given deeply felt expression by Pascal, himself a devout Catholic as well as a distinguished mathematician. Pascal attacked the condemnation of Galileo. "The earth will not halt for a decree," he wrote, "and if there are constant observations which show that it turns, not all the men in the world can stop it from spinning or themselves from spinning with it." Nevertheless, he was torn between his respect for truth and the anguish he felt at the diminution of human beings implicit in the new science. His concern inspired some of his most poignant reflections on the human condition. He was struck by the paradoxical and frightening situation of mankind, suddenly projected into a universe now revealed as infinitely large by the telescope and by the microscope as infinitely small. He saw himself as lost

> in wonders as amazing in their littleness as others in their vastness. For who will not be astounded at the fact that our body, which a little while ago was imperceptible in the universe . . . in the bosom of the whole, is now a colossus, a world, or rather a whole, in respect of the nothingness which we cannot reach? He who regards himself in this light will be afraid of himself, and observing himself sustained in the body given him by nature between those two abysses of the Infinite and Nothing, will tremble at the sight of these marvels.

He recognized that, "in comparison with these Infinites, all finites are equal."[10] The universe, now infinite in all directions, had become infinitely disorienting.

Shakespeare had already suggested the effect of the new science at more popular levels. In declaring his love for Ophelia, Hamlet contrasted the certainty of his affection with the dissolving certainties in the heavens:

> Doubt thou the stars are fire,
> Doubt that the sun doth move,
> Doubt truth to be a liar,
> But never doubt I love.

For Hamlet, only his own subjectivity, unsupported by anything external, was beyond doubt.[11] His lines reverberated in more directions than he perhaps knew.

CHAPTER SIX

The Liberation of Politics

Social and political order had traditionally been validated by an appeal to *nature*. But nature for this purpose was understood in two somewhat different ways. One was the familiar structure of the cosmos, perceived as a unity and internally organized as a hierarchy, the whole ruled by God. This meant that the proper form of government in this world should be a universal monarchy presiding over an internal set of hierarchies. Whether pope or emperor should head it had been inconclusively disputed for centuries.

Another conception of order was based on biological nature. As Aristotle had taught, human society was derived from the union of male and female for procreation, which created families. These found it necessary to come together for mutual assistance, and such groups eventually united to form states. The natural superiority of male to female also implied patriarchy, which pointed to monarchy, just as the qualitative differences among humans pointed to hierarchy. God, kings (or popes), and fathers constituted, in turn, a hierarchy of rulers. The monarch was seen as a kind of father of the extended family of his people, his rule as absolute as that of God the father above and the fathers of families below.

Both models provided an ontological foundation for political and social order and thus also legitimated power. To invoke a distinction made by Pope Gelasius I at the end of the fourth century, the natural basis of power, otherwise naked, clothed its exercise with authority.

All of this was threatened by the new politics of the Renaissance, which had come to a head in Machiavelli. Before Galileo secularized the cosmos, Machiavelli had secularized politics and society, and in much the same way: by rejecting any ultimate model of organization, and thus rejecting unity and hierarchy. The supposedly universal institutions of papacy and empire were, for him, irrelevant to the real world, except insofar as they interfered with its operation; they were powerless to provide order. His political world consisted simply of separate entities, however they had come into existence—"states" as they were now called—that recognized no superior. The problems of politics were, for him, those of attaining and maintaining power sufficient to insure the survival of these states, which alone could provide at least a degree of social order. The only "nature" of importance for him was human nature, which, like Augustine, he considered unpredictable and generally bad. Like Augustine he also rejected the possibility of permanent peace and order in the earthly city. Politics was, for him, an art of the possible, a constant adaptation to challenge and change.

Machiavelli thought change in human affairs inevitable, however threatening; change could at best be minimized. And his principle for maintaining the best order possible was quantitative rather than qualitative; it thus paralleled—indeed anticipated—the new cosmology. It substituted for the static ideal of hierarchy, both within and among states, a flexible equilibrium, constantly adjusted to the changing realities of existence: constitutional arrangements within states to maintain the shifting balance among interests, and among states a balance of power. The old models for peace and order were, for Machiavelli, literally utopian. In this respect he had something in common with his contemporary Thomas More, who also knew what the real world was like.

It is hardly surprising that, long after his death, Machiavelli was attacked by idealists, both Protestant and Catholic. Nevertheless, in spite of his condemnation by moralists and the prohibition of his works in Catholic countries, Machiavelli's major writings were read throughout Europe; even in Italy they circulated in manuscript. The French Calvinist Innocent Gentillet testified disapprovingly to his European influence, reporting that his works "could rightly be called the Koran of courtiers, so much do they esteem them, following and observing his teachings and maxims, no more or less than the Turks use the Koran." His views were also spread by other writers. Among these were Giovanni Botero, who shared much in Machiavelli's thought but made it more acceptable to Catholics; and Trajano Boccalini, whose satirical *Reports from Parnassus* (1612–13) were popular everywhere. Ralegh agreed with Machiavelli that "a Foxe-taile doth sometimes helpe well to peece out the Lions-skinne, that else would be too short." Descartes had a "grudging respect" for Machiavelli; he was also respected by Bacon, Montaigne, and Milton.

In fact, much in the society and culture of the period was being, in various senses, "secularized." With the emergence of relatively well-organized states ruled by secular princes, and of towns dominated by an increasingly assertive middle class, laymen were taking over responsibilities previously assumed by the church, such as education and poor relief. In France, the Parlement of Paris supervised hospital administration. In churches in the Dutch republic, images of the Madonna and Child were replaced by paintings of ordinary nursing mothers. In England, parishes administered poor relief, and time became more secular as religious festivals and holy days in the old church year were replaced by commemorations of important events in the nation's history. Increasing numbers of people now lived compartmentalized lives, ruled by religion in fewer and fewer aspects of their experience: by reason in science; by worldly calculation in economics; and by common sense in daily life. As the English physician Thomas Browne recognized, man had become a "great and true *Amphibium*, whose nature is disposed to live . . . in divided and distinguished worlds."

Secular attitudes toward politics can be found in many, sometimes unexpected places. The "best advice on matters of state" from Cardinal Richelieu's "gray eminence," Père Joseph, was that it "be based on special knowledge of the state itself." Sincerely religious men, troubled by the realization that religion itself was often becoming chiefly a political tool, had reluctantly to accept the new realism. The advice of Sarpi to the rulers of Venice was based entirely on interest of state. Hobbes wrote the epitaph of the old order in his *Leviathan* (1651). Nature, he proclaimed, far from being the source of order as once claimed, was utterly amoral: "The notions of Right and Wrong, Justice and Injustice have there no place. Where there is no common Power, there is no Law; where no Law, no Injustice. Force and Fraud are in warre the two Cardinall vertues." Life in the state of nature, from this standpoint, far from providing a norm for politics, was merely "nasty, brutish, and short." Hobbes thus inverted the golden rule into a principle of survival: "Do not that to another, which thou wouldest not have done, to thy selfe." As Machiavelli observed, earlier writers on politics had been chiefly concerned with what should be rather than with what was. Now, in a period of widespread disorder, much writing on statecraft was concerned not with the legitimacy of governments but with their effectiveness and survival.

In politics, reason of state promoted flexibility and practicality; the tension between the useful and the good was increasingly resolved in favor of utility. Bacon's *Essays* described for rulers points of "cunning" like those taught, he believed, by the Jesuits. Even those who, in principle, believed in the inseparability of politics and morality could not resist distinguishing them. This was the case with Lipsius, the most influential writer of the time on politics. Hooker, an observer of practical politics as well as a theoretician, remarked that "devotion and the feeling sense of religion are not usual in the noblest, wisest, and chiefest Personages of State, by reason their wits are so much imployed another ways, and their minds so seldom conversant in heavenly things."

Montaigne's reflections on his own time recapitulate this development. He had been converted by experience from an idealistic ethic appropriate only to private life to an ethic required by public service: "I once tried to employ in the service of public dealings ideas and rules for living as crude, green, unpolished—or unpolluted—as they were born in me or derived from my education, and which I use, if not conveniently, at least surely, in private matters: a scholastic and novice virtue." But he had found this both inappropriate and dangerous; what was required was a special kind of decorum, i.e., appropriateness to the times:

> He who walks in the crowd must step aside, keep his elbows in, step back or advance, even leave the straight way according to what he encounters. He must live not so much according to himself but according to what others propose to him, according to the time, according to the men, according to the business. . . . Whoever boasts in a sick age like this, that he employs a pure and sincere virtue in the service of the world, either does not know what virtue is, since our ideas grow corrupt with our conduct . . . or, if he does know, he boasts wrongly, and, say what he will, does a thousand things which his conscience accuses.[1]

What was required in public life was reason of state, whatever one's personal misgivings.

Machiavellianism found expression in the Italian notion of *opportunità*, i.e., opportunism or expediency, the recognition that effective political action invites disaster when it ignores time and circumstance. Indeed, it had figured in scholastic discussion. Giovanni Botero, as an apologist for the papacy, recognized its value: a statesman, he affirmed, must

> learn to recognize the critical moment in war and affairs, and to seize opportunities as they appear . . . [for] there is a certain point of time when a fortunate combination of circumstances favors some kind of business which both before and after that moment would be most difficult. This is *opportunity*, and it is of supreme importance. . . . Might and cunning are of little avail if they are not aided and guided by opportunity.[2]

The practicality of the Society of Jesus sometimes tended in this direction. It was also a common attitude among opponents of the papacy. "Many times occasions are born sufficient to produce notable results," Sarpi wrote, "and they are lost in the absence of men who do not know how to make use of them." This was no mere abstraction. During the interdict of 1606, the doge of Venice, Leonardo Donà, defended himself for having changed his mind as circumstances changed:

> Let us not deem it the duty of a prudent man always to have the same opinion, but that which the accidents and rather variable conjunctures of human affairs counsel. Thus he who otherwise might pretend to the title of consistency and constancy in his opinions should rather deserve a reputation for imprudent pertinacity and unconsidered obstinacy, since everyone, even of superficial intelligence in things of state, knows that civil matters are variable and subject like the sea to the diversity of the winds, to the violence and diversity of accidents. For this reason man should regulate his opinions exactly as on a sea voyage, according to the quality of the winds. Nor is he obliged always to have the same opinion, but rather the same end: the good and safety of the Republic.[3]

The imagery here is Augustinian, the conclusion Machiavellian.[3] Sarpi himself waited for the *occasion* to publish his *History of the Council of Trent*, a devastating contribution to the Venetian cause against the papacy. Bacon agreed that

> Occasion *turneth a bald noddle, after she hath presented her locks in front, and no hold taken*; or at least turneth the handle of the bottle first to be received, and after the belly, which is hard to clasp. . . . The ripeness or unripeness of the occasion must ever be well weighed; and generally it is good to commit the beginnings of all great actions to Argos with his hundred eyes, and the ends to Briareus with his hundred hands; first to watch, and then to speed.[4]

The French lawyer Guillaume Du Vair condemned those who, "starting from a fixed principle, are determined to deduce from it a mode of action applicable in all circumstances." This "opportunism" even entered into Hooker's conception of law. One of the "knowne lawes of making lawes," he stated, is "that lawemakers must have an eye to the place where, and to the men amongst whome; that one kind of Lawes cannot serve for all kindes of regiment." He accordingly denied, against the universalism of Rome, that Christ had ordained immutable laws for the church; he defended episcopacy on practical rather than biblical grounds.

Underlying such views was a growing pessimism, like Machiavelli's, about human nature. For Sarpi, fear of punishment could alone keep societies in order. Bodin generally agreed:

> The nature of man, as of all other worldly things also, is most slippery and unconstant, running still headlong from good to evil, and from evil to worse: vices little by little still increasing, not unlike evil humors, which without sensible feeling increase man's body until it be so full of them, breeds in it many most dangerous diseases, and so at length brings it to utter destruction.[5]

All great states, he believed, had been "established through violence by robbers."[6] Other thinkers may have expressed themselves less strongly, but differed chiefly in degree. Montaigne thought the defects in human nature made all political calculation uncertain, realism on this point being crucial in creating "a workable and regular society." Hooker thought governments always defective. Such general views shaped the interest in faction and conspiracy, usurpation and tyranny, not only in Machiavelli but also in Elizabethan drama and the theater of the French writer Corneille.

Much political writing emphasized the reality of power and the need for it in government. As Marlowe observed in the persona of "Machiavel,"

> Might first made kings, and laws were then most sure
> When like the Draco's, they were writ in blood.

Richelieu remarked grimly in 1625 that "in matters of state the weakest are always wrong." Hooker recognized the importance of power, if in a somewhat abstract tone:

> This order of thinges and persons in publique societies is the work of politie, and the proper instrument thereof in every degree is *power*, power being that abilitie which we have of our selves or receive from others for performance of any action. . . . And if that power be such as hath not any other to overrule it, we terme it dominion or power supreme, so far as the bounds thereof do extend.

Sarpi noted that anyone with power seeks to increase it; he studied the process in the history of the papacy and presented the Council of Trent as a struggle for power waged in and by the church. He could at times hardly conceal his admiration for the *virtù*—in Machiavelli's sense of power—with which the popes had managed the council. Bacon saw arms, the instruments of power, as basic to the greatness of states, and war as necessary to maintain it. Lust for power, he argued, is the basic human passion; although there are passions for wealth, knowledge, and honor, all three, produced by the insecurity of the human condition itself, "may be reduced to the Desire of Power," which "ceaseth only in Death."

That power is the basic reality of this world was not easily accepted, and the practical adjustments it required were regularly denounced in the name of piety. Those who sought peace during the civil wars in France were known pejoratively as "*politiques*" for putting peace above "true religion." The *politiques* were opposed to what might be called "reason of religion," which in practice justified the subordination of individual morality to the interests of the religious community. But, as it turned out, only a peace based on compromise—i.e., on grounds other than ultimate principle—was eventually able to end the wars.

Secularization also found expression now in the conception of sovereignty. This meant the absolute independence of the state: put negatively and in terms of the past, having no political superior. This was now claimed by all states, regardless of size or form of government. The conception was enshrined in the Peace of Westphalia in 1648, with its principle of *eius regio, eius religio*, which meant that political power included the right to determine the religion of a state. The idea of Christendom survived, to be sure, as a vague ideal; the papacy made occasional efforts to revive it by proclaiming crusades against the Turks, and even attempted to enforce its authority over churches in such small states as Venice, as in the interdict of 1606. But the inability of Rome to enforce its authority even here only demonstrated its practical impotence. The Venetians—and most of Europe—saw the interdict, indeed, less as an assertion of a traditional universalism than as an expression of the political aims of the papacy. Because the principle of sovereignty was at stake, even Catholic powers tended to sympathize with Venice; if anything, the episode hardened the conception.

The most influential case for it was made by Bodin in his *Six Books of the Commonwealth* (1576), stimulated by his horror at the religious wars and his conviction that they were caused by limitations on the king. Bodin argued for a kingship unhampered by tradition, with full authority to make laws and the power to enforce them, as the only barrier to such disorder. The book met a need widely felt in Europe. It went through ten editions before Bodin's death in 1596, and was translated into every major European language including Latin.

But Bodin's general view of sovereignty can be found in many places, among them the *De rege et regis institutione* (1598) by the Spanish Jesuit Juan de Mariana, which argued that governments exist to meet human needs and that their most effective form is national monarchy. In response to the interdict, Sarpi argued that the sovereignty of Venice was a function of status rather than size, was unqualified and inalienable, and included full authority both to legislate all things necessary for survival and sufficient power to maintain order. Sovereignty, he wrote, "is a power absolute in its nature, from which nothing can be exempted or excepted." Hugo Grotius defined sovereignty a few years later: "That power is called sovereign whose actions are not subject to the legal control of another, so that they cannot be rendered void by the operation of another human will." The establishment of sovereignty meant the definitive collapse in politics of the conceptions of unity and hierarchy.

A further reflection of the notion of sovereignty was an attack on universal empire, regarded as inferior both abstractly and practically to particular states. The most general attack of this kind was the *Political Discourses* of the Venetian diplomat Paolo Paruta, written before the interdict but when Venice was already threatened by the universalist claims of the papacy. This work foreshadowed Gibbon as it emphasized the deficiencies and analyzed the weaknesses of the ancient Roman empire, associating its great size with its transience. The result, for Paruta as for the republican historians of Florence, was a great turning point in world history:

> The stupendous apparatus, constructed [by Rome] over a long course of years through the great virtue and many exertions of so many valorous men, had finally to run the course common to human affairs, that is to be dissolved and to fall to earth; and with its ruin it brought on the greatest revolutions. Henceforth many noble cities were ruined; others were founded that became noble; entire regions, their old inhabitants expelled, were occupied by new. New customs, new laws, new languages, new garments were introduced; and Italy, which had been the seat of so great an empire, was subjected to greater changes and graver calamities than other provinces.

"Governments devoted to empire," Paruta generalized, were usually "destined for a short life."[7] Sarpi shared this view and, like Machiavelli, argued that the collapse of political universalism had been essential to the freedom enjoyed by such states as Venice. He also associated claims to universal authority with the corruption of the church. Montaigne also disapproved of empire.

Even scholastic thinkers generally recognized the impracticality of universal empire now and, at least partially, accepted the sovereignty of particular states. The Dominican Francisco de Vitoria had already admitted earlier in the century that effective imperial authority did not extend beyond Germany; and others went further. The Jesuit Francisco Suarez considered a universal state impossible, and Bellarmine included among the rights of states self-defense and legislation without the possibility of appeal. Although he insisted on the subordination of the state to the religious ends for which, he believed, all human beings had been created, he was criticized in Rome for limiting papal intervention in politics to matters where religious issues were clearly at stake.

Even the claims of the papacy to universal authority could be turned to the uses of political freedom by scholastic thinkers primarily concerned to magnify papal authority. Against the claims of princes to complete authority over the churches in their domains, scholastic thinkers argued that all secular government, in contrast of course to that of the church, depended on the consent of the governed expressed through the incorporation of democratic and aristocratic elements in government to check royal power. Bellarmine argued that, since all men are by nature equal, kingdoms "can be changed by men into other forms of rule"; only the pope ruled by divine right. For Botero, "all legitimate kingdoms originate in popular election, and therefore, at their coronation, kings swear to observe the privileges of the people."

Underlying this line of thought were changing conceptions of society. Traditional notions of status had been challenged by the emergence of new elites in earlier centuries in a process still continuing to challenge the power of hereditary aristocracies. Calvinists like Ramus echoed Calvin's respect for the "mechanic arts," and Burton criticized a nobility that thought it "a disgrace to work, and spent all their days in sports, recreations, and pastimes": what they needed was exercise and employment. He argued, like humanists before him, that true nobility is based on virtue and is therefore possible for everybody. "We are by nature all as one, all alike, if you see us naked," he argued: "let us wear theirs and they our clothes, and what's the difference?" Montaigne thought that "the least contemptible class of people" were those who, "through their simplicity, occupy the lowest rank." He believed "the morals and the talk of peasants commonly more obedient to the prescriptions of true philosophy than those of our philosophers." He recommended, therefore, that noble children should be reared among the common people. The faithful peasant Sancho Panza declined the social elevation Don Quixote proposed for him, but on a rather different ground: that it would be of little use to him.

Protestantism was often at least theologically egalitarian. Luther had attacked, in his doctrine of the priesthood of all believers, both the distinction between learned and unlearned and hierarchies of status and occupation. As the English Puritan William Perkins declared, "If we compare worke to worke," there is a difference "betwixt washing of dishes, and preaching of the word of God: but as touching to please God none at all." The Huguenot Duplessis-Mornay argued in his *Vindiciae contra tyrannos* (1576) that even kingship was "not an inheritance, not a propriety, nor a usufruct, but a charge [and an] office." Such arguments made all social and political distinctions mere human conventions, accidents of history.

Even formal philosophy incorporated this new egalitarianism, if in odd ways. Cartesianism, which begins with the uninstructed self, had egalitarian implications; and Hobbes maintained that every man is essentially equal to every other, since anybody is strong enough to kill anybody else. He also slyly suggested an equality in mind, since "there is not ordinarily a greater signe of the equall distribution of any thing, than that every man is content with his share." The argument may be more witty than substantial, but Hobbes's social contract was based on convention, not nature.

This egalitarianism also pointed to republicanism, as in Machiavelli; it was meanwhile nourished too by admiration for the republics of antiquity and by the remarkable survival of the Venetian republic in an age of often hostile princes. It should be emphasized, however, that none of these models was a democracy; citizenship in a republic, which conferred the right to participate in politics, was usually more or less narrowly defined; even references to "the people" in political discussion generally referred only to those legally entitled to citizenship.

But republicanism provided a more drastic remedy to the abuses of princely rule, at least in theory, than its limitation. Protestants found precedents for republicanism in the polity of the Old Testament Hebrews, but even Botero thought it "politic" to praise republics, which, he observed, often surpassed principates "at once in magnificence of buildings and in beauty of streets and squares, in multitude of people, in variety of arts, in refinement of manners, and in every kind of humanity." He cited as examples the republics of Renaissance Italy. Trajano Boccalini praised Tacitus because he had "no other intention than to teach the Senators of Republics what deplorable Calamities they fall into, when, preferring their private Passions and interests to the public Good, they foolishly suffer themselves to be robbed of their Country's Liberty, which they ought to preserve and guard as their Lives." For Grotius, who saw in the ancient Germans of Tacitus the origin of the Dutch republic, "a people can select the form of government which it wishes by its free choice." Bacon praised democracy as "more quiet and less subject to sedition" than other forms of government. He attributed the excellence of Dutch government to an equality that kept its deliberations less partisan "and the payments and tributes more cheerful." Montaigne claimed to think democracy "the most natural and equitable" form of government.

Underlying these tendencies was the more general shift we have noted elsewhere from hierarchy to balance as the basic principle of order. Machiavelli had earlier employed it in relation to politics, and its identification as the wisest course for states was much repeated. Bodin suggested that peace might be preserved among otherwise militant religious factions if "the groups, each acting as a check on the other, protect the stability and harmony of the state." Sarpi believed that social order depended on a balance between human appetite and the fear of punishment, applying the principle also to international relations, as Venice tried to balance between France and Spain. Bacon noted the workings of the balance of power in Italy and in the relations between the emperor and the kings of France and England, among whom "there was such a watch kept, that none of the three could win a palm of ground but the other two would straightways balance it." Hooker, remarking on the human tendency "to cure one contrarie by another," conceived of the aristocratic and clerical hierarchies in England as checking and balancing each other, "so that the reverend Authority of the one might be to the other as a courteous bridle." There was, perhaps, more than a hint of irony here.

The notion of balance established by contract also served to describe the proper relation between a consenting community and the ruler who served as its agent. Contract theory was not entirely new; contracts had defined the relations among members of the feudal hierarchy, and the conception of a covenant between God and his people had been developed within the nominalist tradition and advanced by Heinrich Bullinger in Zurich as an alternative to absolute predestination. In politics a contract was now understood as an agreement, first among the members of the political community, and then between that community and its ruler.

Contracts were given political form in written constitutions, now attractive to some thinkers. French political thought was much influenced by constitutional theory during the civil wars, when royal authority was challenged from many sides. The *Franco-gallia* (1573) of François Hotman, a Huguenot lawyer disturbed by royal persecution of Protestants, argued on historical grounds for the existence of an ancient French constitution. This, he maintained, made the king, originally elected, responsible to his subjects as represented in the Estates General, which he was obligated to consult.

A corollary of such views was the right of resistance to rulers who violated the contract. Protestants generally defended the right of resistance to Catholic rulers who persecuted them. Hotman argued the point from history; others argued from natural law and the reciprocal nature of contracts. Scholastic thinkers generally taught the right of resistance to secular authority. Even Bodin believed that a tyrant could "be lawfully slain" by "all the people or any of them." Botero described the assassin of William of Orange as "moved by religious zeal and the public good"; and Montaigne sympathized with the assassins of Caesar. Even Sarpi argued for the duty of a subordinate to resist a superior who exceeded his authority.

Finally, the secularization of politics found expression in the concern of many thinkers with the rule of law as a restriction on the power of rulers. The point was emphasized by a contemporary historian:

> Just as little can a people live without law as a body without members, blood, or nerves; and there is nothing so consonant with the condition of nature as law, without which a household, a town, a nation, or all of humankind could not subsist, nor even the nature of things, the world itself. The foundation of liberty, the fount of equity and understanding, the heart, the counsel, and the wills of a state are planted and established upon law.[8]

But there were many ways of understanding law. For conservatives, law, rooted in nature or custom, was an absolute. An alternative view saw law as a human creation adaptable to changing needs. As a French chancellor observed in a speech of 1562, laws should be fitted to circumstances "as shoes to feet." For Bacon, laws existed for "the happiness of citizens" and should be evaluated on this basis. For Sarpi, only religious truths are eternal whereas laws, having to deal with an infinite variety of situations and cases, must be judged for their flexibility and adaptability. Hotman argued that historical conditions must shape the law. Bodin argued that law had no other basis than the will of a ruler; it was "the command of a sovereign concerning all his subjects," dependent on "nothing but his mere and frank good will."

Hooker is of special interest on this subject. He believed in principle that all laws originate with God, and he was deeply concerned to maintain respect for them. But he gave a novel emphasis to the "positive" laws that concern men "as they are linked with others in some form of politique societie"; such laws could be changed because of "alteration of persons or times." God himself, under such circumstances, would change them. Hooker drew on this principle in his opposition to the biblical legalism of his Puritan opponents. He was also aware of the relation of laws to power. "That which establisheth and maketh them is power," he wrote, "even power of dominion the Cheiftie whereof amongst us resteth in the person of the *King*."

But law was finally, for Hooker, a restraint on absolutism. It was, he argued,

> almost out of doubt and controversie that every independent multi-
> tude before any certaine forme of regiment established hath under
> *Gods* supreme authoritie full dominion over it self, even as a man not
> tied with the bond of subjection as yet unto any other hath over himself
> the like power. God creating mankinde did indue it naturally with full
> power to guide it self in what kindes of societies soever it should
> choose to live. . . . the whole body politique maketh lawes which lawes
> give power unto the *King* and the *King* having bound himself to use
> according unto lawe that power, it so falleth out that the execution of
> the one is accomplished by the other in most religious and peaceable
> sort.[9]

Thus all government, both political and ecclesiastical, had originated in the consent of the governed, without which "there were no reason, that one man should take upon him to be Lord or Judge over another." Furthermore, it was "a thing even naturall that all free and independent societies should themselves make their own lawes, and that this power should belong to the whole, not to any certaine part of a politique body, though happilie some one part may have greater sway in that action then the rest." A king, then, may have "universall dominion, but with dependence upon "that whole entier body over the severall partes wherof he hath dominion." This may be represented by "parliaments, councels, and the like assemblies." Thus a state in which "the *King* doth guide the state and the lawe the *King*, that commonwealth is like an harpe or melodious instrument, the stringes whereof are tuned and handled all by one hand, following as lawes the rules and canons of Musicall science."

This chapter has emphasized those aspects of political and social thought in this period that pointed to liberation from the rigidities of social organization and from arbitrary and oppressive government. But, as already for Machiavelli, liberty had two sides. One pointed tø republicanism and the liberty of citizens. The other side tended to free the rules but enslave the people. As we will see in a later chapter, Machiavelli pointed to despotism as well as to republicanism.

CHAPTER SEVEN

The Liberation of Religion

European Christianity after the Protestant revolt in the earlier sixteenth century had been fragmented by national and sectarian interests. But deeper impulses had also been at work even before the appearance of Erasmus, whose influence persisted long after his death in 1536. Reformers, both Protestant and Catholic, sought to liberate Christianity from what they saw as the sterile abstractions of scholastic theology and the externalism that often passed for piety, especially among the laity.

Too much has been made, in treating the history of Christianity in this period, of the divisions between Catholics and Protestants.[1] Catholics, aside from their (often qualified) respect for the papacy, were hardly more united than Protestants and often as likely to "protest" against the papal monarchy as Protestants: the label "papist" was often as pejorative among Catholics as among Protestants. Many in both groups had reservations about the pope's excommunication of Luther and were as hostile to the Society of Jesus as to Protestantism. And while many Catholics continued to look to philosophy to support faith, others had serious reservations about it. Nor were those who agreed on this matter in agreement on others. The Counter-Reformation was not a reaction against later medieval nominalism, in spite of the privileged position eventually achieved by Thomism. William of Ockham's *Opera omnia* was placed on the papal Index of 1557, but its condemnation was soon relaxed. Diego Lainez, professor of theology in Rome and successor to Loyola as head of the Jesuits, admired Gabriel Biel, the most influential nominalist of the fifteenth century. Sarpi's circle in Venice and major figures in the French church were hostile to the whole scholastic enterprise. Indeed, the labels "Catholic" and "Protestant" are themselves misleading; Protestants insisted for many years that they were Catholics, regularly reminding themselves of it by reciting the ancient Christian creeds. There were also confessional ambiguities on all sides. The division between the more pessimistic Baianism and Jansenism, and Thomism, which lasted for decades among Catholics, was paralleled by the division on freedom of the will among Protestants between Arminianism and Calvinist orthodoxy. Nearly a century after the start of the Reformation, important groups of Catholics were pleased by the Synod of Dort, which went beyond Calvin himself on predestination. A "Catholic" in this period was simply a person who insisted on the institutional unity of the church and acknowledged, however tepidly, the leadership of Rome. A "Protestant" was a person who "protested" against papal leadership.

As these examples imply, the basic divisions among Christians were deeper than these common designations suggest. Both Catholics and Protestants differed among themselves over whether faith could be expressed in a systematic, dogmatic, and intellectualized theology or was primarily a function of imagination and feeling. As a religion of the heart, owing much to Augustine's *Confessions* and emphasizing works of love, this kind of Augustinianism among Catholics tended also to be expressed in a radical revulsion against the sinfulness of the world.

Augustinian spirituality, whether Protestant or Catholic, continued to react against scholastic rationalism, opposing to it a simple faith in the teachings of the Gospel. It was a major element in the scholarly "positive" theology of the age, which promoted a religion of personal experience based on the Scriptures and the early church fathers. It had been central to Protestantism, and still influenced the attack of Peter Ramus on Aristotle; among Catholics it influenced such figures as Sarpi and Bérulle. On both sides it rejected a conception of faith as the doctrine to which one adheres; rather, faith—a fundamental distinction—was the gift *by* which one believes: an inward disposition rather than external commitment to a creed. The distinction was not always well regarded by ecclesiastical or ministerial authority on either side, such faith being difficult to identify and control. Its supporters were likely to be laymen and scholars rather than professional theologians. For those who understood faith in this way, true piety was expressed not in doctrine, so often divisive, but in love, the basis of harmony.

This tendency within Christianity continued to reflect the rhetorical theology of Renaissance humanism. It was also basic to Erasmian reformism, still at work in both Protestantism and Catholicism long after the Council of Trent. In Italy, through the movement known as "Italian Evangelism," humanism influenced the Catholic Reformation, and it survived in Venice into the seventeenth century, especially in Paolo Sarpi. In Rome itself, Augustinian spirituality and its biblicism promoted a rhetorical conception of human being and a preference for persuasive rather than rational discourse. Its influence can also be discerned in the Spanish Augustinian friar Luis de Leon, who was close to St. Teresa of Avila. Among Lutherans the followers of Melanchthon kept humanism alive, and Calvin, who unlike Luther never attacked Erasmus, remained a humanist throughout his career. Calvinist educators kept much of Erasmianism, and the influence of humanism was particularly entrenched in theologically Calvinist England, where John Foxe included Petrarch, Lorenzo Valla, and Pico della Mirandola among the faithful few who had remained within the "true church" during the Middle Ages.

It flourished especially among those disillusioned by dogmatic controversy. "It is true," one scholar wrote, "that religion requires knowledge. But it is not enough. For [religion] does not have its seat in the brain but in the heart and affection. The devil himself is very knowledgeable, but he is not religious." A rebel against the dogmatism of Calvinism suggested the skepticism to which this position tended. "I cannot understand or believe that D. Johannes Calvinus, although otherwise most highly gifted and enlightened by God almighty . . . never erred or contradicted himself." Henry Nicholas, founder of the Family of Love, a sect attractive to intellectuals on the continent such as Postel, Lipsius, and the Antwerp printer Christophe Plantin, denounced religious contention as a product of ignorance:

> The mind of man does not understand or comprehend the mind of God rightly out of the letter of the Scriptures, as a result of which there is much contention (such as occurred also in the past among the worldly wise and those learned in Scripture), much disagreement, variance, and controversy among the children of men, who contend about things they do not understand, and appear to know what . . . is not to be known or understood.[2]

Montaigne blamed the religious warfare of his time on "affirmation," "opinionativeness," and "stupidity," by which he meant ignorance of one's own ignorance.

Thus it can hardly be surprising that many on both sides of the major division in Western Christendom, especially among intellectuals, lacked a strong institutional identification. This may help to explain why rulers could see the choice between Catholicism and Protestantism as political rather than spiritual; and "superconfessionality"—participation in the rites of both sides where this was possible—which, though denounced by religious leaders, was common, especially in France and the Netherlands. It is sometimes difficult to determine where to locate individuals. Some wavered, like the King of Sweden, John III Vasa, whom the Jesuit Antonio Possevino tried to convert to Catholicism.

Irenicism among intellectuals was notably represented by Hooker, whose *Laws of Ecclesiastical Polity*, as its title implies, was chiefly concerned with practical problems, not theology. For Hooker, God is mostly unknowable, and Christianity chiefly based on faith:

> Dangerous it were for the feeble braine of man to wade farre into the doings of the most High, whome although to knowe be life and joy to make mention of his name: yet our soundest knowledge is to know that we know him not as in deed he is, neither can know him; and our safest eloquence concerning him is our silence, when we confesse . . . that his glory is inexplicable, his greatnes above our capacitie and reach.[3]

To Bacon, "the more discordant therefore and incredible any Divine mystery is, the more honour is shown to God in believing it; and the nobler is the victory of faith." He vigorously opposed mixing religion and philosophy as an obstacle to the truth-claims of both, denouncing "those who have taken upon them to deduce the truth of the Christian religion from the principles of philosophers," which "disparaged things divine by mingling them with things human."

Some of these tendencies were represented in Catholicism at the University of Louvain, long a stronghold of Erasmianism, by Michel Baius, who revived the anti-Pelagian works of Augustine, and Cornelius Jansen, author of *Augustinus*, a massive work published posthumously in 1640, which emphasized the predestinarian elements in Augustine's thought. Jansen's name was given to a movement—Jansenism—that took root in many parts of the Catholic world, but especially in France under the leadership of Saint-Cyran. Its insistence on the authority of Augustine may seem a departure from Erasmianism, but it looked, if selectively, to Christian antiquity, promoted a biblical and historical as opposed to a systematic and philosophical conception of Christianity, and vigorously opposed scholastic theology.

A biblical fideism was also common among French lawyers. Pierre de l'Estoile confined his beliefs, as he declared, "simply to the words of Jesus Christ"; he rejected "all interpretations or glosses which spoil the text [of Scripture] or are contrary, however subtle they may be." Leaders of the

Catholic Reformation in France, among them Bérulle and François de Sales, rejected scholastic theology for a simple faith conforming to biblical teaching and the ways of the ancient church. Jansen charged that philosophy encouraged contention, error, and heresy.

Montaigne insisted on his own fideism, although basing it chiefly on institutional authority, now often favored in Rome, rather than an internalized spirituality. For Montaigne, human beings are incapable of understanding, for themselves, either God or the world. "Reason," he maintained, "does nothing but go astray in everything, and especially when it meddles with divine things." This meant, for him, dependence on the authority of the church, for the mind of an individual, "when it strays however little from the beaten path and deviates or wanders from the way traced and trodden by the Church, is immediately lost, it grows embarrassed and entangled, whirling round and floating in that vast, troubled, and undulating sea of human opinions, unbridled and aimless." For "as soon as it loses that great common high road, it breaks up and disperses into a thousand different roads." This meant, Montaigne believed, that theology, "as queen and mistress," must be totally divorced from human culture. Faith "must be sovereign everywhere."

In some moods, nevertheless, the inwardness of humanist spirituality can be discerned even in Montaigne, as he emphasized individual transformation and attacked dogmatism and coercion. Faith, he argued, as a gift of God—unlike beliefs acquired by reason—has a unique power. A single drop of faith can "move mountains." With faith human actions "would not be simply human; they would have something miraculous about them," although to support this reflection—a nice humanist touch—he quoted Quintilian rather than Scripture: "Brief is the task of starting an honorable and happy life, if you believe." He also rejected the notion that the truth of Christianity could be demonstrated by its worldly success.

At times he sounded almost Lutheran in his conception of faith as a divine gift. "We are not to think," he insisted, "that it is on us that faith depends, or that our efforts and arguments can attain a knowledge so supernatural and divine." But he differed from Luther by insisting on skepticism as the way to faith:

It presents man naked and empty, acknowledging his natural weakness, fit to receive from above some outside power; stripped of human knowledge in himself; annihilating his judgment to make more room for faith; neither disbelieving nor setting up any doctrine against the common observances; humble, obedient, teachable, zealous; a sworn enemy of heresy and consequently free from the vain and irreligious opinions introduced by the false sects. He is a blank tablet prepared to take from the finger of God such forms as he shall be pleased to engrave upon it. The more we cast ourselves back on God and commit ourselves to him, and renounce ourselves, the better we are.[4]

This position was shared by many others. Bérulle based his conception of reform on the transformation of individuals by faith; and early Jesuit spirituality encouraged inwardness. Loyola's *Spiritual Exercises*, practiced by Jesuits everywhere to the present, required daily self-examination in which an individual recorded his progress—and his failings—in following Christ. The inwardness in humanist piety also nourished a major mystical movement. Michel Certeau, noting the frequency of the word "mystical" in the titles of early seventeenth-century works, has characterized mysticism as "the Trojan horse of rhetoric within the city of theological science." Mystics preferred "spiritual" to literal interpretation of the Bible, prized individual religious experience, and found elements of truth in all religions. This helps to explain the continuing popularity, among Protestants as well as Catholics, of the early fifteenth-century *Imitation of Christ*. In Spain, mysticism flourished in every social group, appealing to the lower classes by its indifference to religious establishments and to intellectuals by its spiritualizing universalism. Its resistance to dogmatism was notably attractive to converted Jews and Muslims.

Another influential work, Pierre Charron's *De la sagesse*, owed much to Montaigne, especially to his emphasis on the weakness and presumption of human wisdom. Charron rejected, like Montaigne, a role for reason in Christian belief, although he acknowledged its value in the ethical life. An effective preacher who had also written against atheism, Charron enabled Montaigne's skepticism to influence a wider circle of readers; and his skepticism, like Montaigne's, raised doubts in some circles about the sincerity of his professions of belief. So his insistence that the immortality of the soul could not be proved by reason—a position condemned by the Sorbonne in 1603—aligned fideism with those who rejected Christianity altogether. Both Montaigne and Charron were widely believed to contribute to radical disbelief. But here we can see again, among both Catholics and Protestants, a holistic understanding of the human personality and its implications for the limits of human knowledge.

This phase in the history of Christianity is often depicted, because of its dogmatic orthodoxies, as singularly arid, and there is much to confirm this view, as we will see in a later chapter. But this is only half true. On all sides we encounter a powerful sense of the divine presence. This is true even of Ralegh's *History*, notable in view of its author's reputation for atheism. For Ralegh

> God worketh by Angels, by the Sunne, by the Starres, by Nature, or infused properties, and by men, as by severall organs, severall effects; all second causes whatsoever, being but instruments, conduits, and pipes, which carrie and disperse what they have received from the head and fountaine of the Universall. For it is Gods infinite power, and every-where-presence (compassing, embracing, and piercing all things) that giveth to the Sunne power to draw up vapours, to vapours to be made cloudes, cloudes to contayne raine, and raine to fall: so all second and instrumentall causes, together with Nature it selfe, without that operative facultie which God gave them, would become altogether silent, virtuelisse, and dead.[5]

In spite of his rather mechanical invocation of secondary causes in the *Laws*, Hooker's God was not a deduction from the physical and metaphysical structure of things but constantly active, intervening and in charge, experienced everywhere. The God of François de Sales was caring and nurturing, like a mother. The Lutheran Johann Arndt's God "possesses man completely, from within and without." His *True Christianity*, one of the sources of pietism, emphasized an inwardness that would eventually challenge both dogmatism and the rationalism of the Enlightenment.

Yet this inwardness was often accompanied by reformism and activism. Calvinists had aimed from the beginning to reshape the world into the kingdom of Christ; and reform went hand in hand with faith for conservatives like Hooker, who was by no means simply an apologist for the English church; he also attacked its ignorance, absenteeism, and clerical ambition. The *Laws* was a reformist document.

Many Catholics, especially outside Rome, were also calling for reform. In Venice, a group of reformers appealed, like earlier humanists, to the decentralized church of antiquity as a model of reform. In France, the Estates General regularly called for reform in the church, demanding more learned and pious clergy, more frequent sermons, and closer supervision of public morals. Gallican lawyers, who tended to regard the decrees of Trent as an instrument of papal control, contrasted the contemporary church unfavorably with the apostolic model. Saint-Cyran and Jansen described the decrees as a "deformation" rather than a reformation.

The horrors of the religious wars combined with reformism to nourish a growing peace movement. Montaigne frequently expressed his outrage at the cruelty of the wars. Burton, when there were already hints that England might not be spared such agonies, thought there could be "no greater discord than that which proceeds from Religion," although he found nearly incredible the reports from France and the related "hurly burlies all over Europe for these many years." Bacon noted the power of religion to incite to evil, giving as examples the St. Bartholomew Massacre in France and the Gunpowder Plot in England. Had Lucretius known of these events, he concluded, "he would have been seven times more Epicure and atheist than he was." The savagery of religious polemic paralleled the cruelty of the wars themselves.

But whatever their similarities, there were also differences among the several versions of Christianity; and the question of the *truth* of religious beliefs, on which so much was believed to depend, was raised directly by their competition. Reflection on this question was also stimulated by a growing awareness of peoples around the world who combined an alien religion with a high level of civilization. This had previously been thought impossible; it was commonly believed that only Christianity could support civilization. Perhaps even more troubling was the supposed discovery in exotic places of ethical practices superior to those of "Christian" Europe; these served reformers as a reproach to Christendom.

The existence of religious division and variety in Europe itself was central to Bodin's *Colloquium*, which brought together a Catholic, a Lutheran, a Calvinist, a Jew, a Muslim, and a skeptic to discuss religious questions. The dialogue ends, in contrast to what was occurring in the world, with general agreement about the desirability for all religions to exist together in harmony, and its participants conclude by singing together "Lo, how good and pleasing it is for brothers to live in unity," followed by fraternal embraces. Henceforth, Bodin remarks, "they nourished their piety in remarkable harmony, and their integrity of life in common pursuits and intimacy." But his final sentence was faintly ambiguous: "However, afterwards they held no other conversation about religions, although each one defended his own with the supreme sanctity of his life."

There were, as this suggests, a few spokesmen for latitude in doctrinal definition, for religious reunion, and even for religious toleration. The more flexible leaders of the early Reformation, Melanchthon among Lutherans and Thomas Starkey in England, had advanced the conception of adiaphora, matters on which Christians could reasonably differ without falling into heresy; and some thinkers in our period accepted and even enlarged on the conception. Hooker distinguished between the substance of faith required by God and other aspects of church and cult; his sensitivity to change here stood him in good stead. "There is no reason in the world," he declared, "wherefore we shoulde esteeme it as necessarie alwaies to doe, as alwaies to believe, the same things; seeing every man knoweth that the matter of faith is constant, the matter contrariwise of action daily change-able, especially the matter of action belonging unto Church politie." This position allowed him, for example, to accept baptism by women. He rejected detailed imitation of Christ in favor of a conception of imitation held by some humanists:

> Our imitation of him consisteth not in tyinge scrupulouslie our selves unto his syllables but rather speakinge by the heavenlie direction of that inspired divine wisdom which teacheth divers waies to one ende, and doth therein controle theire boldnes by whome any prof-itable way is censured as reprovable only under coulor of some smale difference from greate examples goinge before. To doe through-out every the like circumstaunce the same which Christ did . . . were by following his footsteps in that sort to erre more from the purpose hee aimed at then wee now doe by not following them with so nice and severe strictnesse.[6]

Burton was remarkably even-handed about religious difference. "Our Papists object as much to us, and account us hereticks, as we them," he wrote, and "the Turks esteem of both [Catholics and Protestants] as Infidels, and we them as a company of Pagans, Jews against all; when indeed there is a general fault in all, and something in the very best, which may justly deserve God's wrath, and pull these miseries upon our heads."

There are also anticipations of later Quietism in Pierre de l'Estoile's emphasis on the divine will and—along with a hint of Machiavellianism—in Sarpi's doctrine of the occasion, which advocated waiting for the right moment to act: i.e., the "occasion" given by God. Burton observed that God "reveals and conceals, to whom and when he will" and, "to check our presumptuous inquisition, wraps up all things in uncertainty." Calvinist activism was itself restrained by the self-examination so strongly urged by Calvin himself, and in England by the Book of Common Prayer.

The growing centralization of the major religious bodies in this period was thus still everywhere challenged by the lively spirituality to which Augustinian humanism had been central. The centralization of the papal church was often blamed for everything that had gone wrong in religious matters. For Sarpi, the church universal, as in the case of all universals for nominalist thinkers, was only an abstraction; in the real world churches corresponded, at least in principle, to political communities: to urban republics like Venice, or to national monarchies such as England, France, and Spain. This pointed not only to local control but also to a wide range of local variation. It might also suggest, especially in republics, a conception of the church as the whole congregation of believers. It directly challenged both the monarchical and hierarchical models of the church.

This vision underlay Sarpi's *History of the Council of Trent*. The church, in his view, had originated as a decentralized set of local congregations based on political communities, each ruled by the consent of the faithful; and it had degenerated into a tyrannical monarchy claiming a universal and unrestricted power. This vision was partly shared by scholastic writers, who, though disagreeing with its application to the church, followed it in dealing with secular polities. Conversely, Sarpi envisaged the reform of the church as a return to its origins.

These views closely paralleled conciliarism, now reviving in France under Gallican auspices. The conciliar ideal envisaged no more than a limited, constitutional monarchy for the pope, whose authority was based on a general council representing the whole church. In this view the pope was obligated to respect the rights of the church, defined as the whole body of Christians, and to rule it, according to law, for the common good. Such Gallican theorists as Edmond Richer resumed many earlier arguments for the superiority of general council to pope, and especially the view of the council as the only safeguard against "an absolute power" over the church at every level. Jacques Leschassier called on the secular courts of France to reform the church, since they were "the natural and legitimate protectors of ancient right."

Gallicanism had been well represented at the Council of Trent. This explains the silence of the council on the claim of the pope to be *episcopus universalis* (universal bishop), from whom all other bishops derive their power. At Trent, indeed, the papal party had barely prevented the condemnation of the notion. And sentiment for local control in the church was widespread among Catholics. The decrees of Trent met with much resistance, especially those dealing with bishops, a matter on which local ecclesiastics allied with secular rulers. This explains why the decrees were never officially adopted in France. They were also resisted in Belgium as contrary to local liberties, and in Mexico, where the Spanish government jealously guarded its prerogatives. Catholics in England were forbidden by Rome to take an oath of loyalty to James I; but their official superior, the Archpriest Blackwell, not only refused to publish the ban but himself took the oath and exhorted other English Catholics to do likewise.

Given so much confusion about ecclesiastical loyalties, it is hardly surprising that we also find impulses to reunite the separated churches. Protestants as well as Catholics continued to recite creeds that included belief in "one holy, catholic, and apostolic church," and professed an interest, at least in principle, in religious reconciliation. Hooker minimized confessional differences, considering the Roman Church, however misguided, as still Christian, and James I was himself interested in reunion. Meanwhile Calvinist scholars, who increasingly studied ancient Christianity, sometimes promoted reconciliation. François de Sales, its (non-resident) bishop, visited Geneva frequently for discussions with Theodore Beza, Calvin's successor as leader of its church.

Religious pluralism was also sometimes tolerated. Montaigne discovered this in 1580 in Protestant Basel, where he was surprised to learn that its people were "not in agreement over their religion . . . some calling themselves Zwinglians, others Calvinists, others Martinists [Lutherans]," whereas many others "still fostered the Roman religion in their heart." Much also remained there of the pre-Reformation era: images on church exteriors, organs, bells, crosses, and stained-glass windows. The Catholic bishop, though living outside the city, even continued to draw much of his income from it. The populations of the German imperial cities were usually mixed; Catholics and Lutherans lived peacefully together, sometimes even sharing churches. France, though the site of the notorious St. Bartholomew Massacre in 1572, granted a degree of toleration to Protestantism in the Edict of Nantes in 1585.

Thus, in spite of the savage persecution of heresy in some parts of Europe, other places permitted variety. In the Calvinist Netherlands, Catholics were more easily accepted than Arminians; and some theologians in Belgium favored toleration. Intellectuals on the continent admired Stuart England as a haven of toleration. Venice too had a wide reputation for tolerance. Bodin remarked on the permissiveness of its government toward Jews and Greeks, who were allowed to practice their "foreign rites" publicly. The Venetian government resisted pressures from Rome to impose a profession of Catholic faith on students at the University of Padua, many of whom were Protestants. Sarpi thought papal decrees against heresy contrary to the mildness of Venice, especially since they called for the death penalty.

Occasional voices were now heard in favor of general toleration. Burton recommended it as a cure for religious melancholy but also defended it in principle. "Because God is immense and infinite, and his nature cannot be perfectly known," he wrote, "it is convenient he should be as diversely worshipped, as every man shall perceive or understand." He appealed to the new science; an infinite universe, he suggested, implied an infinite variety of religions. The jurist Sir Edward Coke rejected the examination of "the intention and thought" of any man's heart. In the Netherlands, Dirck Coornhert defended toleration against the dogmatism of both Catholics and Calvinists. Postel anticipated Milton in arguing that mistaken belief tested and strengthened the truth. The skeptical currents in the thought of the time also pointed to toleration.

His *Colloquium*, though he did not dare to publish it in his lifetime, gave Bodin an opportunity to present a many-sided argument for it. One of its major themes was the universal harmony of nature, which he took as a model for the harmony of all practical arguments for toleration: the difficulty of imposing a religion, the conflicts that would inevitably result. A contemporary model was "the kingdom of the Turks and Persians," where all religions were permitted. In the end Bodin proposed the Renaissance principle of balance as a practical solution to keep the peace among diverse religions.

The plea for toleration in religion was, however, only a more specific case of a more general value: freedom of expression about all things. This too, almost unknown in earlier periods, was now finding occasional advocates. Sarpi thought such freedom a natural aspiration and an essential condition for all learning; truth would emerge, he believed, only through open discussion. Galileo described one of his pupils as "a man of excellent mind, and free (as one must be) in philosophizing."

Venice was commonly cited to illustrate both the good and evil results of free expression. Subversive literature of many kinds was printed there, as were the *Dialogues* of Galileo. Bodin's *Colloquium* was at least set in this place where freedom of all kinds was thought to flourish. As the English ambassador to Venice wrote home in 1606, Venice was "a State that, whether it be in fear or otherwise, heareth all men speak willingly." The "myth of Venice" gave expression, among other values, to conceptions of intellectual and religious freedom.

The rhetorical conception of human being in this period was thus open at once to reformism, inwardness and toleration.

CHAPTER EIGHT

The Worst of Times

In the earlier Renaissance many thinkers were hopeful. The new monarchies were bringing order to Spain, France, and England. Recently discovered new worlds and the development of new seaways promised both wealth and, with artillery and the printing press, the triumph of European culture and Christianity around the globe. Humanists and reformers foresaw the onset of a golden age ushered in by the new learning, which, under the auspices of the ancient poets and rhetoricians, promised new freedoms.

Yet by the second half of the sixteenth century when, paradoxically, the idea of progress was beginning to emerge, many cultivated Europeans were increasingly anxious and unhappy, even among those we have cited to illustrate the more positive side of the age. Until well into the seventeenth century, the mood of most people who contemplated the current scene was grim. The exhilarating freedom apparent in many aspects of human experience was gradually dissolving. Hope was increasingly rare, despair on the rise; God himself seemed more and more indifferent to the world.

Historians have often attributed this change to developments in the external environment: ferocious wars both political and religious, a depressed economy and social turmoil, the rise of a militant and expanding Islam. These were, to be sure, disturbing realities. But a direct connection between them and the general European mood is difficult to establish. It is not obvious that the times were worse than they had often been before without causing a similar shift in consciousness; indeed, the at least equally unhappy fourteenth century had given birth to the new culture of the Renaissance.

This book argues that a major explanation for this shift in the cultural atmosphere lies in the culture itself, precisely because of the freedoms it promoted. These, to be sure, satisfied fundamental human needs, but at the same time they eroded traditional patterns of order that were equally necessary. The resulting distress, however obscure in its beginnings, afflicted even thinkers who rejoiced in the novelties of freedom. This is why many of the figures whom we have already observed celebrating the novelties of late Renaissance culture can also be cited on the other side. The age was generally ambivalent; it was both the best and the worst of times. Both its brighter and darker sides have long been well known to historians but have usually been treated separately. This study is concerned to connect them by showing how they were two aspects of the same mentality.

Galileo himself, who contributed so much to the great discoveries of the period, by the same token felt dread. In *The Assayer*, in which he reflected on the significance of his work, he hinted at its darker side. A man fortunate enough, he wrote of himself, to escape the "dark and confused labyrinths" in which he would otherwise have been "ever more entangled," might then be engulfed "in a boundless sea" from which he "might never get back to port." Even escape risked "giving rise to a hundred difficulties," as he feared "might have already happened" in his own voyage, though it was "but a little way from shore." The cultural crisis to which Galileo's discoveries contributed had projected Europeans into a predicament somewhat like that of Milton's Adam and Eve after the fall, which resulted in their ejection into the realm of history: "The World was all before them, where to choose their place of rest." Among other things, this novel perspective was supremely discomforting. What Vaclav Havel has described as "the absurd terrain of freedom" was also the realm of anxiety. The period covered in this book was one of an uneasy equilibrium between the exhilaration of liberation and the need to escape its inevitable discontents. As a kind of prolonged crisis, in the original sense of the term crossroads, it was preparing the way for a new stage in European cultural history.

There have always been complaints about the sin and sorrow of life, often expressed in timeless proverbs: "A good man is rare in this life"; "Man is an enemy to other men and to himself"; "Under the skin of a man lurk many beasts." But pessimism has ups and downs, and it was now deepening and spreading. Stimulated by the religious movements of the time, an Augustinian vision of the human condition already at work in earlier humanism was growing. Sarpi thought it a universal truth that, however well all things begin, they will be subverted by human wickedness. Luis de Leon, the champion of St. Teresa, described life as a dangerous journey through "lands inhabited by brigands." Charron saw the world as "a mass of darkness full of pits and prisons, a labyrinth, a confused and highly twisted abyss."

But such views were not confined to the pious. Stoicism was attractive largely because it offered what seemed the only reasonable adjustment to the grim realities of human existence. But, as commonly happens, anxieties deep within the self were attributed to specific causes that, because temporary, might ameliorate. Lipsius recommended Stoicism in his *Politica* (1589) because it could reconcile contemporaries to the disorders of contemporary life. What had driven him to write, he declared, was

> care for the common good and this present condition of Europe, which I cannot look upon without weeping. O [Europe], the better part of the world, what fires of dissension religion has kindled in you! The heads of the Christian states clash with each other, and thousands of men have perished at a time and are still perishing under the pretext of Piety.[1]

Ben Jonson was more terse; he described the best life as the shortest.

Contemporary pessimism was often rooted in a conception of history, ultimately Neoplatonic, as a steady and inevitable decline from an original perfection. For Bodin, nature itself revealed the decrepitude of the world:

> Writers say, continuously complaining, that men cannot be compared with their ancestors in size or strength, as is attested by the remains of their bones and the life of these little men and little lads, when compared with the gigantic size of those who were seven, eight, or nine cubits taller. This fact bears witness to the senility of the world and its future destruction.[2]

Donne described everything earthly as decay and ruin. For the classicist Henri Estienne, his time was "worse than all the preceding." Montaigne described contemporaries as "abortions of men"; everything around him seemed to be crumbling: "all the great states, in Christendom or elsewhere," were threatened by "change and ruin." Ronsard compared France, disordered by the religious wars, to a merchant attacked by a thief who "beats and torments him," and "seeing him dead smiles at his wounds and leaves him to be eaten by mastiffs and wolves." Burton did not know how to react to so mad and confused a world: "I did sometimes laugh, and satirically tax with Menippes, lament with Heraclitus, sometimes again I was bitterly mirthful and then again burning with rage; I was much moved to see that abuse which I could not amend."

The familiar association of ages with the hierarchy of metals was invoked.

Cervantes contrasted "this Iron Age" with the "age of gold." For Donne, the present was an "age of rusty iron." Montaigne went further: the century was "so leaden that not only the practice but even the idea of virtue is wanting." He wished for an even baser metal with which to compare it.

Imagery of disorder proliferated. The world, to cite an Italian book title of 1602, was "overturned and upended," its chaos now, as a result of the new astronomy, disordering and corrupting the heavens. Montaigne, like the surgeon Ambroise Paré, was fascinated with monstrous births, which he interpreted as an irruption of chaos into human affairs; Loy Le Roy read such phenomena as evidence of the "malice and extraordinary changes" of the times. The Spanish Jesuit Baltasar Gracian played with images of disorder:

> All goes backward . . . virtue is chased out, vice exalted, truth mute, three-tongued lies run rampant . . . books are without teachers and teachers without books . . . young people grow feeble and elderly folk rejuvenate . . . beasts play the man and men play the beast . . . young women cry and old men laugh, lions bleat and deer hunt, chickens crow and roosters are quiet . . . those who should be leaders because of their wisdom and knowledge are cast down, despised, forgotten, and humiliated . . . those who should be subjects because of their ignorance and incapacity, incompetent, without knowledge and experience, govern.[3]

Some areas of disorder attracted more attention than others. One of the most troubling for contemporaries was—as more recently—gender. Many difficulties of the times were associated with effeminacy, both as cause and effect. A Spanish moralist attacked the court, where "the vanity of songs and dances entertains the effeminate and makes them waste their time in embellishing their faces, curling their hair, raising the pitch of their voice, in feminine caresses and affectation, and in making themselves equal to women in the delicacy of their bodies." At the French court, it was charged, "men obey women, the wise obey the ignorant, the courageous obey cowards, and courage and military values are held in doubt and suspense." Bodin complained of the decline of paternal authority in families. In the streets of London, it was charged, men wore earrings, women doublets: "it is now come to pass that women are become men, and men transformed into monsters." Bacon worried lest a "slothful peace" might "effeminate" courage. Campanella listed the blurring of gender among the ominous signs of the times.

Rule by women during the later sixteenth century in England and Scotland, and in France under the domination of Catherine de' Medici, was especially troubling, placing whole kingdoms under female dominion. John Knox reacted with his *First Blast of the Trumpet against the Monstrous Regiment of Women* (1558):

> A woman sitting in iudgement, or riding frome parliament in the middest of men, hauing the royall crowne vpon her head, the sworde and sceptre borne before her, in signe that the administration of iustice was in her power: I am assuredlie persuaded, I say, that suche a sight shulde so astonishe them, that they shuld iudge the hole worlde to be transformed into Amazones, and that such a metamorphosis and change was made of all the men of that countrie, as poetes do feyn was made of the companyons of Vlisses, or at least, that albeit the outwarde form of men remained, yet shuld they iudge that their hartes were changed frome the wisdome, vnderstanding, and courage of men, to the foolishe fondnes and cowardise of women.[4]

Joseph Swetnam's *Arraignment of Lewd, Idle, Froward and Inconstant Women* went through ten editions between 1615 and 1634. Bodin was among those troubled by the rule of women because, he wrote, "vigorous action is contrary to the sex, and to the natural reserve and modesty of women." Infringement of the "natural" boundaries of gender pointed to general moral collapse.

The imagery of disease was also common, reinforced by periodic epidemics of plague and the spread of syphilis, so closely associated with immorality. An English almanac warned in 1587 of "disease and unknown maladies." "Now more than ever," it argued, "[God] is preparing to loose his anger upon our vices." Sarpi described Christendom as "a body so full of bad humors that, although its external parts are strong enough to contain them, so that for now no abscess is flowing, it will not long be able to maintain this appearance of health." He feared "that the longer it delays bursting out in some evil issue, the worse it must produce." Burton saw in the world "a vast confusion of hereditary diseases, no family secure, almost no man free from some grievous infirmity or other. . . . our generation is corrupt, we have many weak persons, both in body and mind, many feral diseases and crazed families raging amongst us."

Images of filth and contamination were also common, along with praise of cleanliness. The Dutch were already famous for it; but "purity" was a Catholic as well as a Protestant obsession. Tasso included among the responsibilities of the head of a household taking care "that no dirt be seen in the house or courtyard or on the tables or the cupboards; the walls, floors, ceilings, and all the utensils and implements of the house should be cleaned and shining like mirrors." This had for him social and esthetic, as well as hygienic, significance, since "cleanliness is not only pleasant to look at but also confers nobility and dignity on things that are base and mean by nature, just as, in contrast, filth takes away natural nobility and dignity."

Sin in all its varieties also seemed unusually rife; as Hooker observed, "We all make complaint of the iniquitie of our times, and not unjustly; for the days are evill." Burton pointed to the spread of "wenching and drinking." Montaigne was disturbed at once by the lechery, the judicial cruelty, and the "inhumanity and treachery" of France, his own country. Robert Greene, novelist and playwright, denounced greed: "he is counted the wisest that hath the deepest insight into the getting of gaines."

But if, as Huizinga has suggested, the most conspicuous sin of the earlier Middle Ages had been pride and that of the high Middle Ages cupidity, the sin most widely denounced in this period was hypocrisy. It had for some time troubled humanists, but by the later sixteenth century condemnations of hypocrisy reached a crescendo. "In other centuries," Sarpi lamented, "hypocrisy has had some currency, but in this alone it is dominant and excludes all piety." He interpreted the Council of Trent as a sustained exercise in hypocrisy. Galileo charged his critics with making "a shield of their hypocritical zeal for religion." A French ambassador to Rome associated hypocrisy particularly with Italy, where, he decided, religion was only "a mask," since it consisted chiefly in externals and was "as different from our French devotion as painting from the truth." But Montaigne saw it as far more general, decrying "the new-fangled virtue of hypocrisy and dissimulation" as a peculiarity of his own dismal time. "I mortally hate it," he continued:

> of all vices, I know none that testifies to so much cowardice and baseness of heart. It is a craven and servile idea to disguise ourselves and hide under a mask, and not dare to show ourselves as we are. In that way our men train for perfidy; being accustomed to speak false words, they have no scruples about breaking their word. A generous heart should not belie its thoughts; it wants to reveal itself even to its inmost depths. There everything is good, or at least everything is human.[5]

In England, it outraged Burton to see

a man protest friendship, kiss his hand whom he would wish slain, smile with an intent to do mischief, or cozen him whom he salutes, magnify his unworthy friend with hyperbolical elogiums; his enemy, albeit a good man, to vilify and disgrace him, yea all his actions, with the utmost livor [malignity] and malice can invent![6]

Hooker denounced "the pox of hypocrites and sons of this world" that "spreads in marvelous wise"; and Calvinists everywhere savagely attacked those who, as they insisted, agreed with them but conformed outwardly to Catholicism. Pascal would make a worldly virtue of hypocrisy by observing cynically that, since they are "founded on mutual deceit," few friendships would endure if each knew what his friend said of him in his absence.

Society depended fundamentally, it seemed, on hypocrisy. Boccalini included venerated ancients among the great hypocrites of the world: Seneca because his life was inconsistent with his teachings, Tacitus because "he was admired in an age composed of interest and violence" and extolled "the study of policy." Moral theologians and casuists in this period were concerned to rationalize the dissimulation that had become a necessity of human relations.

The obverse of such attitudes was the idealization of friendship, unusually important when human relations were generally suspect. "Friendship" was ambiguous; it was often the reverse of "disinterested." For Hooker, we need friends because "the actions of life being manie doe neede manie helping handes to further them." But friendship was also valued because it met emotional needs. Friendship, Burton observed, provides comfort, eases the mind, distracts from melancholy: "As the Sun is in the Firmament, is friendship in the world, a most divine and heavenly bond. As nuptial Love makes, this perfects mankind, and is to be preferred . . . before affinity or consanguinity." Bacon wrote that nothing could give such relief as "a true friend, to whom you may impart griefs, joys, fears, hopes, suspicions, counsels, and whatsoever lieth upon the heart to oppress it, in a kind of civil shrift or confession." Montaigne found in friendship "a general and universal warmth, moderate and even, [and] a constant and settled warmth, all gentleness and smoothness, with nothing bitter and stinging about it . . . [in friendship souls] mingle and blend with each other so completely that they efface the seam that joined them." His essay on friendship was admired in Sarpi's circle in Venice. Cervantes suggested, in the amity between the Don and his humble squire, that friendship could cut across barriers of class; and in the friendship between their mounts he saw an example to shame humankind, "who are so little able to preserve friendships for one another."

Protestations of friendship regularly figured in the letters exchanged between the learned, as in the circles of Lipsius and Nicolas de Peiresc. Friendship was Donne's "second religion" and was extolled by François de Sales. Jonson addressed many of his poems to friends in the "tribe of Ben." Friendship was invoked as the bond of unity among the citizens of Orléans, in a document that begins, "All the troubles besetting the city of Orléans were the result of the little intelligence of friendship one towards the other."

Friendship was also recommended as an antidote to "melancholy," that ambiguous malaise of the age and a subject of popular proverbs: "Melancholy makes the healthy sick and the sick to die"; "To be at law or melancholy is to bury life"; "Flee melancholy, sadness, and madness." Melancholy now seems to have assumed epidemic proportions, especially among intellectuals, perhaps because writers and artists were more self-conscious than other people, more self-absorbed and depressed, and more likely to complain. Melancholy was sometimes associated with ecstasy, but also with drunkenness and madness. Doubtless it was sometimes an affectation, as with Shakespeare's Jacques in *As You Like It*; a "melancholy man" was perhaps one who had found a way to express his sensitivity. Burton and Montaigne both suffered from melancholy, and it was fashionable in the circle of Descartes.

But changing fashions are themselves historically significant, and melancholy had a large place in the medical literature of the period. Humoristic medicine attributed it to the predominance in the body of black bile, in which planetary influence played a part, rendering minds subtle if slow and unable to concentrate. It was also associated with earth among the four elements, with the north wind and autumn, with the evening hours, with the onset of old age, and, among the deadly sins, with sloth. Ambroise Paré, who was not given to fads, described the melancholic personality as "sad, annoying, rigid, severe and rude, envious, and timid."

Its best known monument is the massive *Anatomy of Melancholy* (1621) by Robert Burton, not a physician but an obscure Anglican clergyman, who wrote it as therapy for himself. "I writ of melancholy, by being busy to avoid melancholy," he explained, "to ease my mind by writing, for I had a heavy heart and an ugly head." He also hoped that his work might "help others out of a fellow-feeling." The "most grievous and common symptoms" of melancholy for Burton were "fear and sorrow without a cause," which could not be avoided even by "the wisest and discreetest men." It puzzled him that it was so difficult to explain why "melancholy men are witty and all learned men, famous Philosophers, and Law-givers, have still been melancholy." The disease first struck at the imagination, he reported, and then corrupted "faith, opinion, discourse, ratiocination." He rejected supernatural explanations, instead seeking "natural and inward causes." But these were many, including—this gives an insight into what he meant by "natural"—God, angels, devils, witches, magicians, astral influence, old age, heredity, the conditions of conception, diet, constipation, climate, immoderate exercise and idleness, solitude, insomnia, passion, sorrow, fear, shame and disgrace, envy, malice, hatred, anger, pride, and excessive study. Although men were more prone to it than women, women too were sometimes melancholic, and likely to be "far more violent, and grievously troubled." It could afflict "Kingdoms, Provinces, and families as well as private men." Sometimes Burton seems to have thought it universal, "for indeed," he asked rhetorically, "who is not a fool, melancholy, mad? Who attempts nothing foolish, who is not brainsick? Folly, melancholy, madness, are but one disease, *delirium* is a common name to all." At other times he emphasized the special virulence of melancholy in his own time. He also offered some comfort. "It may be mitigated and much eased," he wrote; it was hard to cure, but not impossible for those willing to be helped.

Montaigne began writing his *Essays* after his withdrawal from public life as therapy for his own "melancholy humor": "a humor very hostile to my natural disposition, produced by the gloom of the solitude into which I had cast myself some years ago." Donne admitted to a "sickly inclination" that drove him, "whensoever any affliction assails," to recall that he had the "keyes of my prison in mine own hand, and no remedy presents itselfe so soone to my heart, as mine own sword." One of St. Teresa's greatest problems was the melancholy that afflicted the nuns of her order.

Melancholy often merged into madness, another subject often discussed and a common theme of Italian opera and drama. An Italian work of 1589, *Hospitals of Incurable Lunatics*, classified types of madness; it was promptly translated into English, German, and French. Bodin discovered numerous cases of madness in history; "there are everywhere raving, melancholy, frenzied, and drowsy men," he concluded. Montaigne was sufficiently interested in the reputed madness of Tasso to visit him on his trip to Italy. "What a leap has just been taken, because of the very restlessness and liveliness of his mind," Montaigne lamented, "by one of the most judicious and ingenious of men, a man more closely molded by the pure poetry of antiquity than any other Italian poet has been for a long time." He blamed this sad decline on Tasso's brilliance.

Everywhere madness seemed a problem. Germany had its mad princes. Spain led Europe in establishing hospitals for the mentally ill, and Spanish writers wrote treatises on madness. The lengthy subtitle of one of these suggests Erasmus: the first part demonstrates "that those who are considered by the world to be sane are mad, and therefore deserve no praise. The second part demonstrates how those commonly held to be mad are worthy of great praise. With a great variety of pleasant and curious histories and other things no less useful than delightful." The extended—and surprisingly realistic—treatment of madness by Cervantes displayed familiarity with these works. Burton and Hobbes associated Protestant sectarianism with madness.

But the weightiest evidence that all was not well with the Europe of this time was its profound anxiety, now a commonplace of recent scholarship. Anxiety is by definition diffuse, general, and nameless, and thus, unlike fears, which are specific, difficult to cure; but, by a familiar psychological mechanism, anxiety tends to be transmuted into fears, that, being specific, can be confronted and dealt with, though rarely extinguishing the underlying anxiety. Anxiety lay behind the widespread imagery of disorder, disease, and contamination described above, but more fundamentally in a concern with time and change, with the unknown terrors of the future, and finally with death.

Those who discussed anxiety did not usually distinguish between fear and anxiety, although Montaigne had some insight into the distinction. On one occasion he shifted from his usual French word "*peur*" to "*solicitude*" (a more subjective word) in connection with the paralysis of the will so often associated with anxiety. "The anxiety [*solicitude*] to do well," he wrote, "and the tension of straining too intently on one's work, put the soul on the rack, break it, and make it impotent." These words reflected his own experience. "The thing I fear most," he admitted, "is anxiety [this time, *peur*]." He was appalled by the numbers of those who, "unable to endure the pangs of anxiety, have hanged themselves, drowned themselves, or leaped to their death," thus showing "that anxiety is even more unwelcome and unbearable than death itself." Hooker, too, regarded "fear" as "of all affections (anger excepted)" the least likely "to admit any conference with reason." For Burton, anxiety "makes our imagination conceive what it list, incites the devil to come to us . . . and tyrannizeth over our phantasy more than all other affections, especially in the dark." It is notable that in these passages "fear" is intransitive, not *of* anything in particular: as Hooker saw it, irrational.

Time, as we have noted, was increasingly seen as a valuable but finite resource, and in its passage a source of anxiety. Montaigne, in old age, was concerned to manage his time as carefully as possible in order to enjoy to the full what remained of his life. "The shorter my possession of life," he concluded, "the deeper and fuller I must make it." But he also recognized, in his own preoccupation with the future, a source of anxiety that spoiled the present. "Was I going on a journey," he wrote, "I never thought I was sufficiently provided. And the bigger my load of money, the bigger my load of fear." Such concerns meant, he thought, that "we are never at home, we are always beyond." Galileo worried about having enough time to "leave any trace" of his having passed through the world. Sidney was troubled that, "whensoever you may justly say to yourself you lose your time, you do indeed lose so much of your life." Bacon was anxious about the waste of his time by his "iterations," and his "prefaces and passages and excusations." "To choose time," he wrote, "is to save time." Hooker observed that "what daungers at anie *tyme* are imminent, what evels hange over our heades God doth knowe and not wee." The poet Andrew Marvell's lover hears, at his back, "Time's winged chariot hurrying near."

Jesuits joined Protestants in their concern with time and the need to make it productive, as God required. One of them reported with approval a saying of Loyola "that we should not help our neighbor in slow motion." Another wrote that everyone in his community was in good health, "thanks be to Christ, for we do not have time to be sick." Still another attended to his correspondence at midnight "in order to rob time."

Change, inseparable from time, always identified with this world but now discerned even in the heavens, was a constant source of anxiety. Galileo's discovery of sunspots was especially troubling. These, he demonstrated, "are generated and decay in longer and shorter periods; some condense and others greatly expand from day to day; they change their shapes, and some of these are most irregular; here their obscurity is greater and there less. . . . sometimes many spots are produced, sometimes few, sometimes none at all." This, far more than any scientific—or even biblical—objection, explains the resistance to the new astronomy. The growing acceptance of change was, for many, the reverse of reassuring.

The mutability of all things became an unwelcome commonplace. An Italian music critic declared, "There is nothing under the sun that remains stable and firm; instability establishes laws for everything terrestrial and mortal." In Rome, worry over what might happen intensified espionage in all directions. Even in Venice, in spite of claims for its invulnerability, Paruta acknowledged that all things human were ruled by "variety and change." Montaigne, though compelled to acknowledge its reality, thought "change of any sort disturbing and hurtful." For Bodin, history "ever vacillates and has no objective—nay, rather, each day new laws, new customs, new institutions, new manners confront us," with the result that "human actions are invariably involved in new errors." The French magistrate Pierre de Lancre composed a *Tableau of the Inconstancy and Instability of All Things* (1607), in which he proclaimed that "the past is a dream, the future a dark cloud, the present but wind." Spanish thinkers held that "empires and laws (although Plato and More have greater dreams) grow old like everything else; nature has determined that nothing endures or lasts forever; all things change with time"; the council of Philip III warned him in 1619 that "cities, kingdoms, and monarchies pass away, just as men and all other created things." The Dutch dreaded the sea: sermons in their churches resounded with reminders of the fate of Jonah. The more prosperous they became, the more they worried about the security of their wealth. Even knowledge, in the beginning a forbidden fruit, bred anxiety of a kind that troubled Descartes. The awareness of change also filtered down into popular literature. So Matteo Bandello, whose tales (1554, 1573) were translated and read everywhere, observed that "few ages have seen such sudden changes as we witness daily" and that "things go from bad to worse."

Such distress also pervaded English literature. A figure in Sidney's *Arcadia* observed that in life "there is nothing so certain as our continual uncertainty." Thomas Wilson saw "great alterations almost every year, so mutable are worldly things and worldly men's affairs." Burton used the decline of ancient culture to illustrate the fate of all things:

> Italy was once Lord of the world, Rome the Queen of Cities, vaunted herself of two myriads of Inhabitants; now that all-commanding Country is possessed by petty Princes, Rome, a small village. Greece, of old the seat of civility, mother of sciences and humanity; now forlorn, the nurse of barbarism, a den of thieves.[7]

In his *Defence of Rhyme* (1602) Samuel Daniel saw the mutability of language as "but a Character of that perpetuall revolution which we see to be in all things that never remaine the same: and we must herein be content to submit our selves to the law of time, which in a few yeares will make al that for which we now contend *Nothing*."

Constant, disruptive, unforeseeable, and essentially meaningless, change also explains the perception of "fortune" as a malign and destructive force. Rarely now could human beings, as Machiavelli had done, aspire even half the time to contend successfully with fortune. The possibility of bad fortune, on the other hand, led to an obsession with precaution. It nourished the paranoia of Don Quixote. "Forewarned is forearmed," he declared: "Nothing is lost by taking precautions. For I know by experience that I have enemies visible and invisible, and I do not know when or where, nor at what time or in what shape, they will attack me." But that sanest of men, Montaigne, also knew that "all precautions that a man can take are full of uneasiness and uncertainty," though he concluded all the same that "it is better to prepare with fine assurance for the worst that can happen."

But above all the preoccupation with time and change intensified awareness of human mortality, for in the background of anxiety lurked the fear of death, the ultimate unknown. This period thus brought to a climax a growing concern with death that had been intensifying since the fourteenth century. Bodin noted how men "often die untimely, before they reach old age, in the very flower of their youth or even in childhood." The lawyer Nicolas Pasquier, typically anxious lest he be surprised by the unforeseen, was reminded of death by depictions like those of the elder Pieter Breughel, who balanced his humorous paintings with a depiction of armies of corpses defeating the living. Ralegh ended his history, appropriately enough for an account of the fulness of time, by invoking the triumph of death over all:

> O eloquent, just and mightie Death! whom none could advise, thou hast perswaded; what none hath dared, thou hast done; and whom all the world hath flattered, thou only hast cast out of the world and despised: thou hast drawne together all the farre stretched greatness, all the pride, crueltie, and ambition of man, and covered it all over with these two narrow words, *Hic iacet*.[8]

Religious leaders, of course, emphasized the omnipresence of death. For Bérulle, "the world is the scaffold of our execution; we are not only obliged but condemned to die." Philip Neri, founder of the Roman Oratory, advised the faithful to remember death by looking at corpses as often as possible, and to keep a skull in one's room, to be uncovered only once a week so that death would not be taken for granted. A macabre procession in mid-sixteenth-century Florence emphasized the horrors of death:

> a huge black cart drawn by black bison and crowded with human bones and white crosses, carried an enormous Death wielding a sickle and surrounded by tombs. At each station where the cart stopped, the tomb

slabs parted and the public could see frightening beings simulating decomposing cadavers, emerging from the graves. There followed other terrible personages, or "death masks" who carried torches and sang hymns to intensify the horror of the spectators.[9]

Popular Catholicism in this period has been described as "a cult of the living in the service of the dead"; and in some parts of Catholic Europe the importance of purgatory, through whose torments the dead could be assisted by the prayers of the living, was growing. Theater everywhere was much given to death scenes, and a generation of poets of the macabre emerged in France during the religious wars. Magnificent tombs for the great were tributes to the power of death as well as the importance of the deceased.

In the orthodox view, a good and pious death guaranteed salvation; and the faithful professed to believe it. Its converse stimulated less pious thoughts. Pierre de l'Estoile remarked of "the vilest poet of our time" that he was a man who "died as he lived, without God, thus proving the old proverb, *telle vie, telle fin* [as you live, so shall you die]." But he noted with approval the death of a leader of the Guise faction who "had vices as we all have," but to whom God gave "grace to repent as he died . . . so he must be considered very happy, his sins being covered by the mercy of God." The night before his assassination, the French king Henri IV

was seen on his knees praying to God all night, and when he got up withdrew into his cabinet, and, staying much longer than usual, was interrupted, which annoyed him, and he said, "Will people stil prevent my welfare?" A particular sign of the grace of God, who seems to have warned him of his near end, a thing which comes only to those whom our Lord loves.[10]

The preoccupation with death took various forms. Hooker favored a prolonged death, to allow time for preparation. Don Quixote thought an honorable death "the best fortune of all." However it was regarded, death was very close to the forefront of general consciousness.

People dwelt on its terrors. A growing dualism, nourished by Neoplatonism and Neostoicism, made death more acceptable to intellectuals as the liberation of the soul from the body. This solution to the problem of death was, however, less welcome to most people, for whom the separation of those old friends, soul and body, seemed at least as terrible as the separation by death of husband and wife. The *ars moriendi*, or art of dying, a traditional literary genre intended to reconcile believers to death, had been

declining earlier in the sixteenth century. Now it began to revive, often promoted by the Jesuits. Jeremy Taylor's *Holy Dying* (1651) gave it its classic
form in England.

Efforts to minimize the seriousness of death also suggest the anxieties
surrounding it. The Puritan Thomas Becon maintained that it was given
too much attention. "It is naturall to dye," he wrote, "why then labour we
to degenerate and grow out of kind?" Bacon argued that contemporaries
"bestowed too much cost upon death, and by their great preparations made
it appear more fearful." "Men fear Death," he wrote, "as children fear to
go in the dark; and that natural fear in children is increased with tales."
Sarpi struck a rather different note. Although he was not renowned for
humor, he dismissed life as a frivolity "to be spent in laughing at death."
This seems less Christian than Stoic.

Montaigne wrote often of death, admitting that, from his earliest days,
there had been nothing that preoccupied him more than "images of death."
Far from finding amusement in the prospect, he concluded that "in the last
scene, between death and ourselves, there is no more pretending, we must
talk plain French, we must show what there is that is good and clean at the
bottom of the pot. . . . In judging the life of another, I always observe how
it ended; and one of my principal concerns about my own end is that it shall
go well, that is to say quietly and insensibly." He recalled that Julius Caesar,
when asked which was the best death, replied, "the unexpected, the sudden
and the unforeseen." "Considering human infirmity," Montaigne concluded, "he was right."

The appeal of Stoicism owed much to the belief that it could reduce the
fear of death. In a Stoic moment, Montaigne tried to persuade himself that
"disdain for death" was "among the principal benefits of virtue." It could
give to life "a soft tranquility and a pure and pleasant enjoyment of it," since
"knowing how to die frees us from all subjection and constraint." But
without such tranquility, which he clearly often lacked, "all pleasures are
extinguished" and life becomes slavery. His conclusion to this reflection
seems a bit fragile; but only such thoughts stood between him and "continual fright and frenzy; never did a man so distrust his life [as he did], never
did a man set less faith in his duration." In his last essay he was still
"reconciling" himself to death by thinking of life "as something that by its
nature must be lost."

He also suggested why death was, in this period, increasingly problematic. Traditionally a function of community, the dying person surrounded
by family and clergy, death was now likely to be private. "Dying is not a
role for society," Montaigne declared, "it is an act for one single character."

But again his conclusion was unconvincing: "Let us live and laugh among our friends, let us go die and look sour among strangers." Death was becoming both a solitary and—however difficult to face—a thoroughly *ordinary* event. It was no longer comfortably religious, and there is little evidence that it was often the resigned death of a Stoic. Montaigne's Stoicism did not give him the courage, when plague was raging in Bordeaux, to enter the city to perform his duties as mayor.

One reaction to the growing discontents of the time was reformism. This had also been true in the earlier Renaissance—and of course the Reformation—when most religious and intellectual leaders were, to a greater or lesser degree, reformers. Widespread complaints about the times often implied the possibility, even the urgency, of setting things right. Burton still yearned for

> some general visitor in our age, that should reform what is amiss; a just army of Rosy-Cross men [Rosicrucians]. For they will amend all matters, (they say) religion, policy, manners, with arts, sciences, &c.; another Attila, Tamerlane, Hercules, to strive with Achelous, to clean the Augean stables, to subdue tyrants . . . to expel thieves, to vindicate poor captives . . . and purge the world of monsters . . . to reform our manners to compose our quarrels and controversies . . . alter affections, cure us of our epidemical diseases . . . end all our idle controversies, cut off our tumultuous desires, inordinate lusts, root out atheism, impiety, heresy, schism, and superstition . . . catechise gross ignorance, purge Italy of luxury and riot, Spain of superstition and jealousy, Germany of drunkenness, all our Northern countries of gluttony and intemperance, castigate our hard-hearted parents, masters, tutors, lash disobedient children, negligent servants; correct these spendthrifts and prodigal sons, enforce idle persons to work, drive drunkards out of the alehouse, repress thieves and tyrannizing magistrates.

But Burton knew that these were "vain, absurd, and ridiculous wishes" and that "men will cease to be fools when they cease to be." He would, only to please himself, "make an Utopia of mine own, a new Atlantis, a poetical Commonwealth of mine own, in which I will freely domineer, build cities, make laws, statutes, as I list myself. And why may I not?"[11]

Burton could only take seriously the reform of individual lives, and this was also true for Cervantes, whose great novel suggests something of Burton's state of mind. There was no doubt that the world badly needed mending, and Don Quixote aimed to set it right by himself, moved by "the grievances there were to redress, the wrongs to right, the injuries to amend, the abuses to correct, and the debts to discharge." That these were the aspirations of a madman hardly reduces the accuracy of his vision.

This is not to deny the existence of Europeans who took reform seriously. In Spain itself there was a general concern with reform at both the local and national level, nourished, though with little result, by some hope in its possibilities. In spite of the popularity of Queen Elizabeth, her reign saw a growing interest in republicanism. Humanists had long proposed reform through education, and Johann Comenius, a central European exile in the Netherlands, had fresh thoughts on the subject.

Much reformist sentiment was also still focussed on the church, though, unlike the Protestant reformers of an earlier generation, reform proposals were now chiefly institutional rather than theological, and often politically motivated. Venetians, somewhat like Dante and Machiavelli, attacked the papacy for its greed and lust for power. Sarpi treated the papacy as an enemy of reform, avoiding it by manipulating the Council of Trent; in this sense his *History of the Council of Trent* was a reform document. Meanwhile the young Niccolò Contarini, later doge, gave serious thought to reform, like Gasparo Contarini in the previous century.

Many reformers still looked to the past for models of reform. Bruno looked even further back than others: he proposed to recover the "ancient theology" of pre-Christian Egypt, the oldest civilization and therefore the most sacred source of truth. He depended for his knowledge of Egyptian religion on the writings attributed to Hermes Trismegistus, which in fact reflected Hellenistic gnosticism and later Jewish materials, regarded as authentically ancient and translated into Latin by Marsilio Ficino. Their actual origin was only demonstrated by Casaubon in 1614. Meanwhile the hermetic corpus had provided reformers who conflated antiquity with truth with another model for contemporary reform.

But little reform actually occurred; the reformism of the age was chiefly significant as another symptom of its discontents. An effective antidote for the unhappiness of the period, although it was only temporary and imperfect, would come with the culture of order that was slowly emerging even as Renaissance culture was reaching its climax. Its emergence will be treated in the last section of this book.

CHAPTER NINE

Renaissance Theater and the Crisis of the Self

The discontents surveyed in the last chapter were real, and not unrelated to the material discomforts of the age: to warfare, civil and foreign, now aggravated by religious hatreds and gunpowder, and to the social disruptions caused by the great price rise of the later sixteenth century. But comparable troubles had afflicted earlier periods, and to understand the troubled minds of this age we must look more deeply. A major clue can be found in one of its greatest glories: its importance for theater, the most popular of the arts, which brings into focus a profound set of discontents released by the peculiar freedoms of Renaissance culture. For "art in general," as Vaclav Havel observed, "is a little like playing with fire."

All the arts were now in some trouble. There were hints of disorientation in painting, especially in what its contemporary historian Giorgio Vasari called *maniera*, or Mannerism: an art largely reflecting the virtuosity of the artist. Relativism and skepticism had undermined the traditional conception of art as the imitation of nature; as a result art no longer aimed simply to meet common expectations but looked instead for special effects. At its most extreme it aimed to create what had never existed before, which could be interpreted as blasphemy in a culture that assumed God to be the sole creator.

For there was now a growing sense that the artistic imagination needed no restraints or rules of any kind; that it too should be totally free. The result was such eccentricities as the faces composed of vegetables or fruits by the painter Arcimboldo at the court of Rudolf II, a display of human virtuosity easily interpreted as a distortion, rooted in human presumption, of what God had created. The arts were now increasingly suspect. Botero recognized Michelangelo's talent but criticized him for introducing into churches "an extremely alien form of images." For Pascal, a poet could not be "an honest man." Calvinists, suspicious of anything of human origin, could accept human art only by representing God as its source. But theater, as the most popular of the arts and a special source of corruption, was particularly vulnerable to attack.

Theater differed in two principal respects, both reasons for distrust: it was secular, and it was commercial. It did not aim, at least explicitly, at moral or religious instruction; and—this was symbolically as well as practically significant—its performances were staged in buildings especially designed for the purpose, which anybody could enter for the price of admission. The first such theaters were constructed in London in 1577 and shortly thereafter in Italy and Spain. In France, for the time being, other buildings were converted to theatrical use.

The popularity and profitability of theater attracted the considerable capital it required. The earliest organized theater companies were Italian, and traveling companies of actors brought commercial drama to much of the rest of Europe, helping to demonstrate its profitability and bringing with them plots that could be adapted by native playwrights. The new art caught on rapidly. It has been estimated that in London, by 1594, two theaters alone averaged some 2,500 paying customers a day. One result was to stimulate playwrights, who made theater into an art that attracted audiences both by the quality of their plays and by the novel and daring effects introduced into their production. By the later decades of the sixteenth century hundreds of playwrights all over Europe were composing literally thousands of plays, although many of them have survived only in their titles. In Spain, Lope de Vega, whose plays are still performed today, is said to have written some eighteen hundred plays during his long career. Meanwhile opera—sung drama—after some earlier experiments with the form at the Florentine court, was developed in Venice and exported abroad.

The popularity and relatively rapid diffusion of Renaissance theater throughout much of the continent needs explanation in European and not simply national terms. Nor, in spite of its commercial success, can it be accounted for simply as an economic phenomenon, though theater owners and producers, if not necessarily playwrights, could reap substantial profits from the production of plays because considerable numbers of city-dwellers had both the means and the leisure to attend plays. But a social explanation for Renaissance theater is complicated by the wide variety in the composition of theater audiences, made possible by sliding price scales for admission. The best seats cost the most, but there was usually standing room under the stage, in what was called the pit in England, that cost very little. This is why many playwrights, including Shakespeare, wrote plays designed to appeal to almost everybody. Contemporaries were struck by the variety in theater audiences. As one observer put it,

> For as we see at all the play house dores,
> When ended is the play, the daunce, and song,
> A thousand townesmen, gentlemen, and whores,
> Porters and serving-men together throng.[1]

Foreign ambassadors went to see plays in the great capitals of Europe. So, in London, did law students and apprentices, literate and illiterate alike. Respectable women as well as prostitutes attended plays, even ladies from royal courts—in early Stuart England the Queen herself attended. Theater was thus a force for the breakdown of class distinctions, even for democratization. Conservatives everywhere, in traditionally hierarchical societies, found this disturbing, and it was a major element in the emergence of an anti-theatrical reaction that eventually shut down the London stage.

A satisfactory explanation, therefore, must cut across not only national and linguistic boundaries but also divisions of class. It must consider, in addition to economic causes, the cultural, psychological, and perhaps even religious needs of such varied audiences. What did so many and such different people value in the theatrical experience? On this question there is little direct evidence. We may know what *we* see in such plays of the Renaissance as have survived—chiefly the best—but few contemporary theatergoers tried to explain, or probably could explain, why *they* liked a play, or what they understood it to mean. So here we must try to imagine what theater did for them, in their particular historical situation.

One thing is clear: that they went to the playhouses for all sorts of reasons, notably including pleasure; whatever else they may be, plays are play, and, as we now recognize, play is a vital human need. Renaissance playwrights understood this very well and developed a whole range of techniques for delighting audiences: the imitation of reality to produce wonder, always fundamental to the arts; wordplay, including puns and double meanings; violence, a constant staple of popular entertainment; the use of suspense to manipulate and finally to relieve anxiety; soliloquies to reveal secrets; clowning and magic—fun for both the masses and the classes.

But plays often provide rather complicated kinds of entertainment. Many people, in the long run at any rate and certainly in the Renaissance, wanted more than entertainment or, to put it somewhat differently, they valued entertainment that also stuck in the memory, incited sympathy and admiration, inspired awe and wonder, at the very least related to their own lives and gave insights of various kinds into the human condition. We must explain here not only the quantity of Renaissance theater but also, at its best, its quality, the durability of its appeal. In Renaissance theater, at any rate, bad plays did not always drive out good.

A major clue to the appeal of theater in the Renaissance is that, in addition to being drama's greatest age, the general culture of Europe in this period was probably the most theatrical in its history. The tendency to see life in theatrical terms had deep roots. The ancients had often thought of human existence as a drama played out on the great stage of the world, and the metaphor of the world-as-theater was taken up by medieval thinkers, who depicted the creation as a theater for displaying God's wisdom, power, and love. In this scenario God himself was a kind of casting director, assigning every human being a part in the drama of existence being played out on the world-stage, and God and the heavenly hosts represented its discriminating audience.

This is why early theaters were modeled on the traditional universe: heaven was represented by stars painted on the ceiling above the stage, the actions of this world were depicted on the stage itself, and hell was accessible through a trapdoor from which evil spirits might emerge to bedevil the human actors. It is hardly surprising that a large part of the instruction in schools and colleges in this period was carried on in plays written for educational purposes. Theater taught about the world and how to display oneself in it.

We encounter the metaphor of the world-as-theater only occasionally before this time, but everywhere in Renaissance literature. Machiavelli argued that the prince must sometimes "play" the lion, sometimes the fox. In Erasmus's *Praise of Folly* Folly herself plays a series of roles; she jokingly compares life to theater, both being based on illusion. In the *Anatomy of Melancholy* Burton represented himself as a "spectator of other men's fortunes and adventures, and how they act their parts, which methinks are diversely presented . . . as from a common theatre or scene, now comical, then tragical matters." For Monteverdi, the conception had implications for his own creativity: his great *Orfeo* was composed for "the theater of the universe." Shakespeare was thus drawing on a venerable established image in his well-known lines in *As You Like It* comparing the world to a stage on which we all play our parts.

People in this period commonly thought of themselves and of their own lives as dramas. Role-playing, then as now, was particularly important in politics, in which the theatricality of rulers, their ability to project an "image" of authority and examples of virtue, helps to explain how they could sometimes wield real power even in the absence of reliable standing armies. As Calvin had observed, "Kings are placed, as it were, in a theater, and the eyes of all are turned on them." Image-making, playing the role of monarch convincingly, was especially important for shaky dynasties like that of the Tudors in England or in states ruled by women, as happened almost simultaneously in later sixteenth-century England, Scotland, and France. Queen Elizabeth understood this very well and played to general admiration her role as Virgin Queen. "We princes," she announced, "are set on stages in the sight and view of all the world observed." As a distinguished scholar has remarked, Elizabeth herself may have been "the single greatest dramatic creation of the period." She played her assigned role above all in the city of London, which, as one of her subjects observed, was "a stage wherein was shewed the wonderfull spectacle of a noble hearted princesse toward her most loving people." Her successor, James I, though he played the role less well, understood this too. "A king is as one set on a skaffold," he wrote, "whose smallest actions and gestures all the people gazingly do behold." His successor as "royal actor" was depicted by Andrew Marvell in the role of a martyr on the scaffold. The rulers of the church had an equal awareness of the parts they were seen to play, which was reflected architecturally in the new church of St. Peter's in Rome, designed as a kind of elaborate stage-set for the dramatic processions of the pope, enabling him to move solemnly down a lengthened nave and out to the plaza to bless the assembled multitudes—as he still does.

In a society fragmented by social change, theater, dealing with common experiences and perceptions, also united people. As Havel has pointed out, theater is singularly social in its ability, through the shared experience of the play, to create a small, if temporary, community. This was especially valuable for the urban societies of the Renaissance, populated by alienated, disoriented, and anxious individuals. In Havel's words, theater

is an organism in the larger organism of society and its time, necessarily influenced by everything that influences them. It is a confluence of their currents—be they ever so hidden. Like it or not, theater is always more or less connected to everything by which the "collective spirit" lives—to its hidden and open themes, its dilemmas, to the existential questions that manifest themselves to it or as it manifests them, to the sensibility, the emotivity of the age, its moods, its thought and expression, its gestures, its visual sensibilities, its life-style, [its] fashion.

Theater, by providing "a shared experience, mutually understood," enables the isolated individual both to understand and, if only for a short time, to feel part of the world he or she inhabits.[2] It was all the more important for societies that lacked other media of communication such as the modern world depends on. As Andrew Gurr has noted, it "was the only major medium for social intercommunication, the only existing form of journalism, and the only occasion that existed for the gathering of large numbers of people other than for sermons and executions." And because of its ability to order collective experience through plot and closure, theater also supplied a sense at least of the possibility of a moral order governing the chaos of ordinary experience. This, I suggest, was a major element in the emergence of theater in the age of the Renaissance and helps to explain the concern of those responsible for the maintenance of order to control it.

Theater also met various needs of individual life. Thus it analyzed and helped its audiences to understand the tensions between individual consciences and traditional values. It could also aid reflection about the slippage between social role and the "true self" implicit in the daily life of Renaissance society; and here we are approaching the central problem posed by Renaissance theater. We are now, perhaps, so used to the role-playing needed to lubricate social relations in our own lives that we have ceased to be troubled by it. But as a relatively new development in Renaissance society, it invited attention. The worldly Bacon acknowledged it; though admitting that "some persons of weaker judgment and perhaps too scrupulous morality may disapprove of it," he included it as "no unimportant attribute of prudence in a man to be able to set forth to advantage before others, with grace and skill, his virtues, fortunes, and merits" and "to cover artificially his weaknesses, defects, misfortunes, and disgraces."

On the negative side, it is hardly a coincidence that what for us would be mere tact or decorum, comic rather than tragic, is, in Renaissance drama, usually represented by villains. One of Shakespeare's consummate villains, Richard III, thus describes himself, ignoring the anguish felt by Queen Elizabeth:

> Why, I can smile, and murder whiles I smile,
> And cry "Content" to that which grieves my heart,
> And wet my cheeks with artificial tears,
> And frame my face to all occasions. . . .
> I can add colors to the Chameleon,
> Change shapes with Proteus for advantages,
> And set the murderous Machiavel to school.[3]

Nor was there anything gender-specific here. Lady Macbeth advised her husband that, "to beguile the time," he should

> Look like the time; bear welcome in your eye,
> Your hand, your tongue. Look like th'innocent flower,
> But be the serpent under't.[4]

Iago, another of Shakespeare's villains, is not only a master hypocrite, he also suggests the loss of *any* true self, the terrifying nothingness at the center of role-playing. "I am *not* what I am," he proclaims, in a reversal of God's revelation of himself in the burning bush. Theater, in such passages, was performing a moral as well as a practical function; it both condemned hypocrisy and warned against its dangers.

But, for one reason or another, the self *had* become fluid and problematic, and the denunciation of hypocrisy, which assumed an authentic self that had been concealed, represented a rather superficial approach to the crisis of identity, which now reflected troubling doubts about the shape of the "true" self, even doubts of its existence, perhaps not unlike the doubts raised by the late twentieth-century notion of the self as no more than a social construct. Cressida had an identity problem with which many in Shakespeare's audience might have identified. She admits to Troilus, invoking the fateful Pauline dualism, that she had

> a kind of self resides with you;
> But an unkind self, that itself will leave
> To be another's fool.

Hamlet, too, had lost both his father—symbol of tradition and security—and the throne on which his social role depended; he too faced an identity problem. Indeed, acting itself dramatized the problem of identity. An actor was a kind of professional Proteus, and in the theater the distinction between appearance and reality was constantly threatened, in ways both alarming and instructive. Again and again Shakespeare dramatized this problem in plays about identity: not only with Cressida and Hamlet but with Richard II, who seems constantly aware of merely playing the king and therefore does it unconvincingly; and Lear, who so tragically discovers, in his common, suffering humanity, his own real self.

But concern with the real self lying somewhere beneath the protective layers imposed by the expectations of others also pervades the general culture of the age; indeed, it can be identified at least as early as the confrontation between Augustinus and Franciscus in Petrarch's *Secretum*. It explains the Renaissance discovery of Augustine's *Confessions*, earlier perceived as little more than a conventional work of devotion. As a later humanist proclaimed, if rather tentatively, "It is myself that I express, or so I think." Even the classicist Ben Jonson saw a threat to the self in imitation: "Nay, wee so insist in imitating others, as we cannot (when it is necessary) returne to ourselves." Montaigne saw the problem with his usual clarity: in life, he wrote, "whatever role man undertakes to play, he plays his own at the same time."

The problem of the self had been implicit in the rhetorical tradition from the start; rhetoric, like theater, was in the ambiguous business of multiplying selves, as context and purpose required. The numerous courtesy manuals published in every major language were intended to polish the behavior of the upwardly mobile and further increased the distance between the authentic individual, if such a person still existed, and the self he at least aspired to present. On a deeper level Stoic and other ethical precepts had much the same purpose. Indeed, the Renaissance preoccupation with education can be understood as a concern with shaping and fixing the self in a socially acceptable, agreeable, and profitable mode.

Consciousness that the self might be a problem, however, only fully developed in the later Renaissance. Erasmus worried over the conflict within the self, ascribing it to the tension between soul and body. God, "that greatest craftsman of all," he had written in the most serious of his earlier works, "has joined together in happy concord these two natures," but "the serpent hating peace, again has split them in unhappy discord." For the Calvinist poet d'Aubigné, the self was also divided, but into a sinful and— in the elect—a redeemed self that can repent.

But the most sustained example of self-awareness was Montaigne's *Essays*. Montaigne did not aspire to be a king because a king "exists only as such"; and when he asked his great question, *Que sais-je?*, he could only answer it by looking within himself, a project, complicated by changes in the self from moment to moment, which he continued to scrutinize for the rest of his life. In much the same generation the mathematician and astrologer Girolamo Cardano and the artist Benvenuto Cellini (less reflectively, to be sure) also felt compelled to define themselves in autobiographies; and other works of the period such as Burton's *Anatomy* are filled with self-revelation. Cervantes presented the problem fictionally: in the first part of *Don Quixote*, the adventures of his hero give him an identity that defines and limits him in the second part. But the discovery of the self is clearest in Renaissance theater. As Erich Auerbach pointed out, ancient tragedy was the product of a struggle with fortune; in Shakespeare tragedy results from the predicament of the individual self in an unpredictable world.

But Renaissance drama was concerned not only to represent the *problem* of identity; it also provided examples of fashioning a self in a world in which, it now seemed, anything could happen. Here too theater was useful. The characters in a play gradually reveal themselves, until at last the audience, in the beginning presumably ignorant, "knows" who and what they are. As Havel has also observed, "Taken all round, you realize that in one way or another, every play involves the gradual disclosure of someone's true identity . . . every play raises, in a complex fashion, the question of identity as the most fundamental question of existence." Some of Shakespeare's characters have identities sufficiently positive and fixed to satisfy the most demanding moralist; Desdemona, Cordelia, and Horatio, among others, are role-models as well as role-players. They are, perhaps, too ingenuous to survive in a world pervaded by hypocrisy, and are easily victimized. More complex characters know how to get along in the world by adapting to it, albeit ambiguously—in short, by self-fashioning: Falstaff, for example, and—eventually—Prince Hal. Don Quixote, too, fashioned a self for himself—his enterprise was full of paradoxes—at first "quixotic" but finally possessing a kind of noble grandeur: there was more in him than folly. A primary lesson of Renaissance theater, in presenting to its audiences so many selves—often as explicit moralizing—was the multitude of choices made available by the diverse possibilities of the human condition. Theater can convey a sense of human freedom far clearer than the real lives in which its audience is enmeshed. This is a major reason for the perennial interest of Renaissance theater, which did it so well.

But introspection and the concern with identity were often a source of anguish. A divided self could all too often perceive the flaws in its own performance for, as Stephen Orgel has remarked, the parts we choose to play—too often badly—"are not impersonations but ideals." George Sandys noted this at the time: lack of self-knowledge "hath ruined many: but having it must needs ruine our beautifull Narcissus: who only is in love with his owne perfections." Self-consciousness itself could induce a kind of paralysis. This is suggested in the advice to the young Philip Sidney from his father: "Think upon every word that you will speak, before you utter it, and remember how nature hath rampiered up (as it were) the tongue, with teeth, lips, yea, and hair without the lips, and all betokening reins, or bridles, for the loose use of this member."[5] Subjectivity could intensify, too, the gnawing sense of homelessness implicit in the social mobility of the age. Like the movement of people from small communities close to the soil into novel and bustling cities, it was profoundly disturbing to the sense of personal identity as it exchanged a life requiring neither explanation nor justification for a realm of unlimited contingency, insecurity, and anxiety.

It is thus hardly surprising that, as Renaissance theater developed, a growing reaction against it was also emerging: a reaction accelerated by the tendency of playwrights to compete for audiences by introducing onto the stage increasing violence, shocking situations, moral ambiguity, and melo-dramatic effects, of a kind we know so well in contemporary popular enter-tainment. Plays could be seen as substituting the corrupt works of men for divinely instituted—and sometimes itself theatrical—worship. The reaction against theater, sometimes shallow but much of it profoundly instructive, is, I think, particularly useful to illuminate the deeper problems posed by Renaissance culture.

Theater had almost from the beginning been a special source of uneasi-ness, not only among moralists but even for some playwrights, notably Jonson, so often torn between his love of the entertainments he could contrive and his condemnation of illusion and attraction to the unchang-ing. Some of the hostility to theater arose from the sense that it competed with the church, not least because, as though it represented a rival form of worship, it presented regular performances on Sundays. Hooker implied some rivalry in an attack on those who "esteemed him that erected a stage or theater, more than *Solomon* which built a temple to the Lord." Clergy were especially sensitive to the claim advanced by some of the most serious champions of theater that it competed with the church by offering moral instruction. As one clergyman maintained,

> Players assume an unlawfull office to themselves of instruction and correction. God gave authority to instruct and preach, to correct and anathematize, which is the keyes of heaven, only to the Apostles and their successors, and not to Players. . . . it were most impious . . . to mix Divinity with scurrility on the stage.[6]

An anti-theatrical movement arose on the continent as well as in England. Catholic bishops condemned theater, notably Carlo Borromeo in Milan, who attacked plays as "the source and base of nearly all evils and all crimes." Though the Jesuits sponsored theatricals in their schools, they were respon-sible for the suppression of a secular theater in Venice, promptly reinstated after their expulsion in 1606. Ricci thought the Chinese, otherwise so admirable, far too interested in theater. The Jansenists in France, in this as in other respects like the Puritans in England, were particularly hostile to theater.

The objections were often so general as to suggest that it had become a focus for the widespread anxiety and collapse of boundaries discussed earlier. In London, theaters were literally out of bounds, beyond the boundaries of the city and the reach of municipal law-enforcement. They were also somewhat protected by the court, itself a "theatrical" institution associated by sober Londoners with moral disorder. The Lord Mayor of London complained that theaters were "ordinary places of meeting for all vagrant persons & maisterles men that hang about the Citie, theeves, horse-stealers, whoremoongers, coozeners, connycatching persones, practizers of treason, other such lyke." At the same time the heterogeneity of popular theater audiences—in contrast to theater at court—threatened notions of social order by bringing together all classes of urban society in a "promiscuous mixture." Plays themselves could offend, sometimes unintentionally, for authors could not foresee how they might be interpreted. As the English Puritan Stubbes described them in his *Anatomie of Abuses* (1583), plays are "doble-dealing ambodexters."

Theater was also thought to subvert the economic virtues, especially among the lower classes. Early controls in Spain sought to limit idleness by restricting the number of working days when plays might be performed. In England, theater was associated with waste and luxury. A Puritan preacher called on his listeners to "behold the sumptuous theatre houses, a continual monument of London's prodigality and folly."

Plays were sometimes considered politically subversive as well. The egalitarianism of Lope de Vega in such works as *Fuente Ovejuna* could be overlooked because he depicted the crown as protector of the peasantry against a tyrannical nobility, but Tirso de Molina, whose plays were thought to be critical of the government and especially of corruption at court, was exiled from Madrid in 1625. Even Thomas Heywood's *Apology for Actors* admitted that some plays offended by "inveighing against the State, the Court, the Law, the Citty, and their governements," sometimes putting their criticisms in the mouths of children on the assumption that this would constitute "a priviledge for rayling."

A deeper uneasiness about theater was apparent among those who regarded theater as either (a) a set of lies or (b) too true to life. For the first group, theater was insufficiently serious; it was objectionable precisely because it aimed to amuse. An Elizabethan, himself a reformed playwright, attacked theater on this ground:

Sometimes you shall see nothing but the adventures of an amorous knight, passing from countrie to countrie for the love of his lady, encountering many a terrible monster made of browne paper, and at his retorne, is so wonderfully changed, that he cannot be knowne but by some posie in his tablet, or by a broken ring, or a hand kircher or a piece of cockle shell, what learne you by that? When ye soule of your playes is eyther mere trifles, or Italian bawdery, or cussing of gentlewomen, what are we taught?

Cervantes, himself a playwright, thought most of the comedies of his time "notorious nonsense."[7] Bacon objected to theater as to philosophy for its untruths.

A contrary set of objections was raised by those who believed that theater represented all too well—and made attractive—human wickedness, especially in its treatment of sexual passion. Lope de Vega was criticized for this. Bellarmine thought Guarini's *Faithful Shepherd* (1589) a greater threat to morals than the heresies of Luther and Calvin. For Bacon, love on the stage had done "much mischief, sometimes like a syren, sometimes like a fury"; Jonson recognized that this was often "the only point of art that tickles the *Spectators*." Corneille defended himself against the charge of making love too attractive by arguing that, on the contrary, he purged rather than excited the emotions.

Disapproval of theater was focussed especially on the supposed immorality of actors. Cervantes viewed actors as "as necessary to the republic as flowers and trees," but this was unusual; he wrote plays himself, and in fact no profession was so reviled. Male actors were viewed as vagabonds, actresses as whores—except in England, where women were not even allowed on stage till the Restoration. In France and Spain, actors could be refused Christian burial as public sinners. In England, they were forbidden to use the name of the Lord on stage.

But the supposed irregularity of their lives was not the deepest of the objections to them. More fundamental was the fluidity of the actor's roles, a peculiar threat to the already endangered selves of contemporaries when, in an age of hypocrisy and general distrust, people were already beginning to have doubts about their own identities. In his *Arcadia* Sidney characterized as a villain a man who had previously been an actor in tragedies and had learned from them "besides a slidingness of language, acquaintance with many passions, and to frame his face to bear the figure of them." This Protean quality of the actor also suggested the ambiguity of his sexual identity.

This fluidity figured prominently in attacks on theater. The Puritan William Perkins spelled this out:

> God hath determined what he will doe with every man, and . . . he hath in his eternall counsell assigned every man his office and condition of life. . . . And by his eternall counsell, he separates every man from the very wombe to one calling or other: and accordingly he cals them in time by giving gifts, and will, to doe that, for which they were appointed.[8]

An actor, like a vagabond with no vocation or fixed place in society, was a rebel against his God-given role, a quintessentially masterless man. In addition, his mixture of roles suggested not only a series of deceptions but a basic impurity at the heart of his life.

Acting also implied a lack of seriousness at the center of his existence, already implicit in the ambiguity of "play"—"plot" may have suggested something worse. An actor was a living challenge to all whose lives were *serious*, all who were concerned with personal authenticity. As the reformed actor Stephen Gosson wrote, "If [the actor's] profession were single, hee would think himselfe a simple fellow, as hee doth all professions besides his owne; His owne therefore is compounded of all Natures, all humours, all professions."

Hypocrisy also figured prominently in the charges against theater. In one of the most extreme of the anti-theatrical writings in England, *Histrio-mastix* (1632), so unrestrained that its author lost his ears for it, William Prynne took advantage of the etymology of "hypocrite" to identify hypocrites and actors. He related this coincidence to the larger problem of human identity:

> For God, *who is truth it selfe*, in *whom there is no variablenesse, no shadow of change, no feining, no hypocrisie*; as he hath given a uniforme distinct and proper being to every creature, *the bounds of which may not be exceeded: so he requires that the actions of every creature should be honest and sincere, devoyde of all hypocrisie*, as all his actions, and their natures are. Hence he enjoy[n]es all men at all times, *to be such in shew, as they are in truth: to seeme that outwardly which they are inwardly*; to act themselves, not others.[9]

Burton related hypocrisy, that special vice of the age discussed in the previous chapter, to theater, although his own rhetorical flourishes suggest a degree of posturing even in himself:

To see a man turn himself into all shapes like a Chameleon, or as Proteus transform himself into all that is monstrous; to act twenty parts & persons at once for his advantage, to temporize and vary like Mercury the Planet, good with good, bad with bad; having a several face, garb & character, for every one he meets; of all religions, humours, inclinations; to fawn like a spaniel, with lying and feigned obsequiousness, rage like a lion, bark like a cur, fight like a dragon, sting like a serpent, as meek as a lamb, & yet again grin like a tiger, weep like a crocodile, insult over some, & yet others domineer over him, here command, there crouch, tyrannize in one place, be baffled in another, a wise man at home, a fool abroad to make others merry! To see so much difference betwixt words and deeds, so many parasangs betwixt tongue and heart, men like stage players act variety of parts, give good precepts to others, soar aloft, whilst they themselves grovel on the ground![10]

The combination of indignation and righteousness here reflects the peculiar torment arising out of the disorientation of the self, now aggravated by acting and the theater.

Theater was thus symbol, catalyst, and focus for what was felt—if not understood—to have gone deeply wrong in the culture of the age. In the jargon of contemporary sociology, it had been transformed from *Gemeinschaft* into *Gesellschaft*, from the pattern of open relationships in a simple community into a complex society composed of a congeries of mutually antagonistic special interests. The attack on hypocrisy that the modern world has learned to take for granted reflected distress (as it was supposed) at the erosion of candor and truth. Nothing was quite what it appeared to be; everything had become theatrical. But the reaction against theater was also against the cultural freedoms of the Renaissance: against experimentation with the unlimited and frightening possibilities of the human condition, against a creativity without foundation or limits, against play as well as playing.

CHAPTER TEN

Toward a Culture of Order

Even as the freedom of Renaissance culture was reaching a climax, other developments expressed a growing concern for order, evident in many places and at various levels of experience. Reactions to cultural freedom had always varied, and some thinkers still reveled in it. Bruno was delighted with Galileo's discoveries. There were now, he exulted, "no ends, boundaries, limits or walls which can defraud us of the infinite multitude of things." Burton responded with equanimity to the discovery, as he put it, that the crystalline boundaries of the universe were "penetrable & soft as the air itself & that the Planets move in it, as Birds in the Air, Fishes in the Sea." Montaigne simply shrugged his shoulders. All new doctrines, he thought, should be distrusted, since in each case, "before it was produced, its opposite was in vogue; and, as it was overthrown by this one, there may arise in the future a third invention that will likewise smash the second." He observed that Paracelsus too was "changing and overthrowing the whole order of the ancient rules" in favor of new principles, though these also failed to impress him.

But such insouciance was hardly universal, and it would become increasingly rare. Traditional appeals to nature and reason, to the authority of classical philosophers, and to the literal sense of Scripture all attest now to a growing need for order and certainty. On a humble level, Sir Thomas Elyot's popular *Boke Named the Governour* generalized that "where ordre lacketh, there all thynge is odiouse and uncomly." Henry Peacham, an authority on manners for gentlemen, looked, whatever he meant by it, for a "natural" order in language. Lawyers everywhere—Bartolists in Italy, Gallicans in France, common lawyers in England—were looking for patterns of order, whether in tradition or the cosmos, that might be applied to contemporary needs. Bodin remarked on the need "in all things" to "seek after a convenient and decent order," and deemed "nothing to be more ugly or foul to look upon than confusion and broil."

On his own sublime level, Hooker was made anxious by the very thought of disorder in the cosmos:

> Let any principall thinge, so the sunne, the Moone, any one of the heavens or elements, but once cease or faile, or swarve, and who doth not easily conceive, that the sequeale thereof would be ruine both to itselfe, and whatsoever dependeth on it? And is it possible that man being not only the noblest creature in the world, but even a very worlde in himselfe, his transgresing the law of his nature should draw no maner of harme after it?

He expressed his horror of disorder in a monumental sentence whose impact may be best conveyed by treating it as a kind of poem:

> Now if nature should intermit her course, and leave altogether,
> though it were but for a while, the observation of her own laws;
> if those principal and mother elements of the world,
> whereof all things in this lower world are made, should lose the
> qualities which now they have;
> if the frame of that heavenly arch erected over our heads should
> loosen and dissolve itself;
> if celestial spheres should forget their wonted motions, and by
> irregular volubility turn themselves any way as it might happen;
> if the prince of the lights of heaven, which now as a giant doth run
> his unwearied course, should as it were through a languishing
> faintness begin to stand and rest himself;
> if the moon should wander from her beaten way, the times and
> seasons of the year blend themselves by disordered and contused
> mixture, the winds breathe out their last gasp, the clouds yield no
> rain, the earth be defeated of heavenly influence, the fruits of the
> earth pine away as children at the withered breasts of their
> mother no longer able to yield them relief:
> What would become of man himself, whom these things now do all
> serve?[1]

Pascal too was terrified by "the eternal silence" of "the infinite spaces" in the new cosmos. Even Francis Bacon, usually so bold, was obscurely troubled by the loss of boundaries. "Mixtures," he wrote, "are things irregular, whereof no man can define."

We encounter this mentality now in many places. It found expression in Giovanni Artusi's criticism of the novelties of Monteverdi:

> Has he the permission of nature and art to confound the sciences? To uphold things done in this manner we need one of two things: either the authority of past writers . . . or demonstration. . . . Do you not know that all the Sciences and Arts have been regulated by wise men, and that in each the first Elements, Rules, and Precepts on which it is founded have been set down, so that, not deviating from principles and good rules, one man may be understood by another?[2]

One sign of the yearning for order was a compulsion to make lists, although mere lists of phenomena chiefly testified to the impossibility of assimilating them conceptually. Bodin made an ambiguous advance toward order with his "pantotheca": a system for sorting out all "goods and materials" in the universe, "each in its own class": the heavenly bodies, stones, metals, fossils, plants, and all living things. The sponsor of this system, outlined in the *Colloquium*, was the Catholic Coronaeus, who proposed, in a kind of museum, to display clay and chalk between earth and stones, crystal between water and diamonds, flint and iron pyrites between stones and metals, bats between birds and animals.

More obviously traditional was Bodin's confidence in the existence of a universal and hierarchical order, and his appeal to the great chain of being. Hierarchy had long been central to the ideology of the church, and the conception was reasserted in the bull *Immensa eterna dei* (1588) by which Sixtus V announced his reorganization of the Curia. Its medieval ontology was also reasserted by Cardinal Bellarmine in his *Ascent of the Mind to God through the Hierarchy of Created Being* (1615). Like Bonaventura's thirteenth-century *Itinerary of the Mind toward God*, it described the hierarchy of spiritual beings intermediate to—and mediating between—God and man.

Less philosophically oriented figures also found the conception useful. For St. John of the Cross, the chain of being was a ladder down which wisdom descends to man and up which the soul journeys toward the divine. Bruno appealed to it: wise men rise "to the height of Divinity by means of the same ladder of Nature by which Divinity descends even to the lowest things in order to communicate herself." Recalling this conception in Dionysius the Areopagite, he found its origins in ancient Egypt. Since it supported belief in the influence of the spirit realm over the lower world, this use of hierarchy was also a staple of occultism.

Implicit in the great chain was also a conception of discrete steps between its various levels, which pointed to the recovery of a conception of ordered boundaries traditionally so important for human orientation to the world. The restoration of boundaries was now taking various forms. One was political, expressed in a concern on the part of princes to define as precisely as possible the boundaries of their domains, often obscured by overlapping feudal claims. The notion of natural boundaries was an obvious attempt to base boundaries securely on nature; the Atlantic Ocean, the Pyrenees, the Alps, the Rhine, having been created by God, provided a quasi-ontological foundation for political order.

Boundaries between classes seemed important for social order. After a long period of social mobility, European society was fraught with status anxieties. In the countryside impoverishment by inflation had left the nobility unusually sensitive to questions of status; and at the same time rapidly growing cities were filled with anxious, impoverished newcomers whose volatility posed a threat to the respectable urban classes. The heightened concern about social status was expressed by Philip Stubbes, who was also dismayed by the freedoms of theater. It had become difficult, he wrote, "to knowe who is noble, who is worshipfull, who is a gentleman, who is not." The base-born were now indistinguishable from their betters; they went about daily "in silkes, velvets, satens, damaskes, taffeties and such like." Some writers, like Sir Thomas Smith, took comfort in repeating traditional classifications of society: it consisted, he wrote—implying that this not only was but always should be the case—of four groups: the aristocracy proper; the lesser gentry; citizens, burgesses, and yeomen; and "men which do not rule." But this classification concealed a rapidly changing scene that caused much uncertainty about how individuals might perceive themselves. The result of such uncertainties was increasing class consciousness. Tasso took a dim view of marriage between persons of different status, although he had advice for those involved in such misalliances: he emphasized the obligation of a socially inferior husband to show particular respect in public to his wife.

This concern posed problems of social role that were variously solved. Aristocrats found positions as military leaders and administrators, often going abroad to find suitable posts; but, where they could, they might also contribute by their own magnificence to that of princely courts. Their position was further secured by a change in the conception of nobility itself. Previously understood as based on virtue and so, at least in theory, open to all, nobility was now regarded chiefly as a function of birth and identified with privilege rather than service.

Wealthy merchants invested in land and sought increasingly to identify themselves with aristocracies of birth. This process had begun earlier in Italy, notably in Florence and Venice. Italian merchants took on the ways and values of a landed aristocracy and, as the Medici demonstrated, might ultimately even marry princes. In England, Shakespeare himself bought a coat of arms to establish a claim to gentility. Botero believed that aristocracy was rooted in Christianity itself. "Nobility," he wrote, "is so worthy and such an ornament to one's person that Christ our Lord did not disdain to adorn it with his most sacred humanity, although, to teach us humility, he joined the greatness of the royal blood of David to the poverty of the most holy Virgin his mother and of Saint Joseph her spouse."

The structures of Spanish society also grew increasingly rigid; as Spain's economic plight worsened, nobles were increasingly concerned to protect their status by concentrating land-ownership in themselves. One of the beneficiaries of the system claimed that, since the essential purpose of government was to insure that the nobility were sufficiently rich to preclude aspirations "to change lord or their fortune," the ruler should take care to benefit them. In spite of his camaraderie with his humble squire, Don Quixote paid close attention to social degree. "All the pedigrees in the world can be reduced to four kinds," he observed:

the first are those families which from humble beginnings have extended and expanded until they have reached supreme greatness; the second are those of high extraction who have preserved and maintained their original dignity; in the third sort are those who from great beginnings have gradually dwindled and decayed like a pyramid until, like the point of that pyramid, they end in nothingness. . . . The last sort—and these are the most numerous—have had neither good beginnings nor a respectable development, and consequently will end up without a name, with no better pedigree than ordinary plebeian folk.[3]

The patronage of culture, earlier often provided by towns and townsmen, was increasingly a monopoly of courts. In Italy, the papal court became a major patron of art and literature. The monumental building projects of the popes and their extravagant embellishment used up much of the wealth of Italy. The—by Italian standards—crude French nobility, especially those at court, became more cultivated and even patrons of culture. The most conspicuous literary production of later sixteenth-century France was the poetry of the Pléiade, which, imitating the classics and dedicated to royal and noble patrons, gave esthetic pleasure to a small courtly elite. The nobility who did not frequent the court now praised the pleasures of leisure in the country rather than the active life.

In England, the royal government increasingly supervised much publication by patronage, censorship, or courtly standards that favored hierarchy and controlled behavior. Even the bourgeois Netherlands saw efforts to create a more refined culture. The growing polish, and in some cases esotericism, of cultural expression increasingly divided those who participated in it from the masses. This, indeed, was a source of comfort to the elites, who, it has been suggested, were concerned lest a better-educated lower class might crave power for themselves. As Octavio Paz has remarked, seventeenth-century culture was "for the few."

The family was a particular locus of concern as central to the maintenance of order, its place all the more important because so obviously based on nature. Families were especially glorified in art, their solidarity publicized by family tombs in churches. They were accordingly expected to be based on considerations more solid and dependable than sexual attraction; marriage was not to be entered into out of passion, as Montaigne argued, because its "principal end is generation"; the family was, for him, based on "a religious and holy bond, [and] the pleasure we derive from it should be restrained, serious, and mixed with some austerity."

But since families were thought to depend on the distinction between the sexes, gender roles were a particular source of anxiety; and, then as now, the differences between the sexes were much discussed. Men sometimes took women seriously in every respect. There are many admirable women in plays of this period; indeed, the personalities of women as represented on the stage are often at least as interesting as those of men. Some writers distinguished between masculine and feminine modes of thought: men, they suggested, can achieve by reason one clear truth, the minds of women are less direct and more inclined to recognize variety, but both are valid. Others emphasized the basic similarity of the sexes and the need for the education of both; a change in the Anglican marriage service declared the purpose of marriage to be not only procreation (the traditional formula) but also the "mutual society" of husband and wife. Tasso praised chastity in husbands as well as in wives; and even Montaigne, who did not much practice this virtue, supported it in principle, if tepidly. François de Sales treated marriage as an ideal communion, physical as well as spiritual, between friends and equals. In his much-admired epic poem on the Creation, Guillaume Du Bartas treated women, like Castiglione, as civilizers of men.

Ain erschrockenliche

Newe Zeyttung / So geschehen ist

den 12 tag Junij / In dem 1542 Jar / in ainem Stäct=
lin hayßt Schgarbaria leyt 16 wälsch Meyl wegs
von Florentz / Da haßen sich grausammer Erdbidem
Siben Inn ainer stundt erhöbt / wie es da zü
ist ganngen / werdt ir hyrinn begrif=
fen finden.

Ein andere Newe zeyttung / So ge=

schehen ist / in des Türcken Land / Da ist ain Statt
Versuncken / Das nit ain Mensch darvon ist
komen / die ist von Solonichio ain Tagrayß
da der Türckisch Saffra wechßt auff
der ebne ?c.

1. German announcement of two news sheets, 1542.

2. Protestant martyrs before Windsor Castle, from John Foxe's *Acts and Monuments*, 1563.

3. Paolo Veronese, *Feast in the House of Levi*, 1573.

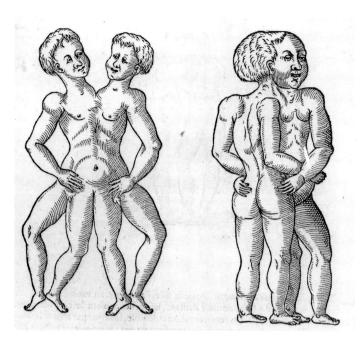

4. Siamese twins from *Les Oeuvres de M. Ambroise Paré* by Ambroise Paré, 1575.

LES
SIX LIVRES
DE LA REPVBLIQVE
DE I. BODIN
Angeuin.

A MONSEIGNEVR DV FAVR,
Seigneur de Pibrac, Conseiller du Roy en son Conseil
priué, & President en la Cour de Parlement
à Paris.

Reueuë, corrigee & augmentee de nouueau.

A PARIS,
Chez Iacques du Puys, Libraire iuré, à la
Samaritaine.

1 5 8 0.

AVEC PRIVILEGE DV ROY.

5. Title page of *Les Six Livres de la République* by Jean Bodin, 1580.

ESSAIS
DE MESSIRE
MICHEL SEICNEVR DE
MONTAIGNE CHEVALIER
de l'ordre du Roy, & Gentil-homme
ordinaire de fa Chambre.

LIVRE SECOND.

A BOVRDEAVS.
Pàr S. Millanges Imprimeur ordinaire du Roy,
M.D.LXXX.
AVEC PRIVILEGE DV ROY.

(Fac-similé d'un second titre des Essais.)

6. Title page of the second edition of
Michel de Montaigne's *Essays*, 1580.

7. Title page to Joseph Scaliger,
De emendatione temporum, 1583, with
annotations by Isaac Causaubon.

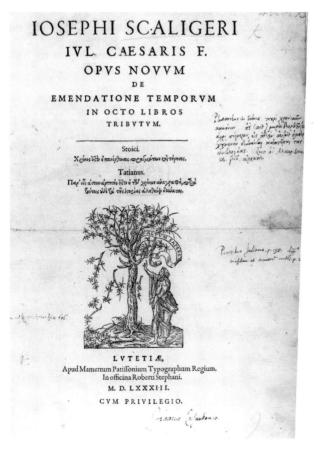

IOSEPHI SCALIGERI
IVL. CAESARIS F.
OPVS NOVVM
DE
EMENDATIONE TEMPORVM
IN OCTO LIBROS
TRIBVTVM.

Stoici.
Χρόνος ἐςὶ ἐπανέρχωσις περιμόντων εἰς τόπους.

Tatianus.
Παρ' οἷς ἀπωφέρεται ἐσὶ ἡ τῷ χρόνοις ἀναγραφή, παρὰ
τούτοις ἐςὶ καὶ τὰς ἱστορίας ἀληθὴῶν δυώατα.

LVTETIÆ,
Apud Mamertum Patiſſonium Typographum Regium.
In officina Roberti Stephani.
M. D. LXXXIII.
CVM PRIVILEGIO.

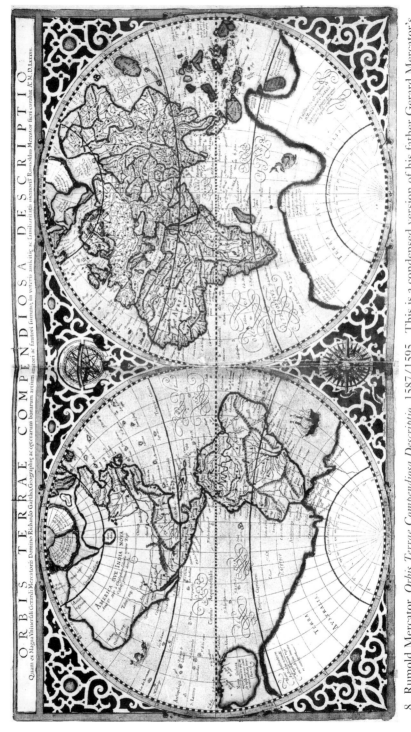

8. Rumold Mercator, *Orbis Terrae Compendiosa Descriptio*, 1587/1595 . This is a condensed version of his father Gerard Mercator's great wall map of 1569 and which appeared in Mercator's *Atlas* from 1595 onwards.

The labels visible in the drawing read: *tectum*, *porticus*, *sedilia*, *orchestra*, *mimorum aedes*, *ingressus*, *proscænium*, *planties sive arena*.

quintum sed disparis et peculiarea, bestiarum conuictati
oni destinatum, in quo multi ursi, tauri, et stupenda
magnitudinis canes, distictis caueis et septis aluntur, qui
ad

9. Drawing of the interior of The Swan Theatre in London by Arnoldus Buchelius, c. 1600 after a sketch made by Johannes de Witt, c.1596.

10. Jan Saenredam, after Abraham Bloemart, *Still Life with a Skull*, c. 1600.

11. Tycho Brahe's quadrant and observatory from
Astronomiae instauratae mechanica by Tycho Brahe, 1602 edition.

12. Adriaen van de Venne, *Fishing for Souls*, 1614.

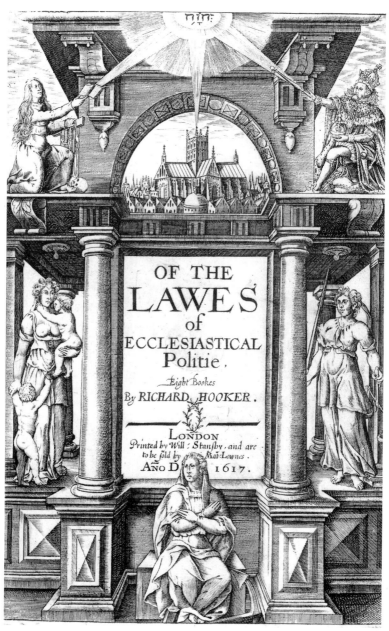

OF THE
LAWES
of
ECCLESIASTICAL
Politie.

Eight Bookes

By RICHARD HOOKER.

LONDON
Printed by Will: Stansby, *and are
to be sold by* Mat: Lownes.
AÑO D 1617.

13. Title page to Richard Hooker, *Of the Laws of Ecclesiastical Polity*, 1617.

14. Jan Breughel the elder, *The Sense of Hearing*, 1618.

15. Prayer book and bishop seal of Saint François de Sales.

16. Scientific instruments belonging to Galileo Galilei, including telescope, magnetic compass, and pendulum clock.

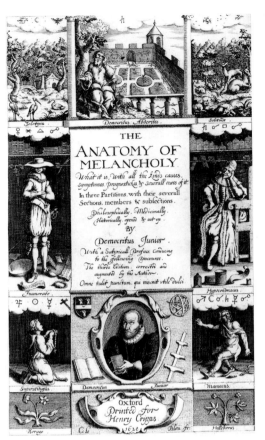

17. Title page of *The Anatomy of Melancholy* by Robert Burton, 1628.

18. Illustration from René Descartes, *Discours de la méthode*, 1637.

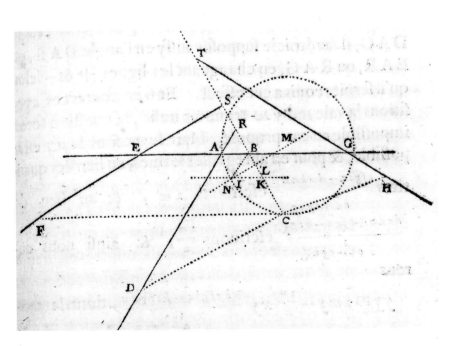

19. Inigo Jones, masquing dress for Charles I,
from *Salmacida Spolia*, 1640.

20. Francis Bacon, engraving by William Marshall, 1640.

21. Title page to Francis Bacon, *The Advancement of Learning*, 1640.

22. Title page of *Leviathan* by Thomas Hobbes, 1651.

But, as contemporary theater also suggests, there were signs that not all was well with the family. Pedro Calderon centered several plays on the murder by jealous husbands of supposedly unfaithful (but in fact innocent) wives; and French theater was fascinated by parents who murdered their children. In England, theater was often concerned with troubled relations between men and women, notably with rebellious or potentially rebellious wives. Shakespeare's Petruchio may have tamed his Katharina, but problems remained for others; John Taylor (1580–1653) struck a popular note with his rhyming:

> Ill fares the family that shows
> A cock that's silent, and a hen that crows.
> I know not which live more unnatural lives,
> Obedient husbands, or commanding wives.

That this was a problem at all levels of society is suggested by court records concerning "unruly women" and the installation in many villages of "ducking stools" to discipline them.

The solution to the problems of the family was thought to lie in a reassertion of the importance and authority of fathers, which were rooted in the order of nature. As *Hamlet* suggests, fatherlessness was associated with disorientation and insecurity; and a husband, as Tasso insisted, must "make his natural superiority felt," for "women are related to men as unbridled desire to reason . . . as desire is to the intellect." Thus, Tasso continued, "just as desire, which is in itself irrational, is informed by many beautiful and comely virtues when it subjects itself to intellect, so a woman who obeys her husband adorns herself with virtues that she would not possess if she were rebellious." Montaigne, in spite of his comradely relationship with Marie de Gournay, advised women generally that it was improper "for them to will and desire; their role is to suffer, obey, consent." Bodin was particularly fierce on the subject, locating the source of all social order in the authority of parents, which of course chiefly meant fathers. "In any rightly-ordered commonwealth," he wrote, "that power of life and death over their children which belongs to them under the law of God and of nature, should be restored." Otherwise "there is no hope of any restoration of good morals, honor, virtue, or of the ancient splendor of commonwealths."

Given the importance of sexuality and its regulation, there was unusual anxiety about the distinction between the sexes. To make this clear was a major function of dress, as the Puritan Stubbes pointed out in his *Anatomy of Abuses* (1583): "Our apparell was given us as a signe distinctive to discern betwixt sex and sex, & therefore one to weare the Apparel of another sex is to participate with the same, and to adulterate the veritie of his own kinde." The depth of his feeling on the matter is suggested by his description of women in men's clothing as "*Hermaphroditi*, that is Monsters of bothe kindes, half women, half men."

Misogyny, not uncommon when masculinity is threatened, was now growing. Paruta thought it particularly widespread among the clergy. But assertions of the superiority of men to women came from many directions. Tasso conventionally compared husband and wife to soul and body, also observing, as though it were a common problem, that if a husband "cannot make his natural superiority felt, he will sometimes find his wife so recalcitrant and disobedient that, in place of the companion whom he expected to help lighten the burden that our humanity brings with it, he will confront a perpetual enemy as contrary to him as unbridled desire to reason." Hooker insisted on the natural superiority of man to woman, who has been "framed by nature not onlie after in time but inferior in excellencie." He was, however, sufficiently "judicious" to admit that the difference between them "might be sooner perceyved than defined," just as "that kind of love which is the perfectest ground of wedlock is seldome able to yeeld anie reason of it selfe." He also held it against the Puritans that they addressed themselves particularly to "those whose judgements are commonlie weakest by reason of their sex." Montaigne thought women incompetent to treat theology, their fittest occupation being housekeeping. He opposed, too, leaving children too long under the influence of their mothers, concluding grandly that "reason, wisdom, and the offices of friendship are oftener found among men, and therefore they govern the affairs of the world." Indeed, women were sometimes considered positively dangerous; it has been suggested that a belief in their special susceptibility to satanic influence contributed to the witchcraft mania of the period.

The growing need for certainty that these various developments reveal helps to explain the renewal of traditional appeals to nature and reason, to classical authority, and to the literal sense of Scripture. As Hooker observed of the Puritans in England, "They hold that one onely lawe, the scripture, must be the rule in all thinges, even so farre as to the *taking up of a rush or strawe*." Some thinkers located the problem of certainty in language and proposed to rehabilitate Latin, the universal language (as they believed) of humanity. Henri Estienne sought "linguistic perfection" in the vernacular. The massive reliance on authoritative quotation in the literature of this period often served to ward off the insecurities of writers.

The quest for certainty had, of course, never ceased in some circles. It had contributed to the new cosmology, although its immediate result had been chiefly to make nonsense of the old system, and it was accompanied by a growing repudiation of skepticism. In spite of the popularity of his *Essays*, Montaigne's radical doubt was shared by few contemporaries; he was generally read as a genial but conventional moralist; few thinkers shared either his profound skepticism or his fideism. Grotius attacked skepticism in the person of Carneades, a Greek of the second century before Christ, whose arguments he ridiculed in his classic treatise *On the Law of War and Peace*. Pascal attacked "probabilism," which made doubt consistent with morality by holding that probability was a sufficient basis for it. Thinkers yearned for systems of thought within which, as Hooker put it, no truth could contradict another truth. The spirit of system, against which Renaissance humanists had revolted, was recovering.

One symptom of this shift was a tendency to find earlier thinkers insufficiently systematic. Calvin was among those who could no longer satisfy later generations claiming to follow him. His successor as leader of the church in Geneva, Theodore Beza, composed tracts in scholastic form rather than in Calvin's own discursive style; and François Turretin, the most prominent Calvinist theologian of the seventeenth century, wrote what was essentially a scholastic *Summa* in three Latin volumes which dealt systematically with major topics, pro and con, in the manner of Thomas Aquinas. Pierre Charron's *De la sagesse* (1601) ordered—and thus totally misrepresented—the thought of Montaigne. The theology of Bellarmine was so dominated by this spirit that he systematized even the views of his opponents in his *Disputations on the Controversies of Christian Faith* (1586–93); he was criticized for this within his own church, for whom system was a virtue: he had, from this perspective, treated heresy too favorably. And whereas humanists had treated the church fathers as individual personalities rather than vehicles of eternal wisdom, coupling their names with their thought, theologians now rarely identified their sources.

But perhaps the most telling evidence of the growing need for certainty was a turn among intellectuals to the consolations of philosophy; if, as Ludwig Wittgenstein suggested, philosophy is symptomatic of a kind of sickness, the gradual recovery of its respectability, long doubted by humanists and some nominalists, was another indication of the discontents of this period. The pursuit of certainty through philosophical demonstration had continued to dominate the universities, especially championed by the mendicant orders and some Jesuits. Now philosophy seemed increasingly attractive, among Protestants as well as Catholics. Prejudice against it persisted, to be sure, among laymen who tended to think of it as the musty and unintelligible preserve of clerical professionals, of little interest to the cultivated public. As Stefano Guazzo declared in his *Civil Conversation* (1574), "The more books of philosophy we have at this day, the fewer [genuine] philosophers we have." But even this hardly suggests a total repudiation of philosophy.

Now philosophy was increasingly praised for its utility. Guillaume Du Vair recommended it for removing "all the false opinions that trouble our brains," for making "our affections kind and natural," and as the source of "all other virtues, as their mother, nurse, and keeper." "We must go to school to Philosophy," he concluded. Bruno advertised his philosophy as a better support for religion than any other. The "philosophy" most invoked was, however, some version of ancient philosophy; until the latter half of the century, the comforts philosophy promised were to be found in the certainties of the past.

There were also major differences between the "philosophy" invoked in this period and the philosophy condemned by the humanists. Medieval philosophy had been studied only by clerical scholars; increasingly technical, it was largely based on Aristotle, *the* philosopher, and the differences among ancient thinkers were often minimized. But generations of philological study had now revealed the variety among the ancients; there could no longer be a single dominant system hallowed by time. There were, in addition, pressures on philosophy, so long embedded in cosmology, to adapt to the new science. It had now to serve many needs for an educated, largely lay public.

The most striking among the philosophies now attracting attention, partly because of their novelty, were what Martha C. Nussbaum has called the "therapeutic philosophies" of later antiquity. Though they may have had systematic implications, these, in their concreteness, corresponded to Cicero's conception of philosophy as "a medical art for the soul." Much in them was congenial, notably their refusal to distinguish clearly between the mind and the passions—now taken more seriously—and the rhetorical strategies with which they gave comfort.

One such therapy was a more formal and systematic skepticism than Montaigne's, which was already attractive to readers because it was thought capable of neutralizing the challenges of reason to faith. Its attraction was enhanced by the discovery of the *Outlines of Pyrrhonism* of Sextus Empiricus, which gave it the sanction of antiquity; it was translated into Latin by Henri Estienne in 1562. Sextus had argued that skepticism gave peace of mind by teaching acceptance of the uncomfortable realities of life. According to Sextus, "Being a lover of humanity, the Skeptic wishes to heal by argument, insofar as possible, the arrogant, empty beliefs and the rashness of dogmatists." This was held to bring "freedom from disturbance through sorting out the discrepancies in impressions and thoughts" after the suspension of belief. Skepticism was given academic form by Francesco Sanchez in *Quod nihil scitur* (1581). In addition to his doubts about knowledge, Sanchez mocked the pomposity of scholastic philosophers who "use for Man the term *Animal rationale mortale*, which is more difficult than what we started with."

Another supposedly comforting philosophy of antiquity was Epicureanism, still often denounced as "atheism": for Hooker, as for Dante, "Epicureans" were enemies of God. The participants in Bodin's *Colloquium* agreed that Epicureanism was little different "from the opinions of beasts" because it relied "only on the senses" and "opened freely all the approaches to sin." The sense of the meaninglessness of human existence in Epicureanism was echoed in John Webster's description in *The Duchess of Malfi* of human beings as "the gods' tennis balls." But Epicureanism also had various, if somewhat contradictory attractions, especially after the printing of the Epicurean Lucretius's great epic poem *Of the Nature of Things*. Lucretius had insisted that philosophy should be useful and had denounced his own times. This made him attractive to reformers, and Bacon defended him against charges of atheism. A group of young poets in France applauded Epicureanism for its description of nature as blind to human wishes, of reason as powerless, and of the passions as irresistible. They also liked it for teaching that competition for honors and wealth is vanity, and that a wise man can believe only in friendship. Sarpi vibrated sympathetically to its rejection of the value of merely abstract principles of justice and morality, and Montaigne was impressed by its "firmness and rigor" and claimed to have based his own calculus of pleasures and pains on Epicurus; he particularly approved of the Epicurean teaching that pleasure is natural.

In addition, the pre-Socratic atomism transmitted by Lucretius interested scientists, partly because it suggested that atomism was older than Aristotle; it was still widely believed that greater antiquity meant a greater likelihood of truth. Bacon thought the pre-Socratics superior to Aristotle because they possessed "some taste of the natural philosopher—some savor of the nature of things, and experience, and bodies." Both Galileo and Gassendi helped to pass atomism along to later scientists.

But Stoicism, known through Cicero, Seneca, and Virgil, though chiefly in fragments, was the most popular of the therapeutic philosophies, much facilitated by scholarship that produced editions of its major sources that made it better understood. The most influential student and popularizer of Stoicism was Justus Lipsius, whose *Six Books of Politics* (1589) spread Stoic doctrine among the ruling classes of Europe. Meanwhile Guillaume Du Vair was making Stoic doctrine available in French in his *Moral Philosophy of the Stoics* (1585), and it was further popularized by Montaigne's *Essays*, although Montaigne used it, as with everything, inconsistently and for his own purposes.

Stoicism was especially attractive because it was thought to give comfort for the disorders and suffering caused by the religious wars. The most popular of Lipsius's works was his *De constantia*, a set of dialogues set in a garden, which here symbolized the private peace and order lacking in public life. For Lipsius, a philosopher was primarily a healer of sick souls who made available "some pleasant and familiar medicines." The philosophical therapist, for Lipsius, after cutting away the illusions of his patients, would help them to descend "from the craggy hill of philosophy into the pleasant fields of philology" and so restore them to health. The basic prescription of Stoicism was on the surface simple: only follow nature, the universal norm of human behavior, the model of order in all things and the best teacher of godliness and duty. Du Vair described nature as "so prudent and provident a mistress that she always disposeth all things unto their greatest good, and unto that end which men should seek and search after: in such sort, that he that will follow after it cannot choose but compass and obtain it." Nature provides, and has imprinted on us all, laws that "teach us what we rightly need," in contrast to the corruption and chaos wrought by civilization. Montaigne, in this tradition, represented nature as "our great and powerful mother," whom we have abused by overloading and smothering "the beauty and richness of her works with our inventions."

Nature thus became a central element in the reformist impulses of the age. It also taught a sterner lesson: that humanity had no privileged place in the universe: Stoic nature was indifferent to human happiness. The best way to "follow" nature was thus to recognize and resign oneself to its sovereignty. Stoic providence rules all things indifferently. In his Stoic mode, Montaigne professed to find comfort in this doctrine:

> In all affairs, when they are past, however they have turned out, I have little regret. For this idea takes away the pain: that they were bound to happen thus, and now they are in the great stream of the universe and in the chain of Stoical causes. Your fancy, by wish or imagination, cannot change a single point without overturning the whole order of things, and the past and the future.[4]

This peculiar optimism was shared by Du Vair, who claimed to believe that grief was intolerable only "to them that think it so":

> If we love our children, let us love them as men, that is to say, as men subject unto infinite casualties of death, and then afterwards when they happen to die their deaths will be neither strange nor grievous unto us. . . . If [your neighbor's] son die, you say, he was of estate mortal, not born to live forever; and I pray why cannot you say as much when your own son dieth, without crying out, tormenting yourself, or accusing God and men for the loss of that which is ordinary?[5]

Lipsius denounced pity (although carefully distinguishing it from mercy) as "neither decent nor right" but mere "softness and abjection of the mind."

The Stoic cure for humanity's distress was thus total resignation to providence, accomplished through the right ordering of the soul by reason, a "lawful Lady," to whom all owe "natural obedience." Such obedience was the essence of virtue; the primary task of philosophy to maintain the obedience of the self to it. It could do so because, for the Stoics, to know the good through philosophy was to do the good. Philosophy was the key to calm acceptance of the inevitable: Lipsius's word for this was "constancy," which he thought a sufficient antidote even to the fear of death. There was nevertheless a hint of magnanimity in Stoic resignation. Stoicism taught that only through philosophy can we recognize the community of the whole human race, and its predicament was terrible but also endurable.

The major task of philosophy in this tradition was thus to evoke a willed resignation. This was the significance of the importance it attached to apatheia, which meant invulnerability to disturbance by sense or passion, calmness through all the adversities of life. "It is a noble and lofty thing," Tasso wrote, "to be both intrepid and constant in meeting the blows of fortune." Montaigne steeled himself by Stoic wisdom to endure the pain of "cutting for the stone" without anesthesia. Indeed, he professed to believe—though he did not claim to have done so himself—that it should be possible for a man to read a book while under the surgeon's knife. The implication here is that pain and grief are culturally determined. If, however, as the Stoics admitted, one reached the limits of endurance, suicide was permissible. God, Montaigne argued, "gives us leave enough when he puts us in such a state that it is worse to live than to die."

This doctrine was related to another: a distinction between what is within our power and what is not. Among the latter were the afflictions of providence or, in its more popular version, fortune. For every person is internally free, whatever the pressures of society or the external constraints of life. These must be accepted but not internalized. "The wise man," Montaigne wrote, "should withdraw his soul within, out of the crowd, and keep it in freedom and power to judge things freely; but as for externals, he should wholly follow the accepted fashions and forms."

This doctrine pointed in two rather different directions. One was an invulnerable, even anti-social, self-sufficiency. Montaigne thus resolved, on retiring from public service, "to live alone and do without company," his happiness dependent only on himself: "let us cut loose from all the ties that bind us to others; let us win for ourselves the power to live really alone and to live that way at our ease." He thanked God for his "idleness and freedom."

But Stoicism might also point to inwardness, understood as a protection for the individual against the demands of a turbulent society. Lipsius aspired to be

> guarded and fenced against all externall things, and settled within myself, careless of all cares save one, which is, that I may bring in subjection this broken and distressed mind of mine to Right Reason and God, and subject all human and earthly things to my Mind. That whensoever my fatal day shall come, I may be ready with good courage joyfully to welcome him, and depart this life, not as thrust out at the windows but as let out at the door.

His ideal was his garden; a "veritable Eden" where he could concentrate his mind, where his reason could make poverty, banishment, even death endurable.[6] Its emphasis on acceptance promised a passivity among subjects that recommended Stoicism to governments. It also promoted discipline in armies, as in France and the Netherlands. More than a century later these doctrines would inform Alexander Pope's *Essay on Man* (1733–34).

But the more traditional philosophies of Aristotle and Plato were also given new life. Available in better texts, they could now be studied more systematically than before. One result was that they were easier to differentiate, both from one another and from other schools of ancient thought.

There were many new editions of Aristotle. Those in Greek prepared by Erasmus and Casaubon were better than anything previously available, and Aristotle was also translated into Ciceronian Latin. Elaborate commentaries were published too, and Aristotelianism flourished in many places. In Italy, it was centered first at the University of Padua, where it was represented both by Jacopo Zabarella, who venerated Aristotle for his consistent rationality, and by the more orthodox Cesare Cremonini, for whom Aristotle was the ultimate authority in philosophy; Cremonini is now chiefly remembered for refusing to look through a telescope because Galileo had used it to attack Aristotelian science. Eventually the Jesuit college in Rome became a center for Aristotelianism, especially in theology and science. In France, the Parlement of Paris forbade, "on pain of death," the teaching of anything contrary to Aristotle. Hobbes would remark that in the universities of Europe one studied "not properly philosophy but Aristotelity." Galileo explained the authority of Aristotle, whose science he rejected, in a speech assigned to Simplicio, the defender of traditional science, in his *Two Chief World Systems*:

Who would there be to settle our controversies if Aristotle were deposed? What other author should we follow in the schools, the academies, the universities? What philosopher has written the whole of natural philosophy, so well arranged, without omitting a single conclusion? Ought we to desert that structure under which so many travelers have recuperated? Should we destroy that haven where so many scholars have taken refuge so comfortably, where, without exposing themselves to the inclemencies of the air, they can acquire a complete knowledge of the universe by merely turning over a few pages? Should that fort be leveled where one may abide in safety against all enemy assaults?[7]

This passage expresses Galileo's perception of Aristotelian science. In fact, although Aristotelian cosmology was eventually if only slowly abandoned, Aristotelianism was increasingly influential in other areas of thought: it remained useful to systematize and integrate various phenomena: logic and metaphysics, biology, politics and ethics, literature, and—above all—theology. Protestants, in the post-Reformation climate, found Aristotle almost as useful as Catholics. Theodore Beza relied heavily on Aristotelian logic and found the Aristotelian conception of "substance" useful to explain the Eucharist. Aristotelianism also became increasingly important in English universities under Archbishop Laud. Puritans venerated his logic, and Thomas Aquinas was a favorite authority of Cotton Mather.

Aristotelianism had, to be sure, changed somewhat. It abandoned much of the technical vocabulary of the schools and gave increasing attention to ethics and politics. And although its utility in physical science was under attack, its influence was growing in biology, in which it had taxonomic uses, and in the arts, for which it provided principles of criticism. But university Aristotelianism also grew more authoritarian, especially to meet the challenge of the new science. And because Aristotle was so widely regarded as an authority, his followers tended to transform even his incidental observations into general laws.

Plato was also widely read, although as in the earlier Renaissance much of what was associated with his name was still an eclectic mix of ideas in which those of Plato were not clearly distinguished from Neoplatonism or even from Aristotelianism; the old notion of the descent of a coherent body of wisdom from the earliest Greeks to Plato and Aristotle persisted. Plato remained a name (almost literally) to conjure with. Hints of his influence appear in many places: in Spenser's *Faerie Queene*, in the notion (used to counter Stoicism) that pleasure might be compatible with virtue, and even in Bellarmine's surprising tribute to Pico della Mirandola for opposing Averroism and materialism. Such a diversity of influence was, indeed, an element in the hostility of orthodoxy to Platonism. Bellarmine also persuaded Pope Clement VIII, who admired Plato, that to introduce the teaching of Plato in Rome would invite heresy. Nevertheless, what passed for Platonism retained considerable interest, partly because Plato had preceded Aristotle in time. Plato also offered a respectable, if sometimes unorthodox, alternative to Aristotle and so appealed to the spirit of opposition, always an element in philosophical discourse. The mystical tendencies in Platonism were helpful to reconcile knowledge and belief, a need felt even by the young Galileo. "The divine Plato" was still envisioned as the great unifier of "things divine and human," especially in his doctrine of ideas, which attached the fragmented and transitory things of this world to divine prototypes. He gave access to a higher, better, morally ordered world without requiring the abandonment of the world of flux. Kepler himself thought of the Creator-God as having "preconceived within Himself the idea of the world, and the idea is prior to the thing." Platonism thus satisfied in its own way the need for coherence and meaning in a disoriented age. Conversely, at a time when rhetoric was increasingly distrusted, Plato's attacks on rhetoricians were often cited.

An inwardness in Platonism also appealed to the Augustinianism of this period. Major figures in France were persuaded that Plato must have had access to the Jewish Scriptures. Bodin's deist, joined by his Jewish colleague, thought Plato vastly superior to Aristotle because of his "much more sure understanding about God and the power of immortal souls"; and

Montaigne believed that Platonism came close to Christianity. In Rome, Philip Neri's Oratory was a stronghold of Platonism. At Cambridge, a group of thinkers identified themselves as Platonists, and the enemies of Hobbes found support in Platonism. Other later readers were fascinated by Plato's account of an aristocratic republic in which a ruling group differed so dramatically in its qualifications to rule from their own upper classes.

Patrizi suggests particularly well what it meant to be a Platonist. In his youth he had improved his Greek in Cyprus and then lectured on the *Republic* and the *Timaeus* at various Italian universities. He demonstrated in his *Peripatetic Discussions* that Plato was right and Aristotle wrong on every point, breaking with the usual effort to establish their agreement. He also translated Neoplatonic writings into Latin and wrote on mathematics, another subject favored by Platonists. In Rome, however, his work came to the attention of the authorities and was placed on the Index.

Platonism (or more accurately Neoplatonism) was another strand among the occult sciences, still often considered a branch of philosophy. One of Bodin's philosophers celebrated "the hidden secrets of philosophy," and another classified "the actions of demons and angels" under metaphysics. For both Platonism and occultism, all similarities, analogies, and parallels were signs of a secret bond in a comprehensive system in which all things had cosmic reverberations, comprehended only by magi who could manipulate the forces they represented. Bacon hinted at a belief of this kind in his concern with the "virtues of things," and it was also given a kind of plausibility by William Gilbert's study of magnetism (1600). Bruno reflected such interests by arguing that all things, both in heaven and earth, are alive and endowed with souls. Much that would eventually be explained by scientists was seen as mysterious; science itself did not exclude but sought to assimilate it. As Celio Calcagnini, a respected humanist, argued, "mysteries cease to be mysteries" once promulgated. He recommended prudence and speaking in riddles because of the hostility of religious authority, which claimed, he thought, an illegitimate monopoly over spiritual matters.

Occult interests could be essentially academic and bookish, a kind of archaeology of ancient mysteries; but they could also express impulses deeply rooted and still vital in popular culture: a feeling for life and nature, a sense of the energies throbbing through the universe. Leonardo da Vinci's conception of the world as an animal expressed this mode of thought. "We can say," he wrote, "that the earth has a vegetative soul, and that its flesh is the land, its bones are the structures of the rocks . . . its breathing and its pulse are the ebb and flow of the sea." Such beliefs were utterly eclectic;

they drew on materials from various systems of thought as well as the popular imagination. But it has also been suggested that the magus, who could understand and manipulate the secret forces of nature, was the ancestor of the modern scientist.

Thus occult beliefs were by no means restricted to the vulgar and illiterate. University students were interested in magic. Court festivities as well as popular entertainments were full of references to the secret connections between ruler and realm. As Thomas Greene has observed:

> The courts of rulers have been perceived from time immemorial as centers of magical power and of magicians. This has been true for two reasons. First, kings have been thought to contain invisible power which emanates from them as an "influence." The royal body was thought to be charged with *mana*. . . . the royal magus tended to surround himself with professional magi.[8]

The emperor Rudolph II was especially interested in the occult. According to a contemporary, he concerned himself only with "wizards, alchymists, kabbalists and the like, sparing no expense to find all kinds of treasures, learn secrets, and use scandalous ways of harming his enemies. . . . He also has a whole library of magic books." Kepler interpreted Copernicanism within a context of dreams, visions, and magic. Along with Gassendi, Mersenne, and other serious thinkers, he also thought it worth his while to engage in controversy with the English magus Robert Fludd.

The most widespread expression of occultism was probably astrology, whose supposed truths were embedded in the pre-Copernican conception of the universe with its heavenly spheres focussed on the earth. Astrology also provided a rationale for other occult arts, including geomancy and palmistry. For most thinkers, astral influence was a branch of science, and the power attributed to the heavenly bodies was increased by general belief in the reality of moral and spiritual influences emanating from above, uniting and shaping all human experience. The English astrologer John Dee expressed the common belief that "man's body, and all other elementall bodies, are altered, disposed, ordered, pleasured, and displeasured, by the influentiall working of the sunne, Mone and other Starres and Planets." Astrology was thought especially important for medical practice. Reservations about heavenly influence chiefly concerned the degree to which it might limit free will; largely for this reason it was not incorporated into scholastic science, even though it reflected the congenial principle of hierarchy. Burton agreed with most contemporaries that the stars could "incline but not compel" the will. The stars may rule us, he concluded somewhat ambiguously, "but God rules all." The author of a popular work entitled *Christian Astrology* argued that there was "nothing appertaining to the life of man in this world which in one way or other hath not relation to one of the twelve houses of heaven." Astrology, in short, was almost unique in its capacity to assure Europeans of the order and coherence of the universe; doubts about it were centered chiefly on its power over human freedom.

Belief in astrology pervaded all classes well into the seventeenth century. Dee cast horoscopes for Queen Elizabeth before traveling to the court of Rudolph II, where he was well received. Even highly respected scientists were influenced by astrology, among them Kepler and Tycho Brahe, whom Kepler succeeded as court astronomer in Prague. The Habsburg military leader Wallenstein wore into battle an amulet inscribed with astrological signs. Postel demonstrated astrologically the right of France to rule the world. Bodin used astrology to explain ethnic differences. Astrology was central to agriculture for Campanella, who also attributed the religious changes of the time to planetary influences. Don Quixote noted its popularity; horoscopes were "so fashionable in Spain," he observed, "that there is not a servant-maid or an old cobbler who does not presume to cast a nativity as easily as pick up a knave of cards from the floor."

Alchemy had more specialized attractions, though it rested on some of the same assumptions. Fundamental to it was a belief in the basic unity of all substances; hence popular hopes for the alchemical production of gold. Alchemy flourished in many of the same centers as astrology, notably the court of Rudolph II, where its operations often employed astrological calculation. Although he rejected alchemy itself, Bacon's conception of "elective affinities" was a close parallel. "It is certain," he wrote, "that all bodies whatsoever, though they have no sense, yet they have perception: for when one body is applied to another, there is a kind of election to embrace that which is agreeable, and to exclude or expel that which is ingrate." Sarpi was reported to have experimented with the transmutation of metals, although his interest was described as purely theoretical. Sidney's many interests included "the starry science, rival to nature."

Hermeticism, which expressed many of the same impulses, claimed to have originated in the writings of one Hermes Trismegistus, thought to incorporate the earliest sacred wisdom of the human race, the original theology of ancient Egypt. The immediate source of its doctrines was a series of Greek treatises supposedly composed by a wise, quasi-divine Egyptian philosopher who had lived, according to a French writer, "long before Moses, and older than Abraham." His teachings were believed to have been the true source of the wisdom of Moses and Jesus on the one hand, and on the other of Pythagoras, Zoroaster, and Plato. The teachings of "Hermes" blended with other currents of occultism, including astrology, which supplied its cosmological framework. These writings were transmitted to the medieval West and were rediscovered by Marsilio Ficino, who published them in a Latin translation (1471); they were given further authority by a Greek version in 1554. Hermetic teachings were propagated by various respectable scholars. Patrizi printed a new translation in 1591; and the Hermetic elements in his own *Universal Philosophy*, which contrasted the piety of Hermes with the paganism of Aristotle, antagonized ecclesiastical authority as a rival to the teachings of the church.

Hermeticism embodied many elements of popular culture—astrology, demonology, alchemy, necromancy and other forms of magic—but it appealed chiefly to the upper classes, for whom it was combined with Neoplatonism in court festivals. In this form it was made to express the centrality of royal power in the political universe, which corresponded to divine power in the cosmos. The emblems employed by printers and artists as trademarks and associated with the hieroglyphs of ancient Egypt were also believed to reveal secret connections holding the universe together. The gnostic doctrine of salvation by secret wisdom in the Hermetic books was particularly attractive to intellectuals. It was paralleled in Hebrew, again because of its supposed antiquity, by cabalism, considered a revelation of ultimate truths older—hence more authentic—than the Christian Scriptures; it was propagated by such learned figures as Guillaume Postel. Books purporting to convey ancient wisdom poured from the presses of Basel and Venice; teachings of this kind were also spread by wandering Italians whose heresies had driven them abroad. Bruno was profoundly impressed by "Egyptian wisdom," which he brought to England and France; his daring *Expulsion of the Triumphant Beast* (1584), which owed much to Hermeticism, was dedicated to Sidney. This "wisdom" was also attractive to Protestants on the continent. Duplessis-Mornay, though doubtful of their authenticity, often cited Hermetic works, seeing in them a possible basis for religious unity.

Some contemporaries were unimpressed by these esoteric materials. Montaigne rejected as presumptuous their lofty view of human understanding, and Burton ridiculed them. Bodin, somewhat inconsistently, generally rejected things "so sublime that they have no utility or purpose for us." But the authenticity of the Hermetic corpus was largely accepted until Isaac Casaubon's attack on the *Ecclesiatical Annals* of Baronius. Following Lactantius, Baronius had listed Hermes among the Gentile prophets of Christ. But Casaubon proved on stylistic grounds, decisively for most scholars, that they were of no great age. After this Hermeticism survived only in fringe movements like Rosicrucianism, whose teachings continued to be disseminated in such works as *The Chemical Wedding* of Johann Andreae.

Sexual polarities also figured in the occultist world-view—above all in the reciprocal yearnings of male and female for union in harmonious marriage—at a lower level among human beings but ultimately as cosmic principles. This conception had its roots in the Pythagoreanism transmitted by Plato, which attributed sexual properties to number, as in cabala. Postel discerned sexual differentiation everywhere in the universe, at all levels of being, as the principle of attraction and unity. Giovanni Battista della Porta claimed that the entire world was "knit and bound within itself, for the world is a living creature, everywhere both male and female, and the parts of it couple together by reason of their mutual love."

Various circumstances help to explain the spread of occult interests among intellectuals. One was the progress of learning about the remote past in a period when antiquity was still thought to guarantee authenticity whereas truth was attenuated by time. Excitement was meanwhile stimulated by new materials, such as the so-called *Chaldean Oracles*, coming in from Byzantium. Printers took advantage of the excitement by producing a flood of exotic works. But even more important, perhaps, was the general hunger for the unity and order of knowledge when the new science was raising far more questions than it could answer, and both humanism and nominalism were hopelessly agnostic. The Puritan Richard Sibbes expressed the yearning of the period. "The people of God," he declared, "are beautiful, for order is beautiful. Now it is an orderly thing to see many together submit themselves to the ordinance of God." He thought an army "a beautiful thing, because of the order and the well-disposed ranks that are within it." Order had been traditionally synonymous with harmony, and it hardly seems an accident that this was also a time when the harmonies of music were especially appreciated.

The need for unity and harmony on every possible level seems to permeate much in the culture of this period. Postel clung, in the amiable madness of his old age, to the *concordia mundi*, the title of his most sane and serious work. All multiplicity, for Bodin, composed a vast harmony; he aspired to "eliminate the disagreement between philosophers and historians," and he compared the political ideal of his *Republic* to the "sweetest and most melodious harmony" of "the treble and bass voices"; a ruler might combine them by bringing together all his subjects, high and low. "Thus," Bodin concluded, "by a wonderful disagreement, concord joins the highest with the lowest, and so all with all." His *Colloquium* was an extended demonstration of the possibility of harmony in religion and philosophy based on mutual good will. As one of his interlocutors observed, "In their myths the Greeks wove the truth which they received from the Hebrews, a truth that had originated in Egypt." And the variety represented by the various points of view among the participants in the discussion is finally made to reveal a broader harmony; the work opens and closes with a song.

In this concern Bodin reflected his time. Kepler climaxed his career with a work dedicated to James I of England encouraging his interest in peace by applying the harmonies of the cosmos to society and politics. Similar impulses were at work in both Bruno and Campanella, who yearned to authenticate their own aspirations by pointing to the harmonies of the cosmos. Because all truths were still seen as mutually consistent and harmonious, such yearnings found wide expression in a syncretism that aimed to encompass even more than Pico della Mirandola had aimed to include a century earlier, for it had now, after the geographical discoveries and the recent triumphs of scholarship, to combine a much broader range of even more exotic materials. Now all the peoples of the earth were widely believed to have participated in the discovery and expression of the basic unity of all things.

The expansion of information and ideas in the earlier Renaissance had been less concerned with intellectual coherence. But its eclecticism was now giving way to syncretism because an unintegrated and chaotic intellectual universe was increasingly unendurable. In the next group of chapters we will examine the results of this distress and the efforts to soothe it.

CHAPTER ELEVEN

The Reordered Self

An earlier chapter showed that, basic to the Renaissance culture of liberation, was a conception of the self quite different from the traditional model of a hierarchy of discrete faculties governed by reason. But increasingly the growing pressure for order aimed to reestablish the old hierarchy. It had, of course, never entirely disappeared; and now it was gradually recovering much of its earlier authority. The passions, to be sure, were more favorably regarded than before, as long as they were kept properly under control. But this anxious age increasingly needed to restore the order of the self as basic to reordering other dimensions of experience.

Hooker, who can so often be cited on the other side, made use of the old hierarchy in a sermon early in 1585. "The orderly disposition of the mind of man," he declared, "should be this: perturbations and sensuall appetites all kept in awe by a moderate and sober will; will in all things framed by reason; reason directed by the law of God and nature." This formulation, which was based on the notion of the "different and distincte partes" in human being, was clear and simple, in contrast to the sometimes baffling mysteries implicit in the alternative, which at times also attracted him. Hierarchy ordered and unified the self again. It was both moral and practical; it gave access to "natures light" and informed us of "the laws of doing well." It also linked the individual to the universe. Hooker contrasted this model with the unrighteous and disordered sinner of Habakkuk, who "had his mind as it were turned upside down," in whom "unreasonable blindnes trampled all lawes both of God and nature under feet, wilfulnes tyrannized over reason, and brutish sensuality over will."

"Soul," "mind," and "reason" were, in common usage, almost interchangeable to designate what was highest in the self, properly located to direct everything below. Burton identified this quality with the brain and described it as "the most noble organ under heaven, the dwelling-house and seat of the soul, the habitation of wisdome, memory, judgment, reason, in which man is most like unto God." Charron regarded it as God's image in man, "a particle of the immortal substance, an emanation of divinity, a heavenly light." For Du Vair, "the good and happiness of man" consisted in the right use of reason, "the source of all virtue." Italian writers joined this chorus, though Tasso sidestepped its dualistic implications by suggesting that sensual pleasure was intensified when guided by reason. Protestants, especially later Calvinists, were moving in the same direction; Beza appealed increasingly to reason, and the Puritan William Ames developed a rational foundation for Calvinist theology.

Many contemporaries would have regarded this anthropology as too simple, but it was increasingly attractive even to such complex minds as those of Jonson and Campanella. It often surfaced in the notion of a struggle between the rebellious body and a soul more or less identified with reason, a theme especially prominent in Stoic thought. Lipsius described the soul as "the nobler part" of the self, whereas the body was the source of its disorders; the soul represented spirit and fire, whereas the body represented earth, the two "joyned together with a iarring concord" and often in disagreement. For Lipsius much was at stake,

> especially when controversie ariseth about souerainty & subjection. For either of them would bear sway, and chiefly that part which ought not. The earth advanceth it selfe aboue the fire, and the dirty nature aboue that which is diuine. Herehence arise in man dissentions, stirs, & continual conflict of these parts warring together. Their respective companions are REASON and OPINION. That fighteth for the soule, being in the soule: This for, and in the body.[1]

He emphasized the divine origins of the soul, and its "excellent power or faculty of vnderstanding and iudgement." It represented the perfection of human being.

Doubts remained, and the perspicacious Bodin saw problems here:

> Since . . . there is no limit to our desire for pleasure, or because this is equally common to man and to beast, the more noble each man is, the further he dissociates himself from the level of the beasts, and little by little he is carried forward by eagerness for glory, so that he may eclipse the rest. From this comes the lust for domination and the violence inflicted upon the weak. Hence also come discords, wars, slavery, and

massacres. But this kind of life is turbulent and full of danger, an empty glory.

This bit of realism was worthy of Pascal and seems consistent with Bodin's later views on princely sovereignty.[2]

The will, as the active agent for controlling the self, was a faculty of special interest to moralists in this troubled age, though often ambiguous and unreliable rather than the automatic servant of reason. Hooker insisted on the importance of "right reason" for the moral life but admitted that "the will about one and the same thinge may in contrarie respectes have contrarie inclinations." Others had a simpler and more optimistic conception. For Du Vair, the will was powerful and free:

The things which are in our power are these: to approve, undertake, desire, and eschew a matter, and in a word, all our actions. For our will hath authority and power to rule and govern them according to reason, till they come unto the place from which our good and happiness must come. As, for example's sake, she is able to dispose our opinion, so that it yield not consent but to that which it is meet she should, and which shall be examined either by sense or reason, that she shall cleave fast unto things which are evidently true of themselves, and keep her self in suspense in things doubtful and utterly reject things which are of themselves plainly untrue and false. Besides, she can so rule our desire, that it shall follow after nothing but that which is agreeable with nature, and eschew the contrary.[3]

Charron too saw the will as a place where "good and virtue lodge." Man, he insisted, is neither good nor bad and can be taught "by understanding and knowing beautiful, good, and honest things to love and desire them." Properly instructed, the will is "guide and light to the traveler." The need for moral order, as it had in the past, was pushing toward optimism about the possibility of control. The pressures for order were so strong that ecclesiastical authorities on both sides rarely took exception to such views, although the Jesuit Luis de Molina produced much controversy by arguing that the will in those predestined to salvation is free to cooperate with or to reject divine grace. Even Puritan preachers, though officially predestinarian, sometimes argued, presumably for practical purposes, for the freedom of the will.

What primarily required control by the will was again the passions, seen as the major source of disorder in human affairs. Burton, in one of his more melancholy moments, admitted that "a few discreet men" might be able to "govern themselves, and curb in their inordinate affections, by religion, philosophy, and such divine precepts of meekness, patience, and the like." But most men, he thought, were ruled by passion. "Bad by nature, worse by art, discipline, custom, education, and a perverse will of their own," they follow "wheresoever their unbridled affections will transport them." What was required was an ethic of control. According to one writer's recipe for a peaceful life, a person should "control himself" and "condemn completely everything having to do with passion." Thus he would "move gently along in all matters, never have cause to repent, to withdraw what he has said, or to change." Sarpi represented the antagonism between the papacy and Venice as a struggle between the intelligence of the Venetian senate and the passionate irrationality of Rome. Pasquier thought himself "king of the Republic God had entrusted" to him, because he knew how to control his passions. Although Puritans applauded "zeal" for the honor of God, they worried lest the "spring-tide of affection" for him should fail to "run in the due channel." The ability to maintain such control was commonly seen as a major difference of men from women.

A more benign and complex view of the passions was sometimes possible. Burton thought that they could be tamed by confiding one's difficulties to a friend. Hooker believed that, although "it is not altogether in our power" whether we will be stirred with affections or no," the actions to which they might give rise were in the power of the will, "to be performed or staied," for "appetite is the wills sollicitor, and the will is appetites controller; what we covet according to the one, by the other we often reject." Only with Descartes were the passions positively regarded. "The customary mode of action of all the passions is simply this," he wrote, "that they dispose the soul to desire those things which nature tells us are of use, and to persist in this desire, and also to bring about that same agitation of spirits which customarily causes them to dispose the body to the movement which serves for the carrying into effect of these things." He concluded that the good as well as the evil in life depends on "the passions alone." But he still insisted that the passions remain firmly under the control of reason.

There was similar ambivalence about the body, of which the clergy took an increasingly negative view. Baronius, interpreting literally the famous Pauline dichotomy, compared the flesh to "an untamable wild beast." He advised a correspondent that "the devil will say, 'Marriage is a holy thing, a sacrament, a state of life established by God himself.'" His response to this wicked suggestion: "Oh what a diabolical deceit! Oh what infernal cunning!" To the Oratory of Philip Neri the body was a "beast" to be subdued. Bellarmine thought celibacy, though difficult, a desirable choice even for the laity. This attitude helps to explain why draperies were chastely painted over the nudes in Michelangelo's *Last Judgment* in the Sistine Chapel. Judicial torture and capital punishment, especially when artfully prolonged, were justified on the ground that they affected only the contemptible body. Lipsius thought its connection with the body "not good for the soule."

Imagination, too, was again increasingly suspect, with support from Aristotle, who had represented it as a function of appetite. Even for Montaigne it was a source of anxiety; his art, he claimed, aimed "to escape, not to resist it." "When real evils fail us," he wrote, "knowledge lends us hers. . . . As if he were not in time to suffer the pain when he is in it, [a man] anticipates it in imagination." When he gave free rein to his own imagination, it produced "so many chimeras and fantastic monsters" that he felt (or thought he should feel) shame. Du Vair identified imagination as the source of the "seditious passions" that "trouble the rest of the soul"; it should therefore be closely controlled by the will. Bacon warned against its intrusion into science and advocated "a religious care to eject, repress, and, as it were, exorcise every kind of phantasm." Richard Sibbes attacked imagination as "a wild and ranging thing" that wrongs "the frame of God's work in us, setting the basic part of man above the higher." For a French Calvinist, "Qui invente ment" (Whoever invents, lies). Bacon, citing Augustine's *Confessions*, condemned all poets as liars. Lodovico Castelvetro, writing on Aristotle's *Poetics* in 1570, denied to poets the freedom to create:

> We cannot create a king who never existed by our imagination, nor can we attribute actions to such a king; indeed we cannot even attribute to a really historic king actions he never performed; history would give us the lie. For if it is permitted to create kings who never existed, and to give them fictitious actions, it will also be permitted to create new mountains, new rivers, new lakes, new seas, new peoples, new kingdoms, and to transport old rivers into other districts, and, in short, it will be permitted to create a new world and to transform an old one.[4]

Burton gave imagination an unusually full discussion, perhaps because of his greater ambivalence. If subject to reason, he agreed that it could be "a man's star, and the rudder of this our ship." But in point of fact, it was a major cause of melancholy, deception, heresy, and schism, and through its distortions "the first step and fountain of all our grievances." Its awesome power, as "the common carrier of passions, by whose means they work and produce many times prodigious effects," usually exceeded the power of reason and became "the first step and fountain of all our grievances." Galileo was relatively temperate, if scornful, in observing that there were but two sorts of "poetic mind": one that could invent fables, the other disposed to believe them.

Some Puritans were even more extreme. For William Perkins, anything of human invention was corrupt, and a work of the imagination, a thing merely "fained in the mind" was "an idol." Any claim to creativity by human beings, indeed, could be seen as an infringement on a major pre-rogative of God, especially if it invented something that did not exist in nature, since only God can create *ex nihilo*. Non-mimetic art verged on blasphemy. Such attitudes could lead to distrust of words like "create" and "creation"; as one of Jonson's characters observes, "Translated thus from a poor creature to a creator . . . now must I create intolerable sort of lies." There may also be a clue here to the significance of such common epithets of the time as "atheist," "Epicurean," and even "Machiavel," which antic-ipated the modern notion, still capable of shock, that "the world" itself, whose shape and existence we assume, may be only a cultural artifact.

The growing reliance on intellect also found expression in a resurgence of respect for the contemplative, as opposed to the active, life, an ideal usually understood as the contemplation of higher things by what is highest in the self. It elevated personal over social values, private over public life. The tension between the active and contemplative life had long been a topos of humanist debate, usually concluding with a reconciliation between them that included much praise of public life. But the balance had been shifting in Italy toward contemplation even before the sixteenth century, a tendency intensified by Neoplatonism. The new mood found expression in a revul-sion against cities and emphasis on the attractions of life in the country. In the later Renaissance cultivated Italians were withdrawing to their country villas, where, as one author put it, you can "cultivate your garden." Even Galileo, who chose to live in Florence, Pisa, Padua, and Venice, was reported to have said that the city was "the prison of the speculative mind" and to have felt free only in the country. French gentry were withdrawing to their country estates. The pastoral, which idealized withdrawal from organized society, was an expression of this mentality, which was related to the increas-

ing absolutism of governments that now preferred more and more to
employ professional administrators. The ideal of the active life open to
talent was less and less realistic.

The question of what constituted the best life was still discussed. Hooker
was ambivalent. He thought "the mind of man by nature speculative and
delighted with contemplation in it selfe," and so depicted rest as the goal
of human existence; but he warned that in this life "God hath created
nothing to be idle or ill employed." Men in public life were themselves often
undecided. Bacon was torn between contemplation and action; men—he
was obviously thinking of himself—were driven, he wrote, by "an ambition
of the understanding," but also, "especially in high and lofty spirits," by
the will to action. In old age he regretted, perhaps chiefly because he had
been disgraced, having given so much of his life to a public career.

Montaigne too was torn between the two ways of life. He claimed that
he valued nothing so much as a life devoted to reflection:

> There is no occupation that is either weaker or stronger, according
> to the mind involved, than entertaining one's own thoughts. The
> greatest minds make it their profession, *to whom living is thinking*
> [Cicero]. Thus nature has favored it with this privilege, that there is
> nothing we can do so long, and no action to which we can devote our-
> selves more commonly and easily. It is the occupation of the gods, says
> Aristotle, from which springs their happiness and ours.[5]

Accordingly he broke off a judicial career for a life of contemplation, which
he considered his reward for public service. "We have lived long enough for
others," he wrote; "let us live at least this remaining bit of life for ourselves."
But he allowed his peaceful life to be interrupted, first by military service
in the civil wars, then by a term as mayor of Bordeaux.

Many thinkers, however, gave themselves more or less completely to the
contemplative life. Lipsius managed to shelter himself from the troubles of
the times (about which he complained) in various universities, where he
composed a philosophy justifying withdrawal from the evils of the world.
His widely read dialogue on constancy is peacefully placed in a garden,
symbol of protection from the tumults of the world. François de Sales, like
many mystics, praised contemplation on religious grounds. It was, he wrote,
"simply the mind's loving, unmixed, permanent attention to things of
God." Burton, a bit daringly, thought the abolition of the monasteries in
England a mistake, for there men might have continued "to follow their

studies (I say) to the perfection of arts and sciences, common good, &, as some truly devoted Monks of old had done, freely and truly to serve God. For these men are neither solitary, nor idle."

But the most fervent advocate of the contemplative life was neither a mystic nor a cleric, but that thoroughly secular thinker Jean Bodin. His early *Method* praised contemplation; it traced the ascent of the mind through natural and human history, thus purified, to the "true wisdom" which is "man's supreme and final good." But he explained the capacity for such enlightenment naturalistically, associating it with southern latitudes, perhaps because a warm climate was less favorable to a life of action. And he viewed his own career somewhat like Montaigne; he had turned to "the contemplation of things natural and divine" after years spent, as he put it, in learning "true wisdom by the managing of worldly affairs." In his *Six Books of the Commonwealth* he described the ascent of contemplation up the great chain of being "from the world of material things forward to the contemplation of the immaterial world of the heavens," until "the ecstasy of this vision inspires [the thinker] with a perpetual longing to penetrate to the first cause and author of this perfect creation" and it "reaches the concept of the one infinite and eternal God, and thereby as it were attains the true felicity of mankind." We are back again close to the spiritual world of Thomas Aquinas and Dante.

These conceptions of the structure and potentialities of human being bring us more generally to answers thinkers gave to the famous question of Socrates: how should we live? As one might expect from a period so uncertain yet so needy, many answers were proposed. It was widely discussed, as in Pierre De La Primaudaye's *The French Academie* (London, 1618), a widely read encyclopedia of ethics, which took a dim view of both variety and change. It was central to the thought of Montaigne, whose "skepticism" can, in this light, be interpreted as an effort to revitalize an ethic that had become external, routine, and ineffective. It helps to explain the Spanish dramatist Calderon's concern with "discretion" as the essential virtue for the improvement of human behavior.

Nobles like Bussy d'Amboise still looked for ethical models in the ancients; he thought constantly of how he would have behaved under circumstances similar to those of the worthies described by Plutarch. Thus in reading of the courage of a Roman, he would say, "There is nothing here that I couldn't do just as well in the same circumstances." Closely related were traditional invocations of "honor" as a guarantor of virtue. Tasso emphasized the pleasure it gave; Montaigne thought its pursuit more effective than utility as a stimulus to action. Bacon recommended it as "the place of virtue." These were residues of an older, essentially military and external shame culture. Another kind of ethical externalism was developed among those Puritans who found detailed prescriptions for human conduct in the Bible, especially in the legalism of the Jewish Scriptures; such concerns were also shared by some Catholics. Hooker criticized them.

But the brutality of both sides in the religious wars stimulated attempts to discover non-religious, or at least non-sectarian, sources for ethics. Charron thought ethics independent of religion and prior in time: "religion came later, and is a special and particular virtue, distinct from all the others." Grotius took issue with Aristotle's notion of virtue as a mean between extremes; there are times, he argued, when it "stimulates to the utmost degree." Tendencies to Epicureanism have been identified in followers of Gassendi, and at a more popular level in pastoral poetry and tales.

But the most important expression of the search for a new basis for ethics was the effort to subordinate human behavior to laws of nature accessible to reason on which all human beings, by definition rational, could agree. Charron defined nature as "the equity and universal reason which illuminates us, which contains and incubates in itself the seeds of all virtue, probity, justice." All the sages, he maintained, had agreed "that to live well is to live according to nature." On the other hand Jesuit and Dominican thinkers attacked—identifying them with one another—Machiavelli and Luther, the two arch-heretics of the century, for rejecting natural law. Bodin suggested the priority of natural law by describing the decalogue as its renewal after a long period of oblivion.

The conception of a natural law both accessible and applicable to every individual was, among other things, the basis for a conception of individual autonomy, since it pointed to the internalization of ethics as a source of order in human affairs. There are suggestions of this conception in Charron's insistence on wisdom as integral to human being. "Inside and outside, in his thoughts, words, actions, and all his movements," he declared: "it is the excellence and perfection of man as man." This sense of interiority was paralleled by appeals to conscience, to the inner man as the source of virtue. As an English Puritan wrote, "Inferior authority cannot bind the superior. Now the courts of men and their authority are under conscience. For God in the heart of every man hath erected a tribunal seat, and in his stead he hath placed neither saint nor angel, nor any other creature whatsoever, but conscience itself, who therefore is the highest judge that is or can be under God."

But the good life was above all seen as dependent on the control of the lower by the higher faculties in the hierarchy of the self. Montaigne argued that "the worst condition of man is when he loses knowledge and control of himself." True virtue depended on control by reason as it empowers the will. Moderation, in its root meaning of control, represented the highest ethical wisdom. As Montaigne wrote of the religious wars, "It is ordinary to see how good intentions, if they are carried out without moderation, push men to very vicious acts." The alternative to moderation could only be enslavement to passion. Thus, Montaigne continued, "we see many whom passion drives outside the bounds of reason and makes them sometimes adopt unjust, violent, and even reckless courses." But Montaigne's ethical conceptions were by no means simple. He recognized the problem of repression, as in the case of anger, which we incorporate "by hiding it, so that it is better to vent it." He was aware too that knowledge did not guarantee virtue, for a man may "see the good and not follow it, and see knowledge and not use it." He also knew that human beings are stimulated by the affections as well as by reverence for virtue, but this meant that the passions should be enlisted to serve virtue; thus "it is the duty of good men to portray virtue as as beautiful as possible; and it would not be unbecoming to us if passion carried us away in favor of such sacred models."

With the possible exception of Montaigne, however, the moral thought of this period often seems oddly general and abstract, in contrast to the concreteness and practicality of much earlier moral discussion. But there were practical consequences of the concern with self-discipline. It had obvious relevance to Renaissance self-fashioning; the formation of an individual and stable self required a sustained effort of the will. To be sure, control was not necessarily relevant to the extirpation of sinfulness in an Augustinian and more inward understanding of that condition. The particular deadly sins were reviewed by Don Quixote in his *persona* as chivalric hero, but by no means inwardly digested:

It is for us to slay pride by slaying giants; to slay envy by our generosity and nobility; anger by calmness of mind and serenity of disposition; gluttony and drowsiness by eating little and watching late into the night; indulgence and lust by preserving our loyalty to those whom we have made ladies of our hearts; and sloth by traveling through all parts of the world in quest of opportunities of becoming famous knights as well as Christians.[6]

And as even Calvinists knew, children could be trained to live orderly lives.

But Bacon was sufficiently a realist to perceive problems in this project. "The stars of natural inclination," he wrote, "are [only] sometimes obscured by the sun of discipline and virtue." Discipline could often be effective, at least superficially and temporarily; this may have been especially important at a time when social hierarchy was crumbling. Discipline was also put to more problematic uses, such as making armies and bureaucracies more efficient instruments of rulers. It can be discerned too in Loyola's famous doctrine of blind obedience. On the other hand it might nourish a self-righteous, sometimes ferocious and insensitive, moralism.

The hierarchical conception of the personality also had major implications for education. Primary schools provided the rudiments of literacy to a minority of the population, chiefly from the middle classes. This might be followed, for a smaller group of adolescent boys destined for responsible positions in society, by education in colleges that aimed to strengthen mental control through instruction in the arts of the trivium (grammar, logic, and rhetoric), but also in the sciences of the quadrivium (arithmetic, geometry, music, and astronomy). Finally, at the most advanced level, there were professional colleges for training in law, medicine, and theology. Young aristocrats were likely to be educated in somewhat the same way by private tutors; although, traditionally contemptuous of book-learning, many now felt compelled to shape their minds by the classics in order to be useful to princes.

But the major purpose of education at all levels was agreed to be the moral and social formation of the young, although there was scarce attention to the lower classes, whose formation was generally left to local clergy who had received little training for the task. As Hobbes put it in another passage in which much is conveyed by his irony:

They whom necessity, or covetousnesse keepeth attent on their trades, and labour, and they, on the other side, whom superfluity, or sloth carrieth after their sensuall pleasures, (which two sorts of men take up the greatest part of Man-kind), being diverted from deep meditation, which the learning of truth, not onely in the matter of Naturall Justice, but also of all the other Sciences necessarily requireth, receive the Notions of their duty, chiefly from Divines in the Pulpit.[7]

The mental education of the populace perhaps seemed less necessary since they were better instructed by the example of the upper classes than by the doubtful formation of their own higher faculties. The Puritan William Ames called for grammar, rhetoric, and above all logic, not to form the self but to grasp the meaning of Scripture and the good of sermons.

Thought about the substance of education was focussed on the arts and sciences, which were generally believed to inculcate both the intellectual and moral discipline required by the times. Bodin described them as "the companions and ministers of virtue," without which "there is no way that life may be lived happily, or lived at all"; the arts and sciences were basic to "a fortunate and flourishing state." For Milton, "a complete and generous education" fitted "a man to perform, justly, skilfully, and magnanimously all the offices, both private and public, of peace and war." Sidney thought poetry most effective for inculcating virtue; for Bacon, too, the end of education was the shaping of "good customs." There was little interest in an education that might (as some earlier humanists had hoped) develop individual potentiality or encourage minds to work freely. Montaigne was not a typical product of the system.

Views of the power of education often ran contrary to orthodox belief in original sin, Catholic as well as Protestant. As Bodin's deist Toralba observed, "To the extent that each pagan or Christian has been equipped with learning and trained from boyhood for true glory, so he excels with distinction in virtues, and the more so if there is a certain innate excellence of soul." He quoted Erasmus, "Holy Socrates, pray for us!" and then asked (but only rhetorically), "Who is so void of understanding as to think that natural goods in men have been corrupted on account of the Fall of the first parent, and supernatural goods completely removed?" Indeed, Protestants so valued education as a barrier against anarchy that they sometimes tended to forget the need for grace. Bacon's view, at least on this point, was more orthodox. "Learning," he wrote, "endueth men's minds with a true sense of the frailty of their persons, the casualty of their fortunes, and the dignity of their soul and vocation: so that it is impossible for them to esteem that any greatness of their own fortune can be a true or worthy end of their being and ordainment."

But the value of education for government and society was clearly recognized. Montaigne, doubtless thinking of his own experience, emphasized its utility in "conducting a war, governing a people, or gaining the friendship of a prince or a foreign nation." Bacon, noting that "only learned men love business as an action according to nature," thought it important for government to employ such persons. And what was appropriate for ruling groups was, of course, also appropriate for the prince whom they served. Botero repeated a common saying, that "an unlettered prince is a crowned ass."

The value of education was occasionally also claimed for the governed, or at least an educable minority. Bacon argued that "learning doth make the minds of men gentle, generous, maniable, and pliant to government"; in short it *civilized* men, a term first current in this period. The notion of civility was given currency in the widely translated *Civile Conversazione* (1574) of Stefano Guazzo, in which it means "the quallities of the minde," especially of "gentlemen" and those who "ought to be put in the middest between gentlemen and clownes." It was given a more overtly political meaning by Henri de La Popelinière, who contrasted being "governed and organized according to certain political forms" with "living in a savage state."

Education could also have less solemn connotations. It could mean polished manners, the subject of numerous courtesy books that taught the upwardly mobile to rise in the world. Baldassare Castiglione's *Courtier* (1528) was still an authority in this area. The *Galateo* of Giovanni Della Casa (1558), addressed to a slightly lower group of gentry, was translated into every major European language, and new translations appeared as late as the eighteenth century. Such polite formation meant, among other things, the inhibition not only of affect but of bodily functions; in short, once again, the rule of higher over lower aspects of the self.

The new refinement can be seen in many areas, to which it contributed distinctions and consciousness of class. Eating, in contrast to medieval feasting, was becoming more refined. The tone of the English court was transformed by a concern for gravity and decorum, partly under the influence of the French queen of Charles I. Theater exploited crudity in speech to suggest the inferiority of some characters to others. "Wheresoever manners and fashions are corrupted," Jonson declared, "language is. It imitates the publicke riot." Montaigne both praised the new manners and showed perspective about them. He appreciated what he called "social dexterity." "Like grace and beauty," he explained, "it acts as a moderator at the first approaches of sociability and familiarity, and consequently opens the door for us to learning by the examples of others, and to bringing forth and displaying our own example, if it has anything instructive and communicable about it." Like Castiglione, he also equated the highest grace in behavior with nonchalance. But when he thought about "civilization" more deeply, he recognized in it a shallowness that had not struck most contemporaries. Montaigne was not only aware of what was happening to the self, he also recognized the superficiality in the shift from virtue to polish, another triumph of society over both community and individuality.

CHAPTER TWELVE

The Quest for Certainty: From Skepticism to Science

The Authority of the Ancients

For centuries it had been assumed that truth was chiefly to be found in ancient writings, the more ancient the better. This conception was natural, given the general sense of decline from the brilliant cultures of antiquity; but it was strengthened by a Neoplatonic belief that the world had steadily declined since its beginnings, which was taken to mean that the discovery of truths unknown to the ancients was impossible. Philosophy, except for Scripture the highest form of truth, was almost completely dependent on the ancients; and contemporary philosophical discourse was largely a commentary on Plato, Aristotle, and the Stoics.

These conceptions were implicit in much intellectual activity in this period. Bodin's interlocutors in the *Colloquium* assumed that certainty depended on the "authority of important men," that is, of the ancients. Jonson's plays followed ancient models and taught classical ethics. Lipsius, to be sure, had made advances in classical philology that promised a new historical perspective potentially subversive of ancient authority, but for him this achievement only pointed to further advances in exploring the wisdom of antiquity. Montaigne, for all his skepticism, deeply venerated the ancients; their writings, he wrote, "not only satisfy and fill me but astound and transfix me with admiration." He thought Plutarch and Seneca "the cream of philosophy" and Caesar still the best guide in war. He praised Epaminondas for his virtues, his knowledge, and his oratory; Homer as "first and last of poets," "master of all things," and the nurturer of "every kind of ability"; and Socrates as "the most perfect" of men. He did not read modern authors much, he claimed, because the ancients were "fuller and stronger." Prose writers studied the style of Cicero; and even Milton, in spite of his belief in the progress of truth through free discussion,

emulated Homer and Virgil in his Christian epic *Paradise Lost* (1667). Latin,
sanctified by the church as well as by ancient usage, was still the language
of the learned. Jesuit schools, in which many leading thinkers of our period
were brought up, promoted its study as required by Ignatius Loyola.
According to a Venetian scholar, contemporary Rome owed such greatness
as it still possessed to its brilliant past:

> It is the metropolitan city of all Christian nations; the Spaniard and
> the Frenchman, every man is at home there. . . . There is no place here
> below that heaven has embraced with such favorable influence and such
> constancy. Her very ruin is glorious and stately. . . . Even in the tomb
> she retains some marks and the picture of empire.[1]

Meanwhile knowledge of Greek and Hebrew, the other languages with
which humanists unlocked ancient wisdom, had also been growing.

Humanism was, however, changing. Though retaining its identification
with the rhetorical tradition, even its rhetorical practice was more and more
subordinated to rules of propriety. Classical culture was increasingly a
badge of status; and the central rhetorical virtue of decorum, in earlier
humanism understood as the appropriateness of communication to its
audience and to the aim of the speaker, was now understood increasingly
—notably in drama—as appropriateness to social status, a function of
hierarchy. Members of the ruling classes were supposed to speak with
dignity, discipline, and restraint; only the lower orders could speak famil-
iarly and freely, a distinction commonly made in theater. Scaliger preferred
Virgil to Homer not because his language was more expressive but because
it was more refined. At the same time, as if to restrict the subversive power
of rhetoric, a point was being made of its impression on readers rather
than, as it had been originally, as an instrument for speakers, to persuade
an audience to a course of action. The principles of classical rhetoric were
also increasingly applied to raising the status of the vernaculars, as in
Guillaume Du Vair's *On French Eloquence and Why It Has Remained So
Crude* (1595).

Meanwhile the republican enthusiasm in earlier humanism had largely
disappeared in this age of princes, except in the Venetian republic, where
it was still given expression by such figures as Paruta and Sarpi. Humanists generally ignored politics now, turning instead to a Stoic endurance of
the world rather than to active emulation of ancient virtue, which at best
they only taught about. Their typical achievements now were reference
works for scholars, such as a dictionary of classical Greek by Henri

Estienne (1572) or a concordance to the Septuagint, the ancient Greek version of the Jewish Scriptures (1602). At the same time the apparatus accompanying works of scholarship became increasingly elaborate, as with the indexes to the elaborate second edition of Giorgio Vasari's *Lives of the Most Famous Painters, Sculptors, and Architects* (1568), to this day a major source for studying Renaissance painting.

Philological study particularly flourished in the Netherlands, where scholars published huge anthologies of obscure ancient and medieval texts. The University of Leiden, a major center of Calvinist learning, went in for biblical and other ancient Near Eastern studies. There Thomas Erpenius prepared an Arabic New Testament and an Arabic grammar that remained standard for the next two centuries. His student Jacobus Golius made trips to the Near East to collect old Arabic, Persian, and Turkish manuscripts. The tolerant atmosphere of the Dutch republic also provided a congenial environment for Jewish biblical scholarship.

Reactions to this scholarly turn varied. Burton, like scholars in every age, thought learning too little appreciated; he was inclined to blame this on the unworldliness of scholars: "Your greatest students are commonly silly, soft fellows in their outward behavior, absurd, ridiculous to others, and no whit experienced in worldly business; they can measure the heavens, range over the world, teach others wisdom, and yet in bargains and contracts they are circumvented by every base tradesman." A scholar was not, he thought, a happy man but, like himself, inclined to melancholy.[2] Montaigne, who had no pretensions to scholarship and would probably have thought it beneath him, also took a dim view of this development. "It is more of a job to interpret the interpretations," he declared, "than to interpret the things, and there are more books about books than about any other subject: we do nothing but write glosses about each other. The world is swarming with commentaries; of authors there is a great scarcity." Bacon, on the other hand, used his biblical learning to demonstrate the momentous eschatological significance of the contemporary increase in learning.

In fact, Burton's stereotype of the neglected scholar was belied by the fame of many learned men. The Catholic as well as the Protestant Netherlands was hospitable to philological scholarship. Lipsius, who edited Seneca and Tacitus in addition to propagating Stoic philosophy, had distinguished careers at the universities of both Leiden and Louvain and was courted by other universities and by rulers. Joseph Justus Scaliger, Lipsius's successor at Leiden, used his proficiency in ancient languages to establish new standards of precision in biblical scholarship and the languages of the Near East. His *Thesaurus temporum* (1614) was a permanent contribution to the previously hazy understanding of ancient chronology, and he pioneered in the interpretation of myth for historical scholarship. He also trained a new generation of scholars. Isaac Casaubon was sufficiently esteemed as an editor of classical texts to be pensioned by both Henri IV of France and James I in England. Torn between religious extremists on both sides, he was also deeply interested in theology and church history and in his later years composed a refutation of the *Ecclesiastical Annals* of Baronius.

Another important development can also be traced through the scholarship of this period. Veneration for antiquity had tended to lump together the various traditions of the ancient world, as though they constituted a single body of wisdom within which successive stages could be distinguished. The famous "historical consciousness" of the Renaissance had so far been little applied to the history of thought. Now, with their more intensive scrutiny of texts, scholars were better able to consider the entire works of a particular author, relate them to his times, discern stages and shifts within his thought, and contrast it with that of others. A leading earlier humanist, Juan Luis Vives, had already begun to recognize the difference between the ethics of Aristotle and the teachings of the Gospel, and Protestants had tried to eliminate pagan influence in ancient theology. But without a better grasp of the various traditions that had been compressed together, distinctions among authors and schools of thought were hard to identify. Better texts and closer reading made this increasingly possible.

But philological scholarship, by itself, could do little more than place conflicting texts side by side, a practice that encouraged a growing tendency, stimulated by the vast increases in knowledge and the need to make it manageable, to summarize what was known. To accomplish this printers were bringing out massive encyclopedias, though at first these were little more than disorganized masses of miscellaneous information. Among them were the *Bibliotheca universalis* (1545–55) of Konrad Gesner and the more highly regarded seven-volume *Encyclopedia* (1630) of Johann Heinrich Alsted. An indefatigable Jesuit, Antonio Possevino, composed a *Bibliotheca selecta* (Rome, 1593), which gave bibliographical information on a vast array of subjects; his *Apparatus sacer* (Venice, 1603) also listed and briefly described the works of some eight thousand religious writers. An exception to such amorphous works was Bacon's *Advancement of Learning* (1605), which made a systematic effort to sort out and digest knowledge. After distinguishing divine from human knowledge, Bacon divided the latter into history, as a function of memory, and philosophy, a function of reason. He then went on to subdivide these broad categories.

The Jesuits, whose schools were largely responsible for the education of upper-class boys in Catholic Europe, were also important for the digestion of knowledge. The *De arte rhetorica* (1562) of the Portuguese Jesuit Cyprian Soarez, typical in its systematic approach to the subject, became the standard text for Jesuit instruction in rhetoric, but it also had general philosophical implications. Conceiving of language as an "image of thought" and therefore subject to reason, it emphasized order, clarity, and restraint. "Reason guides our thoughts," it proclaimed; "speech changes the thoughts of others." Under such respectable auspices classical learning, once suspect for its pagan origins, could be welcomed in the service of faith.

Scholastic method was also increasingly respected by scholars in other areas, partly because of its new openness to philological study, especially at the universities of Cambridge and Louvain, but even more because of its value in science, which was included under the rubric of natural philosophy. Loyola had praised scholastic method in his "Rule for Thinking with the Church," and Catholics generally relied on it as a weapon against heresy. In England, Hooker, though not primarily a scholastic thinker, used scholastic arguments against his Puritan enemies, observing that "the moste approved for learninge and judgemente do use them without blame."

Within Catholicism the need for a higher degree of certainty found expression in the growing influence of Thomism as a major influence on theology, and Thomas Aquinas was officially designated a Doctor of the Church in 1567. Thomism was favored by both Dominicans and Jesuits; even Bruno and Campanella, however doubtful their orthodoxy, thought of themselves as Thomists. Thomism was also entrenched in the Spanish universities, especially that of Salamanca, where a series of distinguished Dominicans taught theology, beginning with Francisco Vitoria (1485–1546), best known as a critic of Spanish imperialism and sometimes regarded as the father of international law. At Louvain after 1585 the Jesuit Leonhard Lessius replaced Peter Lombard's *Sentences* with Aquinas's *Summa theologica* as the basis of theological education. Leading theologians at the Sorbonne also published commentaries on Aquinas. Bellarmine in Rome believed the study of Aquinas more profitable than that of the Bible and the church fathers, and in the Jesuit college in Rome Francesco Suarez strengthened the authority of Thomism by adapting its legal, moral, and psychological implications to more modern sensibilities. Theologians of Augustinian sympathies employed scholastic method to harmonize Augustine and Aquinas. Like other theologians of the time, perhaps because educated laymen like Montaigne were reading theology, Suarez also adopted a looser and more readable presentation. But he broke with Aquinas by refusing to identify divine and natural law with reason; law for him had ultimately to reflect the will of superior authority, a view that was related to the growing authoritarianism of the age. Suarez was more widely studied by Catholics than Aquinas himself, or even Aristotle.

But scholastic method was equally important now for Protestant theologians, and for similar reasons. Since Calvin proved too unsystematic to satisfy a new generation, Theodore Beza composed tracts in scholastic style, relying heavily on Aristotelian logic, starting off with *quaestiones*, considering various *objectiones*, and concluding with *responsiones*. François Turretin, the most prominent Calvinist theologian of the next century, was even more indebted to scholasticism. He composed what was essentially a *Summa* in three tomes, in Latin partly because, by this time, Calvinism had become an international movement. Resembling Calvin's great work chiefly in its title—*Institutio theologiae elencticae*—it too consisted of topics divided into *loci* and *quaestiones*, which were discussed pro and con, much as in Aquinas's *Summa theologica*. Calvinism, originally a version of *theologia rhetorica*, was thus made to look more and more like *theologia dialectica*. Under the influence of Pierre Du Moulin, French Calvinism too was increasingly scholastic, and Huguenot political thought shifted into a scholastic style. Scholasticism was also an important influence on Puritanism; Thomas Aquinas became a favorite authority, among others for Cotton Mather in New England. Puritans increasingly venerated logic, sometimes attributing Adam's sin to irrationality. Lutheran theology was developing in similar ways. Aristotelianism invaded even biological science. William Harvey, discoverer of the circulation of the blood, claimed to "follow Aristotle as a leader."

But scholastic science remained largely pre-Copernican, chiefly a metaphysical rather than a physical study, to be dealt with by the verbal logic of Aristotle, which had to do with qualities rather than quantities. This does not mean that it was fruitless. Jesuit astronomers, at least before Galileo, were leaders in the observation of the heavenly bodies. But, as one of the followers of Aristotle explained, they could not abandon the venerable authority of Aristotle, "that great leader of academies, head of so many schools, subject of so many poets, labor of so many historians, [a man] who had read more books than were days in his life, and had written more of them than he counted years." Aristotle's authority lay behind a facetious rendering of Scripture that asked, "Ye men of Galileo, why stand ye gazing up into heaven?"

The Creation of Natural Science

Nevertheless, it was increasingly clear that logic was a linguistic rather than an empirical instrument of inquiry. It could demonstrate whether propositions were internally consistent or consistent with other propositions. But it could not disclose the truths of what contemporaries referred to as "nature": an objective realm supposedly independent both of language and of the human mind. This being so, it is hardly surprising that doubts about Aristotle were growing in some quarters. Vives, still much cited, had disagreed with him on a range of issues, from the value of the syllogism to the paganism of his ethics. In science Bacon attacked him for a dogmatism that had "by hostile confutations" destroyed all schools of thought, "as the Ottomans serve their brothers," and now "laid down the law on all points."

But the attack on Aristotle was only the most notable expression of the reaction against the authority of books. "When we cite authors," Pascal wrote, "we cite their demonstrations, not their names." For Hobbes, "no [written] discourse whatsoever can End in absolute knowledge of Fact, past or to come." Galileo had seen this with his usual clarity:

> If what we are discussing were a point of law or of the humanities, in which neither true nor false exists, one might trust in subtlety of mind and readiness of tongue and in the greater experience of the writers, and expect him who excelled in those things to make his reasoning most plausible, and one might judge it to be the best. But in the natural sciences, whose conclusions are true and necessary and have nothing to do with human will, one must take care not to place oneself in the defense of error.

What was now emerging was an insistence that truth was of several kinds, among which the least certain was that transmitted only in books composed by men.[3] But God, it was increasingly emphasized—this was hardly a new discovery—had revealed not only the way of salvation in Scripture, but also another set of truths in the "book of nature."[4]

Of the authority of Scripture in its own sphere there could still be little question. But, for Galileo, the book of nature also revealed truths, of a different kind but equally awesome. "The glory and greatness of Almighty God are marvelously discerned in all his works, and diversely read in the open book of heaven," he insisted. And this book too had religious value that commanded respect:

For let no one believe that reading the lofty concepts in that book leads to nothing further than the mere seeing of the splendor of the stars and their rising and setting, which is as far as the eyes of brutes and of the vulgar can penetrate. Within its pages are couched mysteries so profound and concepts so sublime that the vigils, labors, and studies of hundreds upon hundreds of the most acute minds have still not pierced them, even after continual investigations for thousands of years.

The book of nature also had the advantage over human books that, when those who tried to read it made mistakes, they could be corrected.[5]

Along with the recognition of "nature" as a realm apart went a growing sense of the value of mathematics. This was also quite alien to Aristotelianism. As one Aristotelian wrote:

Men having no ground in philosophy give themselves over to mathematics and preach that it is sovereign over all other disciplines. In Aristotle's time this was considered a schoolboys' science, learned before any other . . . and yet these modern mathematicians solemnly declare that Aristotle's divine mind failed to understand it, and that as a result he made ridiculous mistakes.[6]

The traditional preference for quality over quantity also had the particular advantage that it was consistent with common sense, in which "up" and "down" were readily understood.

Even more important for the Aristotelians was the value of the traditional hierarchy of the cosmos for uniting the physical and spiritual aspects of human experience into an intelligible whole and a source of comfort.[7] Galileo would recognize the deep roots of the resistance to one, like himself, "who forsakes an opinion imbibed with his milk and supported by multitudes, takes up another with few followers, is rejected by all the schools, and advances what seems to be a gigantic paradox."[8]

Thus the traditional conception of the universe could not satisfy a new generation of thinkers, skeptical of the testimony even of the oldest books and beginning to suspect that physical reality might be quite different from what books had reported or from what met the naked eye. They were ever more dissatisfied with the Aristotelian science of verbal propositions and merely logical demonstrations, and no longer felt it necessary to assume that all aspects of experience must reinforce one another in a single comprehensive system: in this respect they were perhaps more modest than their predecessors. They were ready for a new method, based on clear distinctions between the metaphysical and physical, between traditional philosophy and theology on the one hand and empirical observation on the other.

Words and books having produced only disagreement and confusion, the question now was how to achieve certainty regarding the real truth of things. Preoccupation with this problem had been growing; treatises on "method" abounded. As the author of one such work remarked, "No word is more popular [than *method*] in our lectures these days, none more often heard, none gives off a more delightful ring than that term." One of a group of Aristotelians at the University of Padua, Jacopo Zabarella, wrote a treatise on method, which he defined as "an intellectual instrument bringing about out of the known a knowledge of the unknown." Bodin applied it to legal study, the Jesuits to spirituality, Jonson to poetry, underlining a passage in George Puttenham's *Arte of English Poesie* (1590): "If Poesie be now an Art, and of al antiquitie hath beene among the Greeks and Latines, and yet were none, untill by studious persons fashioned and reduced into a *method*, there may be the like with us." Burton lamented his own lack of method: "I have read many books, but to little purpose," he confessed, "for want of good method." Shakespeare gave examples of its popularity: Viola applied it to love in *Twelfth Night*; Polonius discerned it in Hamlet's "Words, words, words."

Thus it is hardly surprising that some method, more "natural" than Aristotelian logic, was being sought in philosophy. Immediately popular, though in the long run transient, was Ramism, an educational program named after its author, Ramus (Pierre de la Ramée), a Huguenot who perished in the St. Bartholomew Massacre. Ramism aimed to reform dialectic, making it both more teachable and more useful, by basing it on "nature" and simplifying it by division into a number of manageable sub-problems. It was otherwise eclectic, aimed at utility, was open to empiricism, and popular as a pedagogical device among Protestants and other opponents of Aristotle. The works of Ramus had gone through numerous printings by 1650. Ramism has also been seen as mediating between humanism and the scientific movement. But in spite of his appreciation for mathematics, Ramus's system essentially reflected traditional bookish culture and soon disappeared.

More durable was a growing concern with degrees of certainty in knowledge, out of which emerged a doctrine known as "probabilism." This had its origins in humanism, which had always relied on the practical value of a knowledge that might be less than certain, maintaining that the views of well-known ancient authors were at the very least probable. Montaigne thought no knowledge important for human existence could be more than "probable." "Probability" would prove especially useful when applied to ethical and religious belief. It was basic to a doctrine associated with the Jesuits known as casuistry, according to which degrees of probability might be helpful in deciding questions in moral theology. For some Protestants, degrees of probability in theology pointed to the need for religious toleration. The Anglican divine William Chillingworth (1602–44) denied that the theological pronouncements of any church, or even the testimony of Scripture, could claim more than probable truth, but that adherence to a theological position that was probably true was sufficient for salvation. This position, however, usually did no more than increase the hunger for certainty.

But the notion of degrees of certainty itself reflected the growing tendency toward quantification that also nourished mathematics, which was gradually freeing itself of its old Platonic and occultist associations. Its practical value had long been recognized. In the earlier Renaissance its more elementary stages climaxed a schoolboy's education as preparation for business. This period now saw major advances in mathematics, especially in making calculations easier, more rapid, and more precise. Simon Stevin in the Netherlands developed the decimal system as a tool for scientists and engineers. Even more important was John Napier's invention in Scotland of logarithms, which vastly facilitated astronomical computation.

Mathematics rapidly became a part of the general culture of the age. It was further developed in the sixteenth century by the discovery of classical texts dealing with mathematics; these had stimulated Copernicus. Even Burton recognized the value of mathematics; the "modern Divines" opposed to it were, in his opinion, "ignorant and peevish" in their opposition and sought to "tyrannize over art, science, and philosophy . . . all to maintain their superstition, and for their profit's sake." Galileo contrasted mathematics with the methods of the schools: "One learns the method of proof from books filled with proofs, i.e., from books of mathematics and not of logic." The Jesuit Christopher Clavius praised mathematics at the expense of Aristotle in a work of 1611; and Galileo declared that the world could not be understood unless one learned the language in which God had written it, the language of mathematics, "whose characters are triangles, circles, and other geometric figures, without which it is humanly impossible to understand a single word. Without such knowledge," he concluded, "one wanders about in a dark labyrinth." Hobbes would identify "reasoning" itself with "reckoning": "When a man *Reasoneth*," he wrote, "he does nothing else but conceive a summe totall, from *Addition* of parcels; or conceive of a Remainder."

But mathematics still owed much to the belief that it reflected the spiritual quality of the universe. Guidobaldo Dal Monte, writing in 1577, compared mathematical insight to being "suddenly thrust from the darkness and prison of the body . . . into light and liberty." Both Galileo and Kepler believed that God had created the world on a geometrical model comprehensible to human beings, who could thus understand the cosmos exactly as God had made it. Kepler thought mathematical insight close to Platonic recollection. "Just as objects seen from the outside make us remember those we have already known," he wrote, "the mathematics of the senses, if they are recognized, excite an intellectual mathematics previously present to the inner [man], such that there actively shines within the soul what beforehand was hidden beneath the veil of potentiality." Even Hobbes, often considered an atheist by contemporaries, thought geometry "the onely Science that it hath pleased God hitherto to bestow on mankind."

However conceived, mathematics ordered the previously bewildering data provided by the new cosmology. It was widely—if not unanimously—praised. Sarpi applauded its value to science. A Spaniard thought it should be taught "in all the universities and principal places so it might serve to defend the kingdoms and enrich them with all kinds of works and arts." Ramus, equating mathematics with reason, thought it the ideal study for Christians and useful for the spread of Protestantism. Bodin believed it so superior to law that the passage from one to the other was like falling "from the brightest light into the black murk and entangling labyrinth of error."

Mathematics, nevertheless, was finally an abstract science that, by itself, might point away from direct sense experience; indeed, it went hand in hand with skepticism about the senses. Another movement in thought, exemplified by Galileo's use of the telescope, contributed even more to the new science. This was empiricism, the study of the data available to the senses, traditionally viewed as unreliable, which provided another alternative to knowledge drawn from books.

Empiricism had various sources. Humanist emphasis on the active life implied the value of direct experience, and the humanist slogan *ad fontes* (to the sources) might imply the possibility of bypassing literary sources altogether to read the book of nature. The common experience of literate tradesmen, growing in numbers, pointed in the same direction. So the potter and surveyor Bernard Palissy, asked where he had learned that minerals did not grow like plants as had been commonly believed, replied that his only book was "heaven and earth," a book "known to everybody, and [which] has been given to every man to know and to read." Campanella claimed to have learned more by examining the anatomy of an ant or a plant than by reading all the books in the world. Montaigne emphasized the value of ordinary sense experience. The growth of curiosity among persons of means was leading to the collection of miscellaneous items from around the world, another expression of the empirical impulse. The Jesuit *Relations* from various parts of the world included masses of "interesting" detail. Lawyers and antiquarians collected facts of many kinds; this was a major concern of Sarpi's wide correspondence with scholars outside Italy.

But the resistance among Aristotelians to empirical evidence was deeply entrenched. As a leading figure in the Accademia dei Lincei remarked, the Aristotelians would "rather close their eyes and bury themselves in the dark forest of the ancient writers than use their sense organs in the service of the truth." Galileo himself noted their refusal even to look through a telescope to verify his observations. He thought he understood their resistance; they believed, he wrote, that his work seemed "to injure our holy faith and to falsify the sacred Scripture." But Aristotle himself, he argued, would have taken a different view of the heavens "if his knowledge had included our present sensory evidence."

Against this background there emerged three distinguished philosophers who sought to develop the broader implications of the new science and to bring order out of the chaos left in its wake: Bacon, especially in his *Advancement of Learning* (1605) and *Novum Organum* (1620); Descartes in the *Discourse on Method* (1637); and Hobbes in *Leviathan* (1651), a contribution both to scientific and political thought. Although they differed in important ways, the three had much in common. All had received a classical education including Aristotelian philosophy that left its mark on them. Bacon wrote aphoristic essays on classical themes, quite different in their impersonality—and therefore more classical—from the essays of Montaigne. He also translated Thucydides into English. Descartes had been educated in the classics by the Jesuits, although he criticized this instruction because it left him with so many uncertainties. The youthful Hobbes composed conventionally humanistic Latin verses, wrote a discourse on Tacitus somewhat like Machiavelli's on Livy, and translated Thucydides and Homer.

But all three eventually denied the value of this initial formation. Bacon argued that, if "a man look carefully into all that variety of books with which the arts and sciences abound, he will find everywhere endless repetitions of the same thing, varying in the method of treatment, but not new in substance, insomuch that the whole stock, numerous as it appears at first view, proves on examination to be but scanty." In short, traditional learning had failed to "advance." He proposed a comprehensive reform in which what he called its "idols"—i.e., mere human inventions—would be swept away. These notably included all traditional schools of philosophy, especially that of Aristotle, who had "corrupted natural philosophy by his logic, fashioning the world out of categories," and he was equally harsh regarding other ancient philosophies.

Descartes and Hobbes were similarly scornful of past learning. Descartes reported that he had studied, in the best schools, all the venerated books and found them all worthless—histories, poetry, ethics, theology, philosophy. Accordingly, he wrote, "as regards all the opinions which up to this time I had embraced," he could do no better "than endeavor once for all to sweep them completely away, so that they might later on be replaced." Hobbes was at least equally severe. His *Leviathan* included a sketch, withering in its scorn, of all previous philosophy and science. Of scholasticism he asked rhetorically, "When men write whole volumes of such stuff, are they not mad, or intend to make others so?" He was reported to have described Aristotle as "the worst Teacher that ever was, the worst Politician and Ethick—a Countrey-fellow that could live in the World be as good." He admired Aristotle's *Rhetoric* and was himself no mean rhetorician, but he thought oratory likely to subvert political authority.

In addition, all three men seem to have been unusually anxious, even Bacon. Though usually reticent about his own feelings, he was much concerned with "the vicissitudes of things," the title of his final essay, in which he concluded that "it is not good to look too long upon these turning wheels of vicissitude, lest we become giddy." He also insisted that the adoption of his program for learning was of momentous importance for humanity:

> I have made a beginning of the work; the fortune of the human race will give the issue, such an issue, it may be, as in the present condition of things and men's minds cannot easily be conceived or imagined. For the matter in hand is no mere felicity of speculation, but the real business and fortunes of the human race and all power of operation.[9]

Anxiety was also close to the surface in the *Discourse* of Descartes, and central to Hobbes. Descartes was deeply aware of Galileo's troubles with the Inquisition, a circumstance that helps to explain his long residence in the relatively tolerant Netherlands; and various passages in the *Discourse* imply worry about himself: his protestations of orthodoxy, his disclaimer of reformist intent, and his concern that he not be "misunderstood." Hobbes saw fear as a major motive in human behavior. It is certain, he wrote, "by how much one man has more experience of things past, than another; by so much also he is more Prudent, and his expectations the seldomer faile him." "External objects cause conceptions," he declared again, "and conceptions appetite and fear, which are the first unperceived beginnings of our actions." Fear would, for him, be the basis of the covenant on which, he believed, all political authority and order depended. John Aubrey observed the "extraordinary Timorousness" that Hobbes "doth very ingeniosely confess and [he himself] atributes it to the influence of his Mother's Dread of the Spanish Invasion in 1588, she being then with child of him; it is very prodigious that neither the timorousness of his Nature from his Infancy, nor the decay of his Vital Heat . . . shou'd not have chilled the briske Fervour and Vigour of his mind."

The three were also alike in their sense of the urgency of change, which implied the threat hovering over the present. They agreed that the times required a radical shift in knowledge to give it more certainty. They differed, however, on what this method should be. Bacon distrusted both the deductive syllogism and mathematics as "Idols of the mind" and proposed to substitute "experimental," i.e., empirical, knowledge. Descartes, on the other hand, was convinced—paradoxically by empirical evidence—that everything human beings "know" through their senses is distorted and relativized by subjectivity. Certainty, for him, could be acquired only by mathematical reasoning. Hobbes, perhaps coming closer to a modern view of science, proposed to combine empirical evidence and mathematical conceptualization.

Bacon was closer chronologically to the literary tradition, and was in some respects the most complex of the three. He respected traditional modes of transmitting knowledge. "Let there be one method for the cultivation, another for the invention, of knowledge," he suggested. His concern for its practical uses suggests the utilitarianism both of a Puritan upbringing and of the rhetorical tradition. The purpose of science, in his view, should be "the invention not of arguments but of arts . . . of designations and directions for works." He was also stimulated in his early speculations by the occult traditions that were so close to the science of the period. "The aim of magic," he noted with special reference to alchemy, "is to recall natural philosophy from the vanity of speculations to the importance of experiments." In addition, a lawyer himself, he had learned a good deal about how lawyers generalized "from the harmony of laws and decided cases . . . and in fact the general dictates of reason which run through the different matters of law and act as its ballast."

But he was as concerned as Descartes and Hobbes with proper method and, by avoiding "pretty and probable conjectures," with reaching "certain and demonstrable knowledge." For this purpose, he argued, "the understanding must be hung with weights, to keep it from leaping and flying." Investigation required "a sure plan" that would "proceed regularly and gradually from one axiom to another, so that the most general are not reached till the last." His own plan began with what he called "Aphorisms," fragments of knowledge, themselves the products of inquiry, which, by suggesting hypotheses and raising doubts, "invite men to inquire further"; for "if a man will begin with certainties, he shall end in doubts; but if he will be content to begin with doubts, he shall end in certainties." This also comes close to the humanist practice of argument *in utramque partem*. Bacon's method, in contrast to that of Descartes, emphasized sense experience brought into focus by deliberate experimentation. Nature had to be "forced out of the natural state" and, "by squeezing and molding," he thought, forced to give up its secrets.

In spite of his empiricism, Bacon recognized it as "a great error to assert that sense is the measure of things," and he acknowledged that "truth emerges more readily from error than from confusion." But his theory of knowledge was relatively uncomplicated. Science, he thought, held up a mirror to nature and received its images "simply as they are": knowledge was, quite simply, "the image of existence"; and his own project was to build "in the human understanding a true model of the world, such as it is in fact, not such as a man's own reason would have it to be." The scientist, in this view, can only be "the servant and interpreter of nature." His conclusions were thus the product of induction, which he contrasted with the sterility of the deductive syllogism. He compared the mind, in its scientific work, to a machine. Yet, since nature was so diverse, he recognized that science required a division of labor, although its methods were applicable to every branch, including logic, ethics, and politics. With these principles, he believed, he had "established *forever* a true and lawful marriage between the empirical and rational faculty, the unkind and ill-starred divorce and separation of which has thrown into confusion all the affairs of the human family."

The introduction of "marriage" into this context points to a further dimension of Bacon's thought: the relation it posited between the scientist and nature. For Bacon, the scientist was always masculine, nature a female to be subjected to masculine power. This imagery testifies at once to the

growing sense of human potentiality in this period, but also to the traditional pattern of gender relations. Sexual imagery pervades Bacon's discussion of the relationship between the scientist and nature. Inquiry into
truth was in general, for Bacon, a case of "love-making or wooing," and
knowledge of the truth "the enjoying of it." Scientific explanation is thus
"the strewing and decoration of the bridal chamber of the mind and the
universe, the divine goodness assisting, out of which marriage let us hope
(and be this prayer of the bridal song) there may spring helps to man, and
a line and race of inventions that may in some degree subdue and overcome
the necessities and miseries of humanity." Such passages point to the practical uses of science and to the fruitful technology based on it. But Bacon
also suggests both the dehumanization of women and the exploitation and
despoilment of nature.

This was only one aspect of Bacon's thought, however influential. If he
could describe himself as "in very truth leading to you Nature with all her
children to bind her to your service and make her your slave," he could also
describe man as "but the servant and interpreter of nature: what he does
and what he knows is only what he has observed of nature's order in fact
or in thought; beyond this he knows nothing and can do nothing. For the
chains of causes cannot by any force be loosed or broken, nor can nature be
commanded except by being obeyed." His legacy to the future includes both
attitudes.

Earlier thinkers to be sure had distinguished mind (or soul) from body,
though they had insisted on some link between them. But basic to the
thought of Descartes was their absolute distinction. This was a fateful illustration of a growing tendency to clarify boundaries, which had less scientific than psychological significance. For Descartes, the body is material, the
mind not. In accordance with this dualism, he distinguished between the
"primary qualities" of objects, grasped by the mind alone, such as number
and size, which were the only source of clear and distinct ideas, i.e., of
certainty, and the "secondary qualities" deriving from such fallible and
subjective perceptions as color and smell.

Primary qualities, for Descartes, can be described by mathematics, especially geometry; Cartesian method was essentially geometrical. It meant
first the acceptance as true only of ideas with the clarity and distinctness of
geometrical axioms; then the division of a problem into as many parts as
possible; next proceeding from its simplest to its most complex aspects; and
finally care to omit no step in the entire process of thought. With these principles, Descartes insisted, "there can be nothing so remote that we cannot
reach to it, nor so recondite that we cannot discover it." He had only one

caveat: that no one should employ his method before the age of twenty-three, the age, presumably, at which the impetuosity of youth gives way to patience. Cartesians also tended to believe that the clear and distinct ideas from which all else followed were identical with those in the mind of God.

The result was an absolute distinction between philosophy and science on the one hand, which deal with certainties, and ordinary existence, which is necessarily based on probabilities; indeed, for Descartes, "everything only probable" was "almost false." Here we may discern the influence of the nominalist distinction—notwithstanding Descartes's claim to have wiped his mind clean of all he had learned before creating his own system—between ideas and empirical reality. The passions, in this view, are simply functions of the body, which Descartes compared to a machine: things our bodies do to us and, as in so many formulations of the period, which are mostly dangerous, especially to the life of the mind. Although Descartes claimed to have rejected all traditional wisdom, the ethical principles in his philosophy were largely those of contemporary Stoicism: obedience to the laws, customs, and religion of the place he inhabited; moderation in his opinions, since "all excess tends to be bad"; and the adaptation of his own desires to "the order of the world," since only one's thoughts are within one's own power. He thought this ethic based on reason, which "is the only thing that constitutes us men and distinguishes us from the brutes." If Descartes resembled Bacon in his belief in the utility of his method for the mastery of nature, he meant by this chiefly mastery through reason, based on the intrinsic superiority of mind over matter.

Hobbes drew on both the mathematical and empirical traditions, thus coming closer than either Bacon or Descartes to later scientific method. He was fascinated by geometry and even managed to persuade himself that he had squared the circle. He was also skeptical about the value of sense impressions for understanding nature. In his basic rationalism and his concern both for certainty and the proper method for achieving it, he resembled Descartes:

All men by nature reason alike, and well, when they have good principles; [and] the Use and End of Reason is not the finding of the summe, and truth of one, or a few consequences, remote from the first definitions, and settled signification of names; but to begin at these; and proceed from one consequence to another. For there can be no certainty of the last Conclusion, without a certainty of all those Affirmations and Negations, on which it was grounded, and inferred. [This capacity] is attayned by Industry: first in apt imposing of Names; and secondly by getting a good and orderly Method in proceeding from the Elements, which are Names, to Assertions made by Connexion of one of them to another; and so to Syllogismes, which are the Connexions of one Assertion to another, till we come to a knowledge of all the Consequences of names appertaining to the subject in hand; and that is it, men call SCIENCE. And whereas Sense and Memory are but knowledge of Fact . . . *Science* is the knowledge of Consequences, and dependence of one fact upon another."[10]

Hobbes's conception of science was broad, but he applied his method above all to politics. Here he also resembled Bacon, arguing that the purpose of philosophy is "to bee able to produce, as far as matter and humane force permit, such Effects as humane life requireth."

Hobbes was the first thoroughgoing materialist in modern European history, and the view of nature elaborated in *Leviathan* foreshadowed much in future scientific thought. A crucial passage in that work identified everything in the universe as *body*:

The World, (I mean not the Earth onely . . . but the *Universe*, that is, the whole masse of all things that are) is Corporeall, that is to say, Body, and hath the like dimensions; and hath the dimensions of Magnitude, namely, Length, Bredth, and Depth: also every part of Body is likewise Body, and hath the like dimensions; and consequently every part of the Universe, is Body; and that which is not body, is no part of the Universe. And because the Universe is All, that which is no part of it is *Nothing*; and consequently *no where*. Nor does it follow from hence, that Spirits are *nothing*: for they have dimensions, and are therefore really *Bodies*.[11]

Yet there was a dualistic streak even in Hobbes. The universe consisted, for him, simply of bodies in motion, perceived through sense, the foundation of all thought, which represents the objects of sense to the mind. But since these objects, once they enter the mind, are portrayed as inanimate, thought is itself removed from reality. So, Hobbes declared, "The object is one thing; the image of fancy is another. So that Sense in all cases is nothing els but original fancy, caused . . . by the pressure, that is, by the motion, of externall things upon our Eyes, Eares, and other organs thereunto ordained." This reflection seems at once skeptical and a repudiation of Cartesian skepticism. It also has ethical implications. It meant, for Hobbes, the material basis of morality, which is derived from the pleasure or pain caused by external stimuli. This led also to a total repudiation of the freedom of the will; Hobbes, on the basis of the new science, was a consistent determinist. No element of mystery remained in his world-view, either in nature, in religion, or in human creativity and imagination. Hobbes thus helps us to understand more clearly the ambivalence in Western culture about natural science, which was nevertheless one of its greatest creations.

CHAPTER THIRTEEN

The Decline of Historical Consciousness

The period continued to be deeply aware of the importance of time and change. But change was also increasingly perceived as dangerous; it was therefore another source of anxiety in an anxious age. Thus, while it was studied by some and even celebrated, the awareness of change also stimulated resistance and denial. By the later sixteenth century, history, which has usually been understood as an account of times past and therefore of change, was languishing, put to partisan and polemical purposes, or being replaced by mythical claims that supported one or another special interest. The shift was gradual, but the great Renaissance historians, Machiavelli and Guicciardini, had no distinguished successors.

The change is apparent in Montaigne. Although he observed and even relished his own changeability; he otherwise professed to detest change. "In all things," he declared, "change is to be feared," but especially in public affairs. There was nothing "so bad, provided it is old and stable," he believed, "that it is not better than change and commotion." He was well aware of the imperfection of the world, but he emphasized "the difficulty of improving our condition and the danger of everything crumbling into bits." If, he concluded, "I could put a spoke in our wheel and stop [change] at this point, I would do so with all my heart." Fear of change was the only motive he gave for opposing Protestantism. "In the controversy on whose account France is at present agitated," he argued, "the best and soundest side is undoubtedly that which maintains both the old religion and the old government of the country."

Such attitudes were common. Queen Elizabeth's motto was *semper eadem* (always the same), and even Camden, the historian of her reign, viewed any change in law or the social order with alarm. Hooker believed that, since "the custome of easines to alter and change is so evill, no doubt but to beare a tollerable soare is better then to venter on a daungerous remedie." The

English Puritan William Prynne based his conservatism on the fact that in God there is "no variableness, no shadow of change." A Platonic "immutability" was the ideal.

Thinkers praised and studied "nature" because of its supposed uniformity. Hooker was consoled for the unreliability of human affairs by the stability of non-human nature, "than which there is nothinge more constant, nothinge more uniform in all its waies." He took comfort in the rule of the world by eternal law, with the result that, in contrast to human affairs, it "can have no shew or cullor of mutabilitie." Although Pope Clement VIII would have disagreed with Hooker on much, he found in his writings "seeds of eternity" that would endure "till the last fire shall consume all learning." Plato had taught intellectuals that only the unchanging can be known, and knowledge was what they lived for; laments over the instability and meaninglessness of everything in this world were widespread. Webster's Duchess of Malfi, contemplating her sad fate, took such comfort as she could in recalling that

> all things have their end:
> Churches and cities, which have diseases like to men
> Must have like death that we have.

Indeed, much that passed for historical investigation in this period aimed to demonstrate the *absence* of change: to show that the present condition of one or another institution was identical with its beginnings; this was its ultimate justification. Scholars liked to demonstrate that present laws had always prevailed. Protestants responded to the taunting question of their opponents, "Where was your church before Luther?" that their churches had changed in no way from those of antiquity. Similar claims were made for states. French historians argued that the French monarchy and its Gallican liberties had not altered since their very beginnings. As one of them claimed, France had existed twelve hundred years without changing "its laws and form of government." Venice, isolated in Italy by the combined forces of Spain and the papacy, insisted on its eternal destiny. In the words of one strong doge, "This republic, born twelve centuries ago, has always been preserved without change and will be kept so, with God's help, as long as the world will last." For another Venetian, Venice had been destined by God to "imitate eternity here below." Much of what passed for history in this period was at best little more than antiquarianism.

Novelty was almost ritually denounced. Botero, in his *Reason of State*, argued that "novelty is always hated, and any change in old customs arouses resentment." In cities novelty was likely to be blamed on the lower classes, presumably always ready to overthrow their betters; Lope de Vega attributed this tendency to the experience of change among city-dwellers, mostly immigrants from the country and constantly on the move. Hooker explained that "the love of thinges ancient doth argue staiednes, but levitie and want of experience maketh apt unto innovations." The Jesuit *Ratio studiorum* of 1599 laid down the rule that "nobody shall introduce, in matters of importance, new questions or any opinions not supported by reputable authors, without consulting his superiors," and the curriculum in Jesuit schools had little room for history. A scholastic philosopher disposed of his opponents by remarking that "most new opinions are false. Were they true, they would already have been adopted by one of many wise men of past ages."

A renewed interest in philosophy, which had never much concerned itself with history, paralleled the decline of history. Bellarmine, though he listed historians in his account of ecclesiastical writers, gave no indication of having read them. Sidney thought history worse than useless even as a repository of moral examples: a historian, he wrote, was "captived to the trueth of a foolish world" and so could provide no "perfect patterns" on which to mold human behavior. Fulgenzio Micanzio believed that too much knowledge of history made men irresolute. Bacon, though he wrote it himself, had reservations about history, having observed "how much the sight of man's mind is distracted by experience," and Descartes believed that history might broaden but could not deepen the mind; his follower Nicolas Malebranche would distinguish between the genuine sciences and those "simple sorts of knowledge without any rational discourse, like works of history." Conversely, Bodin's *Method for the Easy Comprehension of History* was denounced for its heresies by Antonio Possevino. Interest in the past was directed now chiefly to applauding the unchanging perfections of antiquity, and to the Near East rather than to later periods; historical accounts were chiefly valued not for giving new life to the past but for embalming it.

Historical writings in the earlier Renaissance had had their static side; its histories had often been chiefly examples of virtue and vice, or of political wisdom relevant to all times and places, on the assumption, as in Machiavelli, of the uniformity of human nature. This tendency persisted and, if anything, grew more pronounced in the later Renaissance. On the other hand *The Anatomy of Melancholy* was only one of many works that placed ancient and modern examples of human belief and behavior side by side, thus implying that they had never changed. Casaubon's Latin translation of Polybius (1609) urged on rulers the value of history—he meant chiefly that of antiquity—for providing ethical and political examples instructive for all times. The exemplary value of history was one of the platitudes urged on Don Quixote as an alternative to his beloved chivalric romances, and Sarpi was convinced that "examples move more than reasons." Baronius found in the past rulers who had obeyed the pope and were rewarded for it by God; and Foxe hoped that his *Book of Martyrs* would provide examples of "life, faith, and doctrine" for the emulation of contemporaries. The English statesman Sir Francis Walsingham argued that ancient political practice was "serviceable to our age" by providing both positive and negative examples. Camden claimed to have learned from Tacitus that the purpose of history was "to preserve Vertuous Actions from being buried in Oblivion, and to deter men from either speaking or doing what is amiss, for fear of after-Infamy with Posterity." This was hardly a historical use of the past.

Thus the hints in the earlier Renaissance of something like historical perspective, of the ability to discern fundamental differences between one time and another, were fading. Even more striking was a tendency to see the past as meaningless. Botero was unable to see the past as much more than an accumulation of individual and insignificant details, and the very title of Loy Le Roy's *On the Vicissitude or Variety of Things in the Universe* (1575) suggests the essential meaninglessness of change. Montaigne had little sense of change in the European past; the ancients for him simply differed from, though they were superior to, his contemporaries. "We do not go in a straight line," he observed of the course of history: "we rather ramble and turn this way and that. We retrace our steps." Time, for Montaigne, was largely meaningless. His *Essays* show little interest even in the direction taken by his own thought, fascinated though he was by the changes he perceived in himself; he appears never to have asked himself how he had become both so ordinary (as he claimed) and so individual. He did not even think it necessary to explain the changes in himself represented by the revisions and additions to his *Essays*.

Thought about history was now chiefly an eclectic and incongruous mixture of inherited conceptions and commonplaces. The same historian could combine in one account both nationalism and universalism, random examples of virtue and vice, a conviction that things were getting worse, a notion of cycles, insistence on the universal rule of providence, and hints of the notion of progress. Most of these can be found in Bodin's *Methodus*, a work popular enough to go through thirteen editions by the middle of the seventeenth century. Bodin himself described the past as a flower garden from which a reader might gather "the sweetest fruits," according to his taste. Like many others, he paid his respects to Truth, but his own diffuse and disorderly reflections exemplify the general state of historical thought in his time. His *Methodus* is a hodgepodge of the various, largely incompatible, notions about possible patterns in history that circulated in the period.

Like Machiavelli, Bodin claimed that history "for the most part deals with the state and the changes taking place within it," but the vision of his *Methodus* was universal. Though rejecting the astrological calculations that usually accompanied such productions, he incorporated into the work a "general chart" of all histories, organized on the basis of the traditional Joachimite "world week." He was not alone in his universalism. It also shaped the thought of Bellarmine and of the Jesuit historian of the New World, José de Acosta. Grotius hinted at similar notions in his concern with international law and searched the Scriptures for clues to the origins of the American natives. In this pious age historical events were seen both as inscrutable, i.e., known only to God, and "providential." An English bishop explained that what we call fortune "is nothing but the hand of God, working by causes and for causes that we know not. Chance or fortune are gods devised by man and made by our ignorance of the true, almighty, and everlasting God." Bodin sometimes invoked providence as an explanation for events, though he admitted that he often could not understand it. It "arranges all things in an admirable order, motion, number, harmony, and shape," he wrote, "but it changes these at will, sometimes arbitrarily." His invocation of providence also strengthened his universalism since providence governs all peoples and events.

Occasionally providence was seen as benign. Agostino Valier argued—against all evidence—that the prosperity of Venice was a providential reward for its devotion to the pope. For the Dutch, beleaguered both by the sea and Spanish armies, their successes were a scroll "on which God wrote His providential design." The English felt indebted to providence for the defeat of the Spanish Armada. But while even Machiavelli had allowed for good as well as bad fortune, providence was now chiefly invoked to explain disasters as punishment for collective sins. Donne saw both national and individual histories as illustrations of divine retribution. Richard Knolles's *History of the Turks* (1603) interpreted the recent advance of Islam as punishment for the sins of Christendom. Ralegh's *History of the World* was an extended demonstration of the role of providence, especially in punishing the presumption of the powerful. Botero saw the hand of God in Germany's loss of its military prowess after the rise of Protestantism. But providence was more likely to be seen as mysterious. Sarpi noted with a hint of satisfaction how often providence frustrated human intentions, and Pierre de l'Estoile took a sardonic pleasure in God's laughter "at the great plans of men," which often bring "very different results from what they expect."

The notion of providence was, however, in some tension with another conception, ultimately Neoplatonic and more consistently troubling: that all things deteriorate from an original perfection. Montaigne contrasted his own dwarfish time with that of the giants of antiquity. The ancients' "vigor of soul," he wrote, had been "incomparably greater; and the weaker the soul, the less its power to do either very well or very ill." Palissy made the point more generally; he believed that "everything in this world runs backward." A shepherdess in Tasso lamented that "the world grows old and, growing old, grows sad." This conception was also included by Bodin among his other notions of time.

Bodin also invoked the Stoic notion of cycles. Thus he wrote that the arts will

arise in some place through practice and the labor of talented men. They then develop, later they flourish for a while at a fixed level, then languish in their old age, and finally begin to die and are buried in lasting oblivion by the eternal calamity of wars, or because too great abundance (an evil much to be feared in these times, of course) brings satiety to the frivolous, or because God inflicts just punishments upon those who direct useful knowledge.[1]

But he also believed that "nature is subject to the law of eternal return," so that all things participate in "a circular revolution, such that vice follows upon virtue, ignorance supplants wisdom, evil succeeds honesty, and mere darkness replaces errors."

Bodin recognized, however, that cycles also implied intervals of improvement; hence the Greeks had been followed by the Romans, among whom "talented people were so abundant that almost immediately they excelled all peoples in warlike glory and in superiority of culture," especially in their legal system and language. But the Romans, too, "by a similar fall, also started to lapse into their early barbarity when the forces of the Scythians, pouring into Italy, burned the well-stocked libraries almost everywhere and all the monuments of antiquity."

Such an eclectic confusion about the patterns of history can be found in many places. A classical belief in cycles, inherently ambivalent about the long-run future but also implying the possibility of a better time to come

during difficult times, was widely attractive. Bodin echoed Machiavelli on
the point:

> They are mistaken who think that the race of men always deteriorates.
> When old men err in this respect, it is understandable that this
> happens to them—that they sigh for the loss of the flower of youth,
> which breathes joy and cheerfulness. When they see themselves
> deprived of every kind of delight and instead of pleasure they feel
> sharp pains, instead of having unimpaired senses, they suffer weakness
> in all their members, they fall to these sad meditations and, deceived
> by the false view of things, think that loyalty and friendship of man
> for man has died. As though, returning from a distant journey they
> tell of the golden age—to young men. But then their experience is the
> same as that of men carried out of port and into the open sea—they
> think the houses and the towns are departing from them; thus they
> think that delight, gentle conduct, and justice have flown to the heavens
> and deserted the earth.[2]

For Bruno, too, cycles, at least temporarily, suggested hope:

> We are not the first inventor of this way of teaching, but we are reviv-
> ing it; as in nature we see vicissitudes of light and darkness, so also
> there are vicissitudes of different kinds of philosophies. Since there is
> nothing new, as Aristotle says . . . it is necessary to return to those
> opinions after many centuries.

In a time when all good things had been reduced to the "dregs" of what
they had been, "we may expect to return to a better condition" and there
was now "no good nor honor which we may not promise ourselves."[3]
Although Bacon could sometimes believe in progress through knowledge,
at other moments he was disturbed, like Bodin, by the probability of an
inexorable return to a previous condition, at least for states:

> In the youth of a state, arms do flourish; in the middle age of a state,
> learning; and then both of them together for a time; in the declining
> age of a state, mechanical arts and merchandise. Learning hath its
> infancy, when it is but beginning and almost childish: then its youth,
> when it is luxuriant and juvenile: then its strength of years when it is
> solid and reduced: and lastly its old age, when it waxeth dry and

exhaust. But it is not good to look too long upon these turning wheels of vicissitude, lest we become giddy.[4]

George Hakewill was more optimistic. In his *Power and Providence of God* (1627) he combined the notion of rebirth with optimism about the intent of providence; for him, the modern age, for all its troubles, was "capable of deepe speculations . . . as *masculine*, and lasting [in] birthes, as any of the ancienter times have done." This suggested that history could take the shape of a kind of spiral ascent.

But these various perspectives all piously required history to be true. Thucydides, now much read, had insisted that the utility of histories depended on their accuracy, and Polybius had made the point that, "as a living creature is rendered wholly useless if deprived of its eyes, so if you take truth from history, what is left is but an idle unprofitable tale." Even when they were writing for purposes in which truth was at best secondary, historians continued to pay lip service to truth.

But another attitude toward history, with roots at least as deep, was now in increasing tension with the demand for truth: history in the service of epideictic rhetoric, conferring praise or blame on its protagonists. Patrizi had assumed that history should record the "pious and religious deeds of our ancestors," and Tasso recommended its use to glorify nations and families. Sarpi simply assumed the tension between a reader's desire for truth and the historian's duty to glorify (or in his own case chiefly to vilify) his subject. So he pointed out in advising the Venetian government that the credibility of a historian depends on his appearance of impartiality. Hence a historian of Venice, while emphasizing the positive, should not omit what was discreditable. Guicciardini had benefitted Venice, he suggested, by seeming impartial.

Meanwhile, in an age dominated by princes, Livy, historian of the Roman republic, was being replaced as a model by Tacitus, historian of the emperors. Tacitus also had the advantage of ambiguity: he could be interpreted either as a critic of a vicious age, as a teacher of realistic adaptation to despotism, or as a guide for tyrants. Several historians of the period were considered disciples of Tacitus, including Davila, who had written on the French religious wars, and Sarpi on the Council of Trent. Sarpi himself described the Jesuits as "good observers of all the precepts of Tacitus"; Boccalini, on the other hand, praised Tacitus for telling the truth about a sordid age. But most histories were increasingly partisan.

This was notably true of official histories, but the tendency can be seen everywhere. When Agostino Mascardi lamented the sad state of contemporary histories, what he had chiefly in mind was their failure sufficiently to respect authority in church and state; the deficiencies he lamented were chiefly rhetorical. Bellarmine maintained that any denial of papal claims to universal monarchy was "heresy in history," much as somewhat later he would find Galileo guilty of heresy in science. Catholic authorities repeatedly condemned histories for ideological deficiencies: not only Guicciardini's *History of Italy*, Bodin's *Methodus*, and the Gallican Jacques-Auguste de Thou's *History of His Own Time* (1604–08), but even the *Florentine History* (1600) of the staunchly orthodox Scipione Ammirato. History ranked so low in Rome that it was difficult to find a successor to continue the unfinished work of Baronius.

In fact, religious polemic under the guise of history had a relatively short life; it was increasingly recognized not only that argument based on history was, as a weapon, potentially dangerous to those who used it, but also because it was too indirect. Lutherans under the leadership of Martin Chemnitz, Beza, and François Turretin in Geneva, and Anglicans following Richard Hooker, turned increasingly toward philosophical and even scholastic modes of argument. The seventeenth century and much of the eighteenth were less and less hospitable to history.

What chiefly passed now under its guise were timeless, quasi-historical myths about the past. One, persisting from the earlier Renaissance, was that the present marked the rebirth of antiquity after an age of darkness. This was apparent in many slogans of the time to which the backward-looking prefix re- was attached, among them rebirth, reform, and restoration. Loy Le Roy recalled how the new learning had begun with Petrarch's "restoration of languages and all disciplines," "the opening of libraries," and "the removal of dust and dirt from the good books of ancient authors." Sarpi, in spite of his pessimism, still looked to antiquity for models of virtue, contrasting, like Machiavelli, the passivity of contemporaries with the activism of the ancients. In spite of his professed contempt for book-learning, much in Campanella's utopian City of the Sun was modeled on the ancients. For Lipsius, the government of ancient Rome was a model for contemporary rulers. As a French diplomat exclaimed, "Oh learned, oh calm, oh free antiquity! how lovely you are with all your wrinkles, all your old rags, all your features wholly effaced and almost unrecognizable! Oh sacrilegious hands which have dared to go over them and claim to have formed you again in place of that venerable original!"

Admiration for pagan antiquity was exceeded only by veneration for Christian antiquity among both Catholics and Protestants, each of whom claimed its authority for themselves. The Catholic position was carried to extremes by Baronius, as we have seen; Protestants charged the Roman Church with having departed from its ancient virtues. This was especially true among the reformed, who claimed that the papal church had betrayed the teachings and practice of the first six centuries, divinely appointed as the model for all time. Cranmer had vehemently denounced the papal church on this score:

> As rich men, flying from their enemies, carry away all they can with them, and what they cannot take away they either hide or destroy; so the court of Rome had destroyed so many ancient writings, and hid the rest, having carefully preserved every that was of advantage to them, that it was not easy to discover what they had so artificially concealed. . . . many more things said by the ancients of the see of Rome, and against their authority were lost, as appears by the fragments yet remaining.[5]

Martin Bucer, much read by Anglicans, praised the church under the Christian emperors. "Truly," he wrote, "in that time the churches of Christ experienced that abundant kindness of the Lord toward themselves which the prophets had predicted." English Puritans, too, looked for guidance to Christian antiquity as well as to Scripture.

A related myth described the procession of learning and power from east to west as "natural" because it followed the sun. For Bodin, the east was the source of "letters, useful arts, virtues, training, philosophy, religion, and finally *humanitas* itself [which] flowed upon earth as from a fountain." Bruno looked further, both in time and space, for the origins of this transit: to the Gymnosophists of India, and from them on to Lucretius and Orpheus; his roster of important thinkers ended with Albert the Great, Nicholas of Cusa, Paracelsus, and Copernicus. Some Frenchmen, patriots as well as scholars, thought that this succession pointed to the intellectual leadership of the University of Paris and promised eventual rule over the world to the French crown.

This sort of mythical retrospection was most widespread in the notion of a golden age, a conception itself of ancient origin, which appealed to a past so distant that it had left no record except an ideal of innocence and simplicity. A Stoic component in the conception associated it with life according to nature, but it was also nourished by the biblical account of Eden. Not least among its attractions was its idealization of free and spontaneous love in beautiful surroundings, which implied innocence and simplicity as well as freedom from care and responsibility. Don Quixote delivered a long harangue on the subject to a group of doubtless puzzled goatherds:

> Happy the age and happy the times on which the ancients bestowed the name of golden, not because gold, which in this iron age of ours is rated so highly, was attainable without labor in those fortunate times, but rather because the people of those days did not know those two words *mine* and *thine*. In that blessed age all things were held in common. No man, to gain his common sustenance, needed to make any greater effort than to reach up his hand and pluck it from the strong oaks, which literally invited him to taste their sweet and savory fruit. . . . All was peace then, all amity, all concord. . . . Nor had fraud, deceit, or malice mingled with truth and sincerity. Justice pursued her own proper purposes.[6]

Little known during the Middle Ages, the popularity of the myth now expressed the reaction of townsmen and courtiers to the complexities and constraints of life in cities and courts.

The notion of a golden age lay behind the idealization of primitive peoples in America, and echoes of it can also be sensed in the praise of country life among many of the nobility everywhere. It also nourished Stoic praise of gardens. For Lipsius, the garden represented withdrawal "from the cares and troubles of this world"; in his garden his mind was "busied without any labor and exercised without pain." Cotton Mather combined it with other elements in his thought, remarking that "the first Age was the golden Age: to return unto *that*, will make a man a Protestant, and, I may add, a Puritan." Gardens suggested the primal garden in which mankind might have lived forever, spontaneously virtuous, obedient to "nature" in all its complex meanings.

This ideal was also reflected in pastoral scenes in poetry and painting, which portrayed a life free from the restrictions of custom, law, convention, status, and responsibility. The pastoral romance *Diana* by the Spanish novelist Jorge Montemayor went through twenty-six editions between 1559 and 1600. Cervantes imitated it in his *Galatea* (1584), which was almost equally successful and was said to have been known "almost by heart" by members of the French court. France had its own pastoral novelist in Honoré D'Urfée, whose *Astrée* (1607) was another popular success. Tasso's pastoral play *Aminta* (1573) contributed to the early development of opera. Sidney's long novel *Arcadia* contrasted the pastoral ideal with the disorderly present; and the pastoral continued to be a favorite representation at the court of Charles I, whose queen participated in performances of pastoral plays.

Serious attempts were made to establish the historicity of the golden age. Bodin's Salomon came close to identifying it with the time of the Hebrew patriarchs, whose historicity could not be denied; he argued that "all things which pertain to salvation are contained in the laws of nature," by which "Abel, Enoch, Noah, Abraham, Job, Isaac, and Jacob lived." "What men!" he exclaimed. Burton too placed ancient Israel within the golden age, though on this matter Bodin was more discriminating.

For some groups, the medieval past was the focus of nostalgia. This accounts for the popularity of chivalric romances, published in large numbers, which described the deeds of medieval heroes, real or imagined. Such works had turned the brain of Don Quixote, leading to his attempt "to convince the world of its error in not reviving that most happy age in which the order of chivalry flourished." Both noble and middle-class Florentines engaged in chivalric recreations. In England, Spenser, Hakluyt, and other patriotic writers celebrated the rule of heroic King Arthur; and Camden's widely read *Britannia* (1607) fed local curiosity about the counties of England, showing "who were the ancient inhabitants, what was the reason of the name, what are the bounds of the county, the nature of the soil, the places of greatest antiquity, and most eminent at present; and lastly, who have been dukes or earls of them since the Norman Conquest." At the same time the English were discovering in the myth of Magna Carta the origins of English liberty. Poets set major works in a mythicized medieval past: Tasso with a crusade epic, *Gerusalemme Liberata* (1580), and Spenser in *The Faerie Queene* (1589–96). A nostalgic medievalism contributed to the attempts of the papacy to organize new crusades after the great Christian naval victory over the Turks at Lepanto in 1572.

The various peoples of Europe were meanwhile discovering their own independent origins in antiquity. Sometimes a connection with ancient Rome was itself sufficient to satisfy this impulse. The papacy insisted on its inheritance to the universal claims of pagan Rome, a continuity symbolized in 1586 when a great obelisk erected in Alexandria by the emperor Augustus was imported by Pope Sixtus V and set up again in front of St. Peter's. Jacopo Strada, an antiquarian at the Habsburg court, composed a history of the modern imperial line that carried it back to Julius Caesar. The magistrates of the Parlement of Paris liked to see themselves, in their capacity as law-makers, as heirs to the Roman senate. Even Ivan IV of Muscovy traced his descent from the emperor Augustus.

Other peoples also discovered evidence of their original freedom and independence from Rome. A number of states claimed to have been "founded" by refugees from the fall of Troy, as Rome had been founded by Aeneas: France by "Francus," Portugal by sons of "Lusus," the Habsburg monarchy and even Ireland by other Trojans unnamed. James I identified the Trojan Brute as progenitor of the English, and Thomas Heywood traced for him, in a long poem, *Troia Britannica* (1609), the passage of Brute to England and his establishment as first king of England in a line culminating in James himself.

Some peoples, with encouragement from Tacitus's *Germania*, were also pleased to discover their origins in Germany before the Roman conquest, noting that only some parts of it had been conquered by the Romans and then only with great difficulty. Dutch Protestants found their ancestry in the Batavians, and French lawyer-historians were identifying their fore-fathers in pre-Roman Gaul. This "Germanic" thesis was most fully devel-oped in François Hotman's *Franco-Gallia* and *Anti-Tribonian*, which argued that, before the Romans, Gaul had experienced a golden age of freedom and justice. Hotman also praised French customary law at the expense of Roman law. Another scholar, Charles Du Moulin, declared, "I regard myself as an enthusiast for the Frankish name and for the nobility, dignity, and virtue of the ancient Franks," claiming that he had "been led to this conclusion by judgment rather than by emotion." He also studied what he saw as the degeneration of the Roman Church. Although pure at the beginning, Du Moulin argued, it had been corrupted by theologians, canon lawyers, and the mendicants, and its original purity was now represented by the French church alone.

Meanwhile the warlike virtues of the French nobility were being traced back, not to the Romans, but to the Franks. However mythical, such notions contributed to interest in the medieval past. As Louis Le Caron urged in 1566, "Frenchmen, you have enough in your own history, without search-ing that of the Greeks and Romans."

Myths also gathered around the Venetian republic, some of local origin, others propagated by travelers impressed by the beauty and order of Venice. The myth of its perpetual freedom, even in antiquity, stiffened the resolve of the government to resist the papal interdict of 1606. Its publicists argued that Venice had been originally settled by refugees from the mainland fleeing the tyrannical rule of Rome, and that the Venetian republic, protected by its island location, its republican spirit unchanged from the beginning, was now the only remaining bastion of freedom in Italy. God, according to one author, had revealed to his beloved Venice "the plan of an eternal city, where, in a little cove of the sea, would be enclosed all that Genius, Nature, and Heaven can achieve." Venetian opera, soon to spread throughout Europe, contributed to keep this myth alive.

Other myths gathered around supposedly significant individuals. Thus Protestants attributed reform in the church, largely unaware of greater historical pressures, to the initiative of "heroical Luther." Bacon, juxtaposing Luther with other cultural heroes, saw in him the origin of both the Renaissance and the Reformation; Luther, Bacon argued, had awakened "the ancient authors, both in divinity and humanity, which had long time slept in libraries." The other side of such hero-making was a tendency to attribute unwelcome change in the past to conspiracies. The converse of the heroic Luther, equally inadequate as historical explanation, was, for Catholics, a diabolical Luther, motivated to rebel by his uncontrollable lust.

Such myths proliferated during the period of the religious wars, especially among Protestants. Each side converted rumors of brutality by the other into reports of wanton cruelty committed against the innocent and helpless. Among the more durable of these concoctions was the notion of an international conspiracy to destroy Protestantism that explained the St. Bartholomew Massacre in France. Another concerned the operations of the Spanish Inquisition in the Netherlands and the outrages perpetrated by Spanish armies against helpless civilians during the Dutch struggle for independence. This is not, of course, to deny that both sides during the religious wars committed acts of cruelty.

Religious polemic generally exploited history. A multi-volume *History of the Church of Christ* in Latin (1559–74), the work of Lutheran scholars directed by Matthias Flacius Illyricus, depicted Christianity as having been diabolically corrupted since antiquity by the papacy. At a more popular level was the vernacular compilation of John Foxe, *Acts and Monuments* (1563), commonly known as "Foxe's Book of Martyrs." Much of it described the sufferings of English Protestants under Queen Mary. But in a later edition (1570), Foxe outlined a general view of church history that was taken up by many Protestants. It depicted that history as the record of a cosmic struggle between God and the devil, temporarily won by the latter in about the year 1000. Foxe was particularly concerned to attack claims for the continuity of the Roman Church from the time of Christ. The true church, he argued, had been represented during the Middle Ages by a "saving remnant" consisting of "a poor oppressed and persecuted Church of Christ . . . continually stirred up by faithful ministers, by whom always hath been kept some sparks of his true doctrine and religion," a remnant notably including the major medieval heretics: the Albigensians and Waldensians, Wyclif and Hus. Catholics eventually supplemented Foxe's list by identifying other heretics with whom they believed Luther had affinities. In later editions of the work Foxe added Alexander Neckham and Robert Grosseteste (probably because they were English), Marsilio of Padua, William of Ockham, and Dante, and also more recent Renaissance figures, Petrarch, Valla, and Pico della Mirandola, thereby establishing the venerable link between the Renaissance and the Reformation. Indeed, Foxe eventually emphasized the large numbers composing his "remnant": "What shall need then," he asked rhetorically, "any more witnesses to prove this matter, when you see so many years ago, whole armies and multitudes thus standing against the Pope? Who, though they be termed here for heretics and schismatics, yet in that which they call heresy served the living Lord within the ark of his true spiritual and visible Church." The remnant had now swollen into something very like the mainstream of medieval and Renaissance Christianity.

The major Catholic reply to Protestant versions of church history came from Cardinal Baronius (Cesare Baronio), who developed a Catholic counter-myth, published in a dozen huge volumes (1588–1607) entitled *Ecclesiastical Annals*. Baronius only reached 1198 before he died. He was a respectable scholar, and his extensive quotations from sources have made the work a useful tool for scholars ever since. But the *Annals* largely ignored the theological issues raised by Protestantism; Baronius was chiefly concerned to defend and promote papal authority. Basing his argument on the ancient conception of imperial Rome as divinely ordained to rule the world, he claimed that the papacy had inherited its universal authority, which he traced back through an unbroken succession of popes and their supposed Hebrew precursors before Christ to the creation of the human race. Adam, in this conception, was both the first pope and the first emperor, and later popes were heirs to both aspects of his authority. To the charge of papal corruption he made the curious—and radically anti-historical—response that the papal church had never changed since the creation of the world. Baronius concluded:

> Just as successive links form a single chain, so years joined to years by many cycles of years compose one same work, and reveal that the Church has been always one and the same. . . . nothing can seem more pleasing to a pious mind that desires only the truth, nothing more delightful, than to consider the Christian faith in which it believes to have been the same since the beginning of the church, as

taught, spotlessly preserved, and guarded in sanctity through all the centuries.[7]

To demonstrate this claim, however, he chose to concentrate on the institutional history of the church rather than its beliefs, without replying directly to the major Protestant charges. From a modern standpoint, a demonstration from history that any institution could endure for centuries unchanged seems improbable, but it reflected a powerful impulse in the culture of the age.

But the most effective—and rather more historical—contribution to the debate over papal claims was still to come. This was the *History of the Council of Trent* by the Venetian Servite friar Paolo Sarpi first printed—for prudential reasons—in London in 1619. In the background of the work was the interdict of 1606, imposed on Venice as a result of longstanding controversies about the authority of the Venetian government over the Venetian clergy and the property of the church. Sarpi had served as a legal adviser to Venice during the struggle, which was followed with intense interest by other Catholic states. Like the Gallican lawyers with whom he corresponded, Sarpi looked for historical precedents to support Venetian claims. Meanwhile his close friend Fulgenzio Micanzio was working his way through the *Annals* of Baronius in order to refute him, and this had supplied background for Sarpi's work. Sarpi himself was studying the history of the Council of Trent, the key, as he supposed, to the recent claims of Rome. His *History of the Council* was a detailed account of that event, the outcome of which he depicted as a triumph of the papacy, made possible by deceitful management of the council. Here Sarpi was inconsistent. He had started out by representing the outcome of the council as proof that everything earthly turns out contrary to human designs, and he concluded that therefore we can trust in God alone. But he ended by displaying—and exaggerating—the artful triumph of the papacy. Meanwhile he included much evidence of change in the papal church since its foundation: a position directly contradicting that of Baronius. Sarpi's history eventually drew an extended reply by Sforza Pallavicino (1656–57), which bore the same title and was in fact somewhat more objective. But Sarpi's book was translated into many languages, and was widely read; and it badly damaged claims for the divine inspiration of the council and for broader claims for the immutability of the Roman Church.

In spite of the efforts of historians to make their work as objective as possible, it is by now sufficiently clear that it can never be entirely free from the values, perspectives, and biases of its authors, which, indeed, help to humanize and give it life. But histories were increasingly subordinated to interested and barely disguised motives. The mentality of this period was increasingly ahistorical. Historical composition would not recover its earlier vitality until a new chapter in the evolution of European culture began in the period of the later Enlightenment.

CHAPTER FOURTEEN

Order in Society and Government

Two centuries of rapid change had disrupted traditional patterns of life, causing deep and widespread uneasiness. This was exacerbated by the persistence of traditional and static conceptions of order, against which recent novelties were obscurely measured. The period consequently exhibited an almost feverish interest in how best to improve social and political organization. Various theories were advanced but no consensus emerged.

Much of the problem was located by ruling groups and intellectuals in the lower classes, which everywhere aroused fear. For Bodin in France, the people, "variable as the winds" and without a "sense of judgment," oscillated from one extreme to the other; once a tyrant had been expelled, the hatred of his memory and the fear of once again falling victim to him would "excite them to rush to the other extreme." Only terror, he believed, could control restive peoples. For Bodin, as for many others, democracy was "the most perverted"—i.e., the most disorderly—form of government; subjects should never "be encouraged to entertain political ambitions." Botero associated popular government with Calvinism, another reason to detest it. Jonson, himself of humble origins, denounced the "beastly nature of the multitude," though Burton, more mildly, hoped the populace might be distracted from rebellion by recreations. For the respectable classes everywhere, popular rule meant anarchy, in which, in Bodin's words, "no one rules, no one obeys, no rewards are granted to good men, no punishments for the wicked." Even in the Dutch republic the patrician authorities worried that the populace might withdraw its customary deference.

In this situation political debate tended to oscillate between arguments for hierarchy and for autocracy, between lofty idealism and brutal realism. Both can sometimes be found in a single writer, even in the same work—as in the case of Bodin, who could sound idealistic about what was needed: "an apt and comely order, such that the first may be joined with the last, and they of the middle sort with both; and so all with all, in a most true knot and bond among themselves together." This meant, for him, an amicable hierarchy, as in his *Methodus* where he had argued that only hierarchy could bring harmony to an otherwise discordant world. Much later one of his colloquists put this conception in a cosmic framework. "I believe," he asserted, "that the intelligible or angelic world is governed by the power of God alone, the heavenly world by the angelic, the elementary by the heavenly; moreover I think the higher orders are [always] examplars for the lower orders." Hooker too was committed to the principle that "the better should guide and commaunde the worse," and a hierarchical conception of society permeated the world-view of the French *parlementaires*.

But Bodin also made the same speaker recommend absolutism. "Not only the contrary elements but the stars themselves and also the powers of the angels," he argued, "are subject to the power of one divine majesty," although he gave an idealistic twist to the notion by adding that it was the duty of princes to develop the moral and contemplative virtues by exhibiting the same qualities in themselves. He failed, however, to explain how this was to be arranged. He also made other suggestions. He discouraged excessive familiarity in a ruler lest it decrease the respect of subjects, and he recognized that in politics there were usually "almost infinite degrees of difference and change."

In fact, hierarchy was more common than autocracy in this period. Although government was often arbitrary, it was usually too inefficient for autocracy to be more than an abstract ideal. And much political discussion was highly abstract, based not on history and experience, as for Machiavelli, but on universal truths discovered by reason and confirmed by Scripture or Aristotle, in which the problem of order was often seen as determining the best (usually meaning chiefly the most stable) form of government. Bodin and Hotman reviewed as many legal systems as possible, past and present and with little attention to historical context, to discover which might be "best." Politics was thus likely to be seen as a branch of philosophy or theology, as for Suarez, who began, somewhat like Dante's *De monarchia*, with the general proposition that since "the way of salvation lies in free actions and in moral rectitude and depends to a great extent on law as the rule of human actions, it follows that the study of laws becomes a large division of theology; and when the sacred science treats of law, that science has as object no other than God Himself as Lawgiver."

Abstract and theoretical approaches to politics were widespread. A Venetian writer praised all forms of polity indiscriminately with ancient commonplaces and clichés; another Italian piously asserted that "states are always preserved and conserved by the true and uncorrupted cult of religion"; and even Sarpi could only offer vague generalities in prescribing for the future of Venice: equity in judicial and financial matters, a strong defense, conservation of the arts, benevolence toward the *popolo*, respect for morality, careful observance of commitments, temperance, general esteem for virtue. In England, Burton emphasized, as though this would much concern them, what rulers should contribute to the general welfare. Such idealism also animated Sidney's *Arcadia*, a prolonged exercise in high thinking about politics set within a divine order and an all-controlling providence that promptly punished those who transgressed its laws. Cervantes reproduced satirically the platitudes of political right-thinking in a discussion between the Don and his friends:

> In the course of their conversation they happened to discuss the principles of statecraft—as they are called—and methods of government, correcting this abuse and that, reforming one custom and abolishing another, each one of the three setting up as a fresh legislator, a modern Lycurgus, or a brand-new Solon. To such a degree did they refashion the commonwealth that it was as if they had taken it to the forge and brought away a different one.[1]

Even the Don's fantasies of knight-errantry hardly seem a merely private delusion when compared with the masques at the English court under the early Stuarts, which celebrated Neoplatonic conceptions of order and harmony and depicted a social hierarchy at once embedded in nature and dependent on the crown.

Meanwhile a universalism, reflecting the order imposed on the world by ancient Rome and based on reason, was variously in the air. The famous classical scholar Lipsius contributed to this ideal in his *Six Books of Politics* (1589), intended as a guide for contemporary rulers, just as his ethical writings aimed to guide subjects into passive acceptance of their rule. The work was an anthology of classical writings with a commentary endorsing absolutism as the only basis of political order. Lipsius composed a kind of oration on this theme:

> Firm and stable is the greatness of that [prince] whom all know to be far above them . . . whose care they daily find is to be on guard for the safety of each and all [his subjects]; and when he goes forth among them they do not run away, as if some bad or dangerous animal had burst from its lair; but, as if toward some bright and kindly star, they

eagerly run towards him. They are ready to cast themselves before the attackers' daggers on his behalf and to lay down their bodies before him, if a road to safety must be made through human slaughter.[2]

Living in the Netherlands, long afflicted by religious division, Lipsius also recommended the imposition of a single state religion. Such views became the political orthodoxy of the European ruling classes. Twenty-two thousand copies of Lipsius's book were printed during the first decade after its publication, ten editions in France alone between 1595 and 1613.

Such views were often combined with the idealization of political universalism. Lipsius deplored patriotism as a product merely of local custom rather than nature and reason, and directed only to a part of the world rather than the whole. Botero attributed the "multitude of princes" to sin, noting that Christ had been "born when the world enjoyed a most happy peace under the Empire of Augustus Caesar." Bellarmine at least knew that no such universal empire had ever existed, but he would have preferred it to a world of particular states. The Society of Jesus promoted an ideal of Christendom governed by a common law that reflected universal patterns of justice. Though in maturity his views changed, the youthful Bodin's universalism was emphatic. He wanted all humans to feel (even, apparently, if they were not) that they were "of the same blood and allied by the same bond of race," the basis of human community, and by "the good will and friendship of mankind." Particularity violated "the very bond of human society":

> Hence come those implacable and threatening words of the Egyptians against the Jews, of the Greeks against the Latins, when one called the other barbarian with scornful disrespect. If the natives are better, they ought to train strangers through their own virtues and make them happy, not keep them away. No region is so fecund that it does not need the resources of others. Peoples should unite their possessions and ideas in mutual commerce and thus strengthen their peace and friendship.

He knew enough about Roman law to dismiss it on the ground that, far from expressing universal principles, it was no more than "the legislation of a particular state" whose imperfections were evident in its changes over time. His own prescription was for "wise men to bring together and compare the legal framework of all states, or of the more famous, and from them compile the best kind."[3]

Campanella consistently advocated a universal state, first under Spain and later, like Postel, under France. His utopian *City of the Sun* (1602) envisioned a universal theocracy based on a mixture of traditional ideas, Platonism, various occult motifs, and numerological correspondences. It would guarantee peace by community in wives and property, institutions otherwise likely to stimulate self-love and rapacity.

Universal aspirations, drawing on memories of antiquity, persisted among some existing states. Spain still nourished vague expansionist ambitions, stimulated by papal bulls conferring lordship on it over all newly discovered lands to the west. France, too, where the empire of Charlemagne had not been forgotten, was hospitable to ambitions of this kind. Nor had claims to universal rule been forgotten by the Habsburgs, still officially Holy Roman emperors.

But the primary claimant to universal rule was still, as during much of the Middle Ages, the papacy, whose actual influence had been somewhat enhanced by its ability to balance between the Habsburg rulers of Spain and Austria and the French crown. The eternal destiny of Rome was emphasized as never before, and its universalism was stimulated by missionary expansion in the New World and Asia. The Congregation for the Propagation of the Faith, established in 1622, gave new impetus to papal universalism, and the Society of Jesus expressed it around the world. A sermon addressed to the pope expounded the conception:

> The whole world owes you servitude. You owe the world your supreme authority to rule over it. Certainly Christ, the king of kings and lord of lords, entrusted the earth to the Holy Spirit and to you with the highest commission. Whichever way you lift your eyes and spirit, North and South, East and West, the earth you see is yours. Everywhere the Lord has subjected the peoples to you and the nations below your feet.[4]

As Botero put it, "Other princes have had their authority from the people, who have chosen them for their government and rule, and since then it has passed through blood and heredity to their successors. But the pope has his greatness and superiority over the human race immediately from God. Therefore it cannot be restricted or altered by anyone." Botero also argued that God had regularly punished rulers who defied the pope, among them various medieval emperors and Philip the Fair of France. Papal universalism nourished, too, the attempts of popes to mobilize the powers of Europe in new crusades against the Turks.

This idealism was complemented by a vigorous, if ultimately equivocal, reaction against Machiavellianism. In Rome, the increasingly open secularism of the European states was attributed to Machiavelli. His works were regularly listed on the Index, and none was printed in Italy, Spain, or Catholic Germany in this period. This did not prevent his being widely read and his more notorious passages often quoted.

A small army of writers, both Protestant and Catholic, attacked Machiavelli, and "Machiavellian" became a common term of abuse. Each side applied it to the other during the Venetian interdict. Any tendency toward a secular politics, as among the *politiques* in France, who sought to end the wars of religion by compromise, was denounced as "Machiavellian." Indeed, "politics" and "political," previously respectable terms, now acquired their dubious modern connotations. Protestants attributed the St. Bartholomew Massacre to "Machiavellianism," and Richelieu was attacked by his critics as a disciple of Machiavelli. Machiavelli's supposed deviousness and lust for power also became a stereotype of theater. Marlowe used him to speak the prologue to his *Jew of Malta* (1594), which attributed Machiavellianism to the pope himself:

> Admir'd I am of those that hate me most,
> Though some speak openly against my books,
> Yet they will read me, and thereby attain
> To Peter's chair.

Among the more prominent adversaries of Machiavelli were Jesuits: Antonio Possevino, though he had not read a line of Machiavelli; and Juan de Mariana, a more equivocal foe. Botero and Lipsius attacked Machiavelli, and Campanella charged that "all the actions of men" were now "directed to the state [*regnum*], as there is nothing that man does not do for its sake, since every prince transgresses religion and virtue, as they say for *ragion di stato*, because domination compensates for all evils." Bodin's affinities with Machiavelli were noted and held against him. Hooker viewed his own *Laws* as an antidote to Machiavellianism. Attacks on Machiavelli were well represented in the libraries of rulers. The Venetian Paruta, on the other hand, objected to Machiavelli on quite different, and perhaps more modern, grounds; he thought his views too philosophical because of his attachment to the political cycle of Polybius (perhaps also because this implied the transience of Venice) and his sweeping generalities.

Nevertheless, the practical reality of European politics was a congeries of increasingly assertive particular states, whose need for internal order required a realistic politics of the kind toward which Machiavelli had pointed. "Necessity" thus loomed as large as ever in this period, and even for his critics Machiavelli remained pivotal. Primarily disturbed by his secularization of politics, they absorbed as much from his thought as they could to develop a kind of "Christian" Machiavellianism. Since, the general argument went, government itself has been instituted by God and princes are his delegates, their rule ought to be as effective as possible; indeed, political success was taken as itself a sign of divine grace. Thus the useful was made to seem almost as important as the good.

Bodin, rejecting the utopianism of Plato and More, came to share something of Machiavelli's realism. Laws and institutions, he argued, must be suited to "the nature of the people" and to "the requirements of time, place and persons." He enjoyed attacking the political myths of contemporaries, pointing out that the German emperor was not a true sovereign and that there had never been a society in which all persons were equal. Although he argued for the power of rulers, he realized that they could not be expected "to be content with what they possess and refrain from encroaching on their neighbors, when frontiers coincide and opportunity offers."

Other writers equivocated. Botero, although he attacked it as contrary to the common good of Christendom, praised balance of power as a lesson taught by nature. And the tension between realism and idealism produced a compromise. Reason of state, it was widely agreed among Catholics, was legitimate where rulers professed Christianity and maintained the true church. On this basis Lipsius thought that "some kinde of persons rage too much against Machiavell" and defended dissimulation: a prince, "in desperate matters, should always follow that which were most necessary to be effected, not that which is honest in speech." Botero was prepared to defend anything that promoted the power of the Habsburgs. Bodin criticized Machiavelli only for his inadequate knowledge of antiquity and his republicanism, "in opposition to the approved opinion of philosophers, historians, and all great men"; he also argued for "the principle to which there is no exception, *salus populi suprema lex esto.*" Roger Ascham argued that "those words which are not in themselves true, are not alwaies lies; For they are directed to a Morall and to a pious end, and therefore by that intention are not contrived to deceive or abuse." Sir Henry Wotton, English ambassador to Venice, "called that honest which tendeth to the discovery of such as are not so, by what means soever." On this basis he supported a proposal to kidnap an Italian refugee in England who might then be exchanged for an English refugee in Italy.

That Europe was now largely ruled by princes also led to some shifts in the uses of antiquity. Aristotle was still important for those concerned to identify the best form of government, but he was less useful for the practical problems of contemporary politics. The major shift in the uses of the past, as already noted, was from Livy, historian of the Roman republic, to Tacitus, historian of imperial Rome. Marc-Antoine de Muret in Paris, a professor of rhetoric and jurisprudence and student of Tacitus, emphasized in 1580 the similarities between the condition of the European political scene and the world of Tacitus. Since modern states were now ruled by absolute monarchs, he observed:

> It is profitable for us to know how good and prudent men managed their lives under them, and how to and to what extent they tolerated and dissimulated their vices; how, on the one hand, by avoiding an unseasonable frankness they saved their own lives when they would have served no public end by bringing themselves into danger, and on the other hand they showed that baseness was not pleasing to them by not praising things in the conduct of princes which a good man cannot praise, but which he can cover up or pass over in silence. Those who do not know how to connive at such things not only bring themselves into danger, but often make princes themselves worse.[5]

In fact, the political lessons supposedly taught by Tacitus were ambiguous. His *Histories* could be read as a satire on imperial guile, or again he could be seen as a pagan teacher whose Machiavellianism could therefore be forgiven.

Various prescriptions for the restoration of order in the disorders of the time were proposed. Aristotelians recommended greater respect for Aristotle. Montaigne invoked the power of custom, though he warned of its ability "to seize and ensnare us." "Infused into our soul by our father's seed," he wrote, its power seems "universal and natural," even when unreasonable. For Bacon, custom was "the principal magistrate of man's life." Burton believed it could "mitigate or make all good again." Hobbes testified to its ability (for him a virtue) to justify self-interest. Du Vair thought it served "unto the common sort of people, the same [that] meditation bringeth unto a Philosopher."

Much thought was also given to law as the basis of order. But there were many kinds of law in Europe: customary and common law, differing from place to place and derived from community practice and long usage; canon law for the church; and "positive" law, which depended only on the will of the ruler. Roman law, hallowed by antiquity and often assumed to be based on reason, now prevailed in most of Italy and Germany. Efforts were also being made to strengthen law by systematization and enforcement. Lawyers were examining existing bodies of law, ancient and modern, local, national, and foreign, with an eye to the improvement of legal systems, though with uncertain results.

A systematic classification was provided in Hooker's *Laws of Ecclesiastical Polity*: "Lawes, being imposed either by each man upon him selfe, or by a public society upon the particulars thereof, or by all the nations of men upon everie severall societie, or by the Lord him selfe upon any or everie of these, there is not amongst these foure kinds any one but containeth sundrie both naturall and positive lawes." But the most important distinctions for Hooker were between divine, natural, and positive law.

Divine law, revealed in Scripture, was universally considered authoritative, though some biblical injunctions, such as the ritual law of the Hebrew Scriptures, were considered (except by some radical sects) as applying only to a particular people long in the past. Divine law, though generally believed consistent with reason, was understood to draw its force from God's will.

Closely related to it was natural law, the expression of the divine will in the natural order, whose regularities, accessible to human observation, were interpreted as obedience to the will of the Creator so sadly neglected on earth. Aristotelians added to the laws of physical nature, which they deduced from the inclination of human nature to society, further principles governing human relations; for Bellarmine, both society and government were based on the common "nature" of man. As Hooker argued, all laws implicit in nature could be ascertained by reason, "without the helpe of revelation supernaturall and divine." They "are investigable, the knowledge of them is generall, the worlde hath alwayes beene acquainted with them." Their existence was "not agreed upon by one, or two, or few, but by all. . . . this lawe is such that being proposed no man can reject it as unreasonable and unjust." He regarded natural law as a precious gift of God which, by linking human beings to the universe, provided them with the deepest existential security. Such views were common among scholastic theologians and philosophers, both Protestant and Catholic.

Most thinkers believed that law was, as Suarez put it, "written in the hearts of men," i.e., implicit in human nature itself and comprehended by "right reason." This testifies whether "a man does ill or well when he resists or obeys its natural dictates," whether the law has a written form or not. Reason also testifies that law "be enacted for the common good." In

substance, this view resembles medieval natural law theory, but for Suarez
it had lost its cosmic foundation and was based on reason alone. For Bodin,
"a true king" was a ruler who observed "the laws of nature as punctiliously
as he wished his subjects to observe his own laws, thereby securing to them
their liberty, and the enjoyment of their property." Montaigne suggested
that "the laws of nature as shown by the Golden Age" provided the best
model for legal reform, though he failed to specify their content. A Spaniard
worried that unidentified persons were seeking to turn Spain "into a nation
of enchanted people who live outside the natural order." Paruta assumed
an immutable "nature" as the basis of politics, and for Campanella, offended
by Venetian particularism, true liberty depended on universal conformity
with nature. Indeed, for all the skepticism underlying Calvin's own thought,
Puritans never gave up trying to identify the laws of nature. Because natural
law theory was assumed to reflect the order of the cosmos under the monarchy of God, it led some theorists generally to favor monarchy; but it could
also be cited to support republicanism, as in the *Politics Methodically
Digested* (1603) of the German Calvinist Johannes Althusius.

The most fruitful conception of natural law, largely because of its flexibility, was that of Hugo Grotius, worked out in *On the Law of War and Peace*
(1625), which would set the agenda for political thinkers through the
eighteenth century. Grotius gave a more realistic account of natural law by
basing it on self-interest as implicit in human nature. He agreed to this
extent with the Aristotelians on the natural sociability of human beings. But
he also recognized that self-interest is variously conceived, and that legal
systems differ and change over time; these realities needed to be taken into
account, and this required flexibility. In addition, Grotius contributed to the
secularization of political thought. "What we have been saying," he insisted,
"would have a degree of validity even if we should concede . . . that there
is no God, or that the affairs of men are of no concern to him."

Hobbes's *Leviathan* stretched natural law theory beyond what most contemporaries could accept, but his version was driven by the same, indeed
by an even greater, concern for order. For Hobbes, who had lived through
the civil wars in England, the state of nature would by no means be the
golden age idealized by some of his contemporaries. Life without the protection of laws and government would be "nasty, brutish, and short." Under
such conditions the only right implicit in nature would forbid doing "that
which is destructive of [one's] life, or taketh away the means of preserving the same; and to omit that, by which he thinketh it may best be preserved," for "Right consisteth in liberty to do, Whereas LAW determineth,
and bindeth to one of them." Under these conditions self-preservation

dictates to everyone "to endeavor peace." Hence all should be "willing, when others are so too, as farre-forth, as for Peace and defence of himselfe he shall think it necessary, to lay down this right to all things: and be contented with so much liberty against other men, as he would allow other men against himselfe." Hence Hobbes's highly original conception of the social contract: it was not an agreement between governor and governed but agreement only among the governed to subordinate themselves unconditionally to the ruler. This was the most extreme expression of this common need of the age.

Custom and customary law were also expected, ideally, to mirror nature and reason. Aldo Manuzio represented the customary law of Venice as an expression of "civil reason." In France, Du Vair treated custom as the equivalent, for common folk, of rational thought for Stoic philosophers. For Sir Edward Coke, its systematizer, the common law of England had its source in "sages," a word that hinted at an origin in nature:

> to the end that all the Judges and Justices in all the several parts of the realm, might, as it were, with one mouth in all men's cases pronounce one and the same sentence . . . wherein if you observe the unity and consent of so many several judges and courts in so many successions of ages, and the coherence and concordance of such infinite, several, and diverse (one, as it were with sweet consent and amity, proving and approving another) it may be questioned whether the matter be worthy of greater admiration or commendation, for as in nature we see the infinite distinction of things proceed from some unity, as many flowers from one root, many rivers from one foundation, many arteries in the body of man from one heart . . . this admirable unity and consent in such diversity of things, proceeds only from God the fountain and founder of all good laws and constitutions.[6]

Basing law on unchanging reason and nature had the advantage of making it immune to alteration. Montaigne, though arguing the point, believed variability in the law more dangerous than any benefit of reform:

> The worst thing I find in our state is instability; and the fact that our laws cannot, any more than our clothes, take any settled form. It is very easy to engender in a people contempt for their ancient observances; never did a man undertake that without succeeding. But as for establishing a better state in place of the one they have ruined, many of those who have attempted it have achieved nothing for their pains.

Quite different, though at least as useful for the maintenance of order, were what Hooker called "positive" laws, which, lacking such foundations, were neither universal nor immutable. A positive law, for him, bound "them that receyve it in such thinges as might before have bene either done or not done without offence, but not after during the time it standeth in force. . . . But there is no person whom nor time wherein a law naturall doth not bind."[7] Positive laws were adaptable to the varying needs of time and place and also—usually—had the virtue of simplicity. Theoretically dependent only on the will of the ruler, they did not require approval by any other agency, although their enforcement was another matter. Hobbes's whole view of law was of this kind. "Nature" itself, for him, knew no laws; it could not be depended on to distinguish between right and wrong. He attacked Coke for thinking that law could be based only on custom and precedent.

But laws could not, by themselves, order society; they had to be enforced by rulers with sufficient power to maintain order. The effectiveness of positive law especially depended on this. In addition to laws, therefore, the times were widely thought to call for an unprecedented empowerment of princes, and the justification of such power was now a major concern of political thought. Every sort of model and argument was exploited to this end, including the traditional analogies with a cosmos unconditionally ruled by God and the family under the absolute rule of the father; a king was father of his country. All these were exploited by Bodin, in his *Six Books of the Commonwealth*, in which nature figures again:

> Seeing that the family, which is the true image of the commonwealth, has only one head . . . all the laws of nature point towards monarchy, whether we regard the macrocosm of the body, all of whose members are subject to a single head on which depend will, motion, and feeling, or whether we regard the macrocosm of the world, subject to one Almighty God. If we look to the heavens we see only one sun. We see that even gregarious animals [are] never subject to many leaders, however good they may be.

Bodin also emphasized the difference between the sexes: so, he argued, the father of the family has a natural right to command, first "in the literal sense of marital authority, and second in the moral sense of soul over body and reason over concupiscence, which the Scriptures always identify with the woman." But the father also possesses "a natural right of command" as "the image of Almighty God, the Father of all things." For Bodin, public order had its foundation in the reverence of children for parents, a reverence whose decline had destroyed the Roman empire. Children "who stand in little awe of their parents and have even less fear of the wrath of God," Bodin argued, "readily set at defiance the authority of magistrates."[8] The patriarchal case for absolute monarchy would be developed most elaborately in Robert Filmer's *Patriarcha* (1680, but preceded by earlier works), which argued that, "as the father over one family, so the King, as father over many families, extends his care to preserve, feed, clothe, instruct, and defend the whole commonwealth." The king's subjects were presented in such discussions as weak and helpless, like children but hardly childlike. In France, similar arguments were presented in coldly rational rather than sentimental terms.

Since the father represented divine authority, patriarchy was closely related to the notion of the divine right of kings, a status that also countered papal claims to ultimate sovereignty. The traditional argument from the two swords, originally intended to separate church and state, was now losing ground, as princes, Catholic as well as Protestant, increasingly interfered in the administration of churches. Even Bellarmine had admitted that all political power came "immediately from God," a position that temporarily discredited him in Rome. Hooker, too, citing the standard Pauline text, insisted that

> power is of divine institution when either God himself doth deliver or men by light of nature finde out the kinde thereof. So that the power of parentes over children and of husbandes over wives, the power of all sortes of superiours made by consent of commonwealths within themselves or growne from agreement amongst nations, such power is of Godes own institution.[9]

Princes were now commonly described as "images" of God. Christophe de Thou, president of the Parlement of Paris, spoke in an address to Charles IX of the joy of the court "at seeing before them the image and power of God represented in their king, seated in the throne of his majesty." Even the Huguenots supported the divine right of the French king. James I compared kingship to divinity:

> Kings are iustly called Gods, for that they exercise a manner or resemblance of Divine power upon earth. For if you will consider the Attributes of God, you shall see how they agree in the person of a King. God hath power to create, or destroy, make or unmake, at his

pleasure, to give life, or send to death, to iudge all, and to be iudged nor accountable to none: To raise low things, and to make high things low at his pleasure, and to God are both soule and body due. And the like power have Kings.[10]

Italian writers, however, so close to Rome, rarely asserted notions of the divine right of secular rulers.

But divine right was also claimed for every government, including republics such as Venice and that of the Dutch. Sarpi considered the authority of the Venetian republic to be as unrestricted as that of the most absolute kingdom. He argued that every aspect of Venetian life, including private property, was under the jurisdiction of the government and that no private person could challenge it. Every state, he believed, whatever its size, can claim all powers necessary to maintain order.

Otherwise there was general agreement that monarchy alone could maintain order. Bodin believed that "the right to command on one side, and on the other the obligation to obey" were the essence of social order. Bellarmine condemned both aristocracy and democracy as contrary to the basic principle of order that "some should command and others should obey." Botero argued, more pragmatically, that monarchies lasted longer than republics—a major consideration in an anxious age. Sidney's *Arcadia* described the chaos resulting from the absence of a monarch.

The authority of rulers was also strengthened by a novel conception of sovereignty. Bodin defined it sweepingly as "the most high, absolute, and perpetual power over the citizens and subjects in a commonwealth." Whatever the form of government and whatever its size, it was its own *summum imperium*, i.e., without a superior, its authority limited only by natural law. This meant that a state consisting of only three families had as much authority as an empire: the elephant, as Bodin put it, was "no more an animal than the ant." He admitted that sovereignty might originally have been conferred by popular choice, but that the choice once made—here he anticipated Hobbes—was unconditional. It created "a sovereign and perpetual power to dispose of property and persons, to govern the state as [the sovereign] thinks fit, and to order the succession in the same way that any proprietor, out of his liberality, can freely and unconditionally make a gift of his property to another." More generally it included the right to issue laws binding on all but itself. Bodin was aware of his own originality; no thinker, he claimed, had brought forth such a doctrine before. Its significance was dramatized throughout Europe when it was challenged by the papal interdict imposed on Venice in 1606; and Venetian resistance to Rome created sympathy even among the major Catholic powers. The papacy would not again make such a mistake; the principle of sovereignty had triumphed.

Bodin's position was in some respects developed after the fact; the kind of absolutism that he described theoretically was generally in the air. Patrizi had recognized that in Italy a prince, whatever his title, "is called absolute who is unrestricted lord over laws and arms." Botero conceived of politics as little more than an expression of the will of the prince. Gallican theorists were moving from an emphasis on the autonomy of the French church to claims of royal sovereignty that, in important matters, excluded intervention by the pope. Jean Du Vergier de Hauranne, the future Abbé de Saint-Cyran, even argued that in some circumstances it might be the duty of a subject to commit suicide for his king. In England, James I believed in his own absolute power over the lives and property of subjects; and the autocratic claims of Charles I, vividly dramatized in court masques, were making English lawyers increasingly uneasy; eventually they would provoke a civil war between factions representing the rival claims of royal absolutism and the power of custom. In Campanella's City of the Sun there were no private rights, whether in property, family or household; even procreation was regulated.

An unqualified doctrine of princely sovereignty transformed entire populations, who in another political context might have been citizens, into subjects. It meant a total repudiation of the Renaissance ideal of the active life of political responsibility. The prince, elevated far above his subjects, was now responsible for every aspect of government; the subject could only obey. It is hardly surprising that Bellarmine, the loyal servant of the ruler with the most autocratic claims in Europe, saw little value in public life. For secular polities, the rule of the prince meant the withdrawal of his subjects, or at least those sufficiently affluent, into a life of contemplative repose, the ideal represented by Lipsius's *On Constancy*. Among other Stoics only Du Vair still believed in the responsibilities of citizenship. Charron took no interest in the public sphere. Bodin was ambivalent about whether civic responsibility extended to subjects. A prince could hardly do without the help of ruling elites, but, transformed into courtiers, they served only at his pleasure.

It is not clear that European society was better ordered by this doctrine, which (at least theoretically) vested all power in central government. Hierarchical conceptions by no means disappeared. The main result was perhaps that everywhere individuals and such intermediate bodies as guilds and ecclesiastical organizations, although they clearly persisted, were vulnerable to the pressures of central government.

Meanwhile the empowerment of rulers seems chiefly to have given them the resources to engage in wars with one another. The problem was not simply that some rulers were moved to conquer others; as J.G.A. Pocock has remarked, rapid change had made all princes insecure and likely to act aggressively. The results included constant tension between France and the Habsburgs in Spain and central Europe that culminated in the Thirty Years' War; the prolonged struggle of the Netherlands for independence from Spain, known in Dutch history as the Ninety Years' War, in which France and England were occasionally involved; and constant friction between England and Spain both in Europe and overseas, punctuated by such great actions as the defeat of the Spanish Armada in 1588.

In some measure these were also religious wars, not altogether independent of the civil wars in France, in which political and religious conflict were hopelessly entangled. Religious passion contributed to the cruelty of warfare. Meanwhile competition for control of the seas, increasingly a source of wealth, also played a part in international conflict. The lawyer John Selden was developing Britain's claims to control the surrounding seas. The general belligerence was only temporarily relieved by peace agreements worked out around the turn of the century: between France and Spain in 1598, Spain and England in 1604, the Habsburg monarchy and the Turks in 1606, Spain and the Netherlands in 1609.

The wars stimulated among thoughtful men a profound and widespread yearning for peace. Their country having long been ravaged by outsiders, Italians particularly longed for peace. Stoic love of personal peace was paralleled by Lipsius's hatred of the wars that disturbed it. "If I love quietness and rest," he wrote, "the trumpets and rattling of armor interrupt me. If I take solace in my country gardens and farms, the soldiers and murderers force me into the town." His admiration for ancient Rome was driven by a "sincere desire to teach students and educated readers the meaning of the *pax romana* and *power* as the only deterrent to revolution and anarchy in Europe." Montaigne, deeply troubled by the civil wars in France, suggested that "peccant humors which contaminate our body at the moment may keep our fever still at its height and in the end bring on our total ruin"—again the imagery of disease. The only remedy he could think of was to deflect the warring factions into foreign campaigns. The savagery of warfare had increasingly troubled idealists, among them Giordano Bruno, who had coupled a plea for peace with an argument for religious toleration:

There are vicissitudes of light and darkness and the present time of darkness is afflicted by quarreling sects. Breaking the law of nations and consequently the order instituted by the true God, these dissolved the bonds of society, being moved by misanthropic spirits, ministers to the infernal furies, who put the sword of discord between the peoples, as though they were mercuries descending from heaven, imposing all kinds of impostures. They set man against man and break the law of love. . . . True religion should be without controversy and dispute, and is a direction of the soul. No one has a right to criticize or control the opinions of others, as today, as though the whole world were blind.[11]

A near-contemporary, the Duc de Sully, outlined in his *Memoirs* a project to bring peace to Europe by the impractical suggestion that it be reorganized under the hegemony of France.

This period also saw, therefore, the development of interest in the regulation of warfare by a body of international law already developing in Spain, where theologians had been troubled for some time by the conquests of native peoples. The most influential figure among those who sought to regulate and reduce the horrors of war was Hugo Grotius. Grotius called for limits to what was permitted in war. "Least of all should it be admitted," he argued, "that in war all laws are in abeyance. On the contrary war ought not to be undertaken except for the enforcement of rights; when once undertaken, it should be carried on only within the bounds of law and good faith." And in spite of his readiness to take up arms for others, even Don Quixote deplored war, especially since it now employed artillery. Bodin himself called attention to the practical benefits of peace by attributing the prosperity of Venice to its pacifism. But such sentiments had little effect, though they would be repeated again and again for centuries.

CHAPTER FIFTEEN

Order in Religion

That this period was one of religious ferment, both Catholic and Protestant, is well known. The result had been a division that fractured the unity of Christendom, undermined old religious beliefs, and compounded political and social conflict. Consequently, there was a reaction toward stability, order, and control closely related to the movements in politics reviewed in the last chapter. It can be discerned in all parts of Western and central Europe and in most communities of faith, new as well as old; Protestants as well as Catholics participated in a "counter-reformation" directed against uncertainty and change.

It was facilitated by a general assumption that churches, whatever their beliefs, should function as agencies of social control; religious conformity was commonly identified with respect for political authority, religious deviation with rebellion against social order. Thus the persecution of religious minorities was commonly justified, as by Thomas More, not on religious but on political grounds. Botero argued that without religion a state would "have little strength and stability" and that of all religions Christianity served this purpose best, Catholicism best of all. No state, he insisted, could prosper without religion; for this reason, even an Indian prince had been known to promote Christianity. Religions were commonly described as "laws," and their political value was emphasized. Mariana praised religious unity as essential to the order and survival of states, and a learned friar depicted Christ as the legislator *par excellence* described by both Plato and Aristotle. One Englishman argued that, since Christianity supports civil authority, the best way to bring people to obey their betters is "to plant the gospel." Hobbes treated all religions in this way, Christianity being exceptional for him only because ordained "by Gods commandement and direction." Grotius emphasized God's concern, as ruler of the universe, to maintain the good order of states by punishing disobedience to his laws.

Conversely, in religious polemic crass political motives were commonly discerned in the views of one's opponents. As Wotton remarked of Italy, "He that taketh religion in these countries to be anything else than a point of state may peradventure be deceived."

The argument for the political use of religion was usually associated with an insistence on unity of religion within states. For Bellarmine, "freedom of belief" was "nothing but freedom to err," so that rulers, "if they wish to be faithful to their duty, must not in any way concede this liberty." This concern was often supplemented by the identification of all free expression with error. In a legal opinion submitted to the Venetian government, Sarpi pointed out that words may seem "of little moment," but "from words opinions come into the world that cause partisanship, seditions, and finally wars." For Hooker, disputes about religion were "not onely the farthest spred, because in Religion al men presume themselves interested alike, but they are also for the most parte hotlier prosecuted and pursued then other strifes, for as much as coldnes which in other contentions may be thought to proceede from moderation is not in these so favourably construed." Bacon thought religion the chief bond of human society, so that it was "a happy thing when itself is well contained within the true bond of Unity." Bodin believed that the discussion of religious issues should be discouraged because it led to social division. Even Montaigne, however freely he expressed himself, had reservations about such freedom for others:

> Our mind is an erratic, dangerous, and heedless tool; it is hard to impose order and moderation upon it. And in my time those who have some rare excellence beyond the others, and some extraordinary quickness, are nearly all, we see, incontinent in the license of their opinions and conduct. It is a miracle if you find a sedate and sociable one.

It was right, therefore, "to give the tightest possible barriers to the human mind."[1]

Governments, even if little concerned with the substance of faith, were thus likely to identify religious dissent with rebellion. The French *parlementaire* Étienne Pasquier summed up common opinion on this point:

> The general foundation [of a state] is principally dependent on the establishment of religion, because the fear and reverence of religion keeps all subjects within bounds more effectively than even the presence of the prince. Therefore the magistrates must above all other

things prevent the mutation of religion or the existence of diverse religions in the same state.

Religious diversity was thought to lead only to "partisanship and internal discord, which turn into civil wars, which in turn bring about the decline and fall of republics."[2] Such considerations also lay behind the arguments of Lipsius, chiefly expressing his concern with peace, for enforcing religious uniformity; this explains why, in spite of his conversion to Catholicism, his *Politics* was put on the Index. Hooker saw the first duty of government as the maintenance of religion because religious men made the best subjects.

But the major pressure for religious uniformity was the deep need of contemporaries for certainty; any wavering from orthodoxy provoked profound insecurity and charges of insincerity. Sarpi was convinced that his opponents were either hypocrites or lunatics. Bullinger's relaxed view of predestination was under growing attack in Zurich; and even in Basel, whose tolerance of religious diversity so struck Montaigne, a printer was fined and imprisoned in 1577 for publishing works advocating it.

This helps to explain why each of the major religious groups in spiritually divided Europe felt compelled to define its position in official creeds. Catholicism had the decrees of the Council of Trent, confirmed by Pius IV in 1564. Lutheran orthodoxy, after a period of struggle among conflicting parties, was defined in the Formula of Concord (1577). The reformed churches generally accepted the decrees of the Synod of Dort (1619), where—it had not been so earlier—an extreme definition of predestination was made official. Although it was intended for the Calvinists of the Dutch republic, the synod was attended by delegates from other reformed churches, including the Church of England; subsequently even Zurich, which had not formally endorsed predestination, went along with it. The Church of England, meanwhile, had an additional doctrinal standard in the Thirty-Nine Articles, promulgated by Queen Elizabeth in 1563, in theology basically Calvinist. Catechisms to accompany these creeds served to educate the faithful in all major groups.

None of these efforts to standardize religious belief was immediately or more than locally successful; even the decrees of Trent were opposed by many Catholics, in France primarily on political grounds as limiting the power of the king. But the various creeds nonetheless contributed to a profound change in the understanding of Christian belief. It had doubtless often been grasped mechanically, as a list of dogmas to be affirmed. But at deeper levels faith had never been mere assent to propositions. Faith was not so much that *in* which one believes, which might find expression in dogma, but that *by* which one is empowered to believe, a divine gift. Now creeds tended, for the sake of uniformity and order, to convert it from the internalized ground of belief into dogmas identified with and holding together particular religious bodies. Thus among Protestants, "justification" could be understood as the result of a correct *doctrine* of justification, and "religion" as a set of propositions was identified as the "faith." Hobbes, always primarily concerned with order, made the point: "by *Believing in,* as it is in the Creed, is meant not trust in the Person; but Confession and acknowledgement of the Doctrine." This was to reverse what had been central to earlier Protestantism.

The results for understanding Christianity were major. Scripture and the church fathers were transformed from wellsprings of faith into sources for proof texts of dogma, as in the teaching of Philippe de Gamaches, a theologian at the Sorbonne. The sense of mystery receded in the face of formulas. Miracles were increasingly understood not *in* faith but as proofs *of* faith. Belief itself was no longer a gracious gift but a dutiful and passive acceptance, or even an act of will. "Since I am not capable of choosing for myself," as Montaigne wrote, "I accept other people's choice, and stay in the position where God put me. Otherwise I could not keep myself from rolling about incessantly." He was a Christian, he observed, because of an accident of birth. Pierre de l'Estoile was both flippant and poignant in explaining his remaining in the old church: "Though she be a whore, still she is my Mother!"

Many in this period were fideists in the sense of accepting the faith proclaimed by their own group, personally unexamined and taken on the authority of its tradition and leadership. On this basis earlier Protestants had tended to a biblical fideism; Catholics invoked the authority of the church, usually identified with the papacy, which promoted fideism at least among the laity as protection against criticism. Ignatius Loyola supported it; his "Rule for Thinking with the Church" included a resolution to believe "that the white that I see is black, if the hierarchical Church so defines it." The professed fideism of Hobbes may have been chiefly prudential. This radical rationalist observed that much in Scripture was "above reason," and he compared "the mysteries of our Religion" to "wholsome pills for the sick, which swallowed whole, have the vertue to cure; but chewed, are for the most part cast up again without effect."

But although uniformity of belief could be proclaimed, it could not always be maintained, especially in Protestantism, which had after all originated in the defiance of higher authority and continued to splinter into sects that abandoned state churches. Even in Catholicism there was resistance to the decrees of Trent, in spite of—sometimes because of— their promulgation by Rome; submission had political as well as religious implications. The result was to externalize beliefs that for earlier reformers resided in the "hearts" of the faithful, but were from the standpoint of orthodoxy too likely to be variable and uncontrollable.

Meanwhile increasing attention was given to Scripture and the teachings of the church fathers, though chiefly to confirm the correctness of the creeds. Thus the kind of scholarship represented by Erasmus persisted, though in a different spirit. Its description of the historical foundations of Christian belief was described as "positive theology" to distinguish it from scholastic theology. It was subdivided in turn into biblical exegesis, patristics, the history of dogma, and ecclesiastical history, and was now promoted by the papacy. Gregory XIII and Sixtus V were both patristics scholars. In 1592 Sixtus sponsored a major revision of the Vulgate, to which Bellarmine contributed. Paul V decreed that every religious order should establish professorships in Hebrew, Greek, and Latin, the languages needed for positive theology. The University of Louvain was a major center for such study, and Catholic scholars produced vast works of biblical and historical scholarship. Denis Petau and Cornelius à Lapide prepared massive biblical commentaries. Meanwhile Bellarmine, who, though primarily a scholastic theologian, was also steeped in the methods of positive theology, reviewed all of Christian literature in his *De scriptoribus ecclesiasticis*, from antiquity to the sixteenth century, with special attention to the fathers. Protestant scholars too drew on his patristic learning.

Protestants were also devoted to positive theology. Their emphasis on *scriptura sola* (Scripture alone) guaranteed continued study of the Scriptures, although Protestant exegesis now tended to transform them into an objective record to be grasped and ordered intellectually. Hooker argued for more systematic exegesis based on learning and diligence rather than imagination and claims to personal inspiration.

> I holde it for a most infallible rule in expositions of sacred scripture, that where a litterall construction will stand, the farthest from the letter is commonlie the worst. There is nothinge more dangerous then this licentious and deludinge arte, which chaungeth the meaning of wordes as alchymie doth or would doe in the substance of meatals, maketh of any thinge what it listeth and bringeth in the ende all truth to nothinge.[3]

The Anglican bishop John Jewel, author of an influential *Apologia ecclesiae anglicanae*, celebrated his church's reliance on the fathers. He praised patristic learning and its value for interpreting Scripture, describing the fathers as "instruments of the mercy of God, and vessels full of grace." "We read them," he continued, "we reverence them, and give thanks unto God for them." The Lutheran theologian Johann Gerhard, who depended heavily on Bellarmine, provided a critical introduction to patristics. Bacon suggested how useful such products of clerical scholarship were, even for cultivated laymen. "That form of divinity which in my judgment is of all others most rich and precious," he wrote, "is positive divinity collected upon particular texts, not dilated into commonplaces, nor reduced into method of art." Such material, he thought, was the basis of "the best work in divinity since the Apostles' times."

But after the turn of the century, as theological polemics grew more intense, biblical and patristic studies were inadequate to provide the certainties so many needed. Biblical authority was all very well, but it sometimes could not, even for Protestants, resolve disagreements over interpretation. And as knowledge of the church fathers deepened, it was increasingly apparent that they too differed in emphasis, sometimes even in substance. Positive theology was also eventually discredited among Catholics by its association with Jansenism; and in relatively tolerant Belgium the trilingual college at Louvain was closed for many years after 1590. Positive theology was never supplanted, but it was forced to give way before systematic theology, which aimed to strengthen faith with rational proofs, for Protestants as well as Catholics.

The two approaches to religious truth were in some degree complementary; the demonstrations of scholastic theology were generally based on first principles ostensibly derived from Scripture, and on the conviction that reason, guided by faith, could illuminate its content. On this basis speculative and metaphysical thought became an integral dimension of theology, imposing on it an order and system that lasted into the twentieth century. A devout French physician testified to the value of such theology. It was not an art, he argued, but a true *science*, and not a fallible "human science" like medicine, "but purely divine; not invented by man but infused by God, concerning souls rather than bodies. It is eternal, infallible, immutable, having for object or subject Almighty God . . . having as its principal aim the soul, and, as its next object, moral philosophy."[4]

Scholastic procedures were reinvigorated and to some extent modified to suit new conditions. Its major representatives were Spanish followers of

Thomas Aquinas, beginning with the Dominican Francisco de Vitoria in the earlier sixteenth century, in a tradition carried on by Jesuit theologians, especially Luis de Molina and Francesco de Suarez in the seventeenth. Thomist Scholasticism was also influential at the University of Louvain, where it was represented by Leonhard Lessius, and at Rome by Bellarmine. By the early seventeenth century it was also dominant in Paris.

Thomists aimed for a total vision of God, man, and the universe based on both revelation and reason. According to Suarez, "Our philosophy must be Christian and the handmaiden of Divine Theology"; but it could also accommodate "metaphysical principles" provided they were "set forth and adapted in such a way as to confirm theological truths." Loyola required the dismissal from the Society of Jesus of any member hostile to Aquinas. The mentality scholasticism brought to theology is also suggested by a discussion of the phrase "necessary to salvation," which, by itself, seemed ambiguous to the French cardinal Du Perron, "for there is absolute necessity, and conditional necessity, necessity of means, and necessity of precept, necessity of special belief and necessity of general belief, necessity of act and necessity of approval," all requiring discussion and clarification. Pierre de l'Estoile reported Du Perron's boast that he could prove equally the existence and the non-existence of God. When the influence of Thomism began to recede, it tended to be replaced among Catholics by the new rationalism of Descartes.

Scholastic method was also increasingly attractive to Protestants as the biblicism of Calvin gave way to a growing rationalism. Grotius sought to provide a rational foundation even for the atonement. François Turretin brought the systematization of Calvinism to a climax in his *Institutes of Theology*, published in 1680–83, which, in spite of a title recalling Calvin, was very different from his *Institutes*. Turretin distinguished between religious and scientific truth on the ground that "theology and faith" were more certain, since they depended "on indubitable principles and self-evident truths." Lutheranism had its scholasticism in the essentially Aristotelian formulations of various theologians, among whom the most prominent was Martin Chemnitz. Among Anglicans, Hooker, though his affection for it has been much exaggerated, praised "the light of reason" for determining "what lawes are expedient to be made for the guiding of his Church, over and besides those that are in Scripture." Many Puritans depended on rational argument, regarding fideism as "a papist trick."

These various efforts to establish the certainty of Christian belief, whether through a willed act of faith, the authority of the church, of Scripture and of Christian antiquity, or rational demonstration, may have quieted the doubts of individuals. They were not sufficiently reassuring, however, to quiet the anxiety of the authorities of church and state. Thus, along with efforts to lift the truths of religion above all doubt, institutional means to enforce conformity also seemed necessary; and creeds provided a means for evaluating orthodoxy, among both Protestants and Catholics. As Puritanism fragmented into a variety of sects, some socially as well as theologically radical, the Calvinism of the Church of England grew increasingly clerical and conservative; ministers told their congregations what to believe and dominated disciplinary proceedings, and there was growing pressure for conformity in English universities. Even in the relatively tolerant Nether-lands, the mathematician Simon Stevin, who recognized that the majority of his compatriots did not share its theology, endorsed conformity to the state church because he thought religion indispensable to social order. In the absolutist states of Germany, churches, both Catholic and Protestant, were largely assimilated into state bureaucracies. Although Copernicanism had been as abhorrent to Luther and Calvin as to the papacy and remained so to most Protestants, everywhere a conservative reaction to the disorders released by the reformations had begun. Church leaders affirmed the hier-archical organization of religious communities.

The reform of religious life may have been more effective in Catholicism, with its tradition of authority and organization, than in Protestantism. The Council of Trent, to be sure, had decreed that

> the clergy should feed the people committed to them . . . by teaching them those things that are necessary for all to know in order to be saved, and by impressing upon them with briefness and plainness of speech the vices that they must avoid and the virtues that they must cultivate, in order that they may escape eternal punishment and obtain the glory of heaven.[5]

But much of the impetus for Catholic reform came from bishops at the local level who transformed their dioceses from what had been chiefly administrative entities into instruments for the instruction and shaping of the lives of the people. The religious obligations of Catholics even in the countryside were enforced as they had not been before, aided by an increase in the numbers and authority of the lower clergy; and the rival authority of families over children was weakened. Church buildings, once places for eating and drinking, gossip and assignations, became specialized places of devotion. Confessions became more serious and searching with the intro-duction of the confession box and insistence on sincere repentance before absolution. Communions were more frequent, and adoration of the reserved sacrament became common. Devotion to Mary also grew, stimulated by the use of the rosary. The Jesuits aided in much of this reform, busying themselves with the preparation of writings for the religious instruction of the laity.

Meanwhile papal authority was growing, aided by the defeat of conciliarism, especially after the Council of Trent, where it had still been strong. Sarpi's interpretation of Trent as a great victory for Rome was misleading; the triumph of the papacy came chiefly in the following decades. While churches elsewhere were being subordinated to secular rulers, the papacy was imposing an increasingly absolute rule over the church in Italy that had long-range implications for Catholicism elsewhere.

The papal monarchy was promoted by various champions of the papacy, notably Bellarmine. "The Roman pontiff," Bellarmine insisted in an attack on conciliarism,

> has been established by Christ as pastor and head, not only of every particular church, but also of the whole assembled universal church. . . . Supreme ecclesiastical power is not in the church of the council if the pope is taken away. . . . The Roman pontiff is above the universal church and the general council without any exception, in such a manner that he recognizes no judge over him on earth.[6]

Bellarmine's arguments were equally directed against the claims of secular rulers over the church: "What has been offered and consecrated to God," he wrote, "what has thus become the possession of God himself, is absolutely outside the power of the secular prince." Support for the claim of papal infallibility, though still widely contested, was also growing; some theologians now argued that the pope alone had been given the privilege of defining the faith of the church, and even of settling matters of fact. The sensitivity of the papacy to criticism was displayed by the execution in Rome of a writer who, influenced by Tacitus, had dared to compare the pope to the emperor Tiberius. Claims of papal authority were also expressed in sermons delivered before the pope which purported to describe the order God had decreed for this world. According to one preacher, for centuries kings had "laid down before the most august altar of the Prince of the Apostles their swordbelt, sword, military cloaks, golden bracelets, royal diadem and scepter."

This vision of the past was accompanied by the consolidation of papal power both in Rome and, insofar as possible, throughout Europe; the papacy equated reform with uniformity in administration and obedience to the pope. An essential step in this direction was the conversion of the College of Cardinals into an instrument of papal governance. The college had developed, in the earlier Renaissance, into a kind of self-appointed aristocracy divided into factions which, in the later sixteenth century, had come to represent the rival interests of France and Spain. A series of popes after the final session of the Council of Trent in 1567 sought to end this situation. In 1583 Gregory XIII, without consultation or prior notice, suddenly appointed nineteen new cardinals. When the dean of the college, Cardinal Farnese, protested against this novelty, the pope responded that he had simply wanted to avoid long and wearisome discussion. He also revised canon law into a more effective instrument of papal absolutism. Sixtus V (1585–90) continued the work of centralization by organizing the cardinals into groups of bureaucrats with designated responsibilities, stressing that they were subordinate to the pope exactly as the apostles had been to Christ. Meanwhile laymen were officially excluded from the cardinalate, and in 1602 a work appeared with papal approval that, ignoring a major reform of Trent, dispensed cardinals who were also bishops from residence in their dioceses. The college was also weakened by a reduction in its non-Italian cardinals: fewer cardinals from France and Spain meant fewer cardinals independent of the pope. Paruta, as Venetian ambassador to Rome, noted in his dispatches how firmly the popes now controlled the college, ignoring it in making decisions and reproving its members for speaking too freely. The new edition of the Vulgate, revised by the pope himself and published over the objections of scholars, was another expression of this new absolutism.

The papacy also sought, if less successfully, to extend its influence over the church in Europe generally, aided by the Jesuits and other new orders and by its network of nuncios in the major capitals of Catholic states. A papal bull of 1591 insisted on the right of sanctuary in all sacred places, and an attempt was made to control the previously autonomous confraternities that had emerged spontaneously in earlier centuries. The papacy also claimed an exclusive right to designate saints, previously often created locally. There were numerous canonizations and beatifications in this period, including the start of proceedings on behalf of such recent figures as Ignatius Loyola, Carlo Borromeo, the reforming archbishop of Milan, and Philip Neri, founder of the Roman Oratory. Spurred on by a newly militant conception of a diocese—one archbishop of the period thought that dioceses should resemble "well-organized armies, which have their generals, colonels, and captains"—the papacy tried to end the nomination of bishops by secular rulers, required visits by bishops to Rome, and instituted a system of reports by all bishops on the fulfillment of their duties and the condition of their dioceses. By 1621 the papacy felt strong enough to condemn the interference of lay powers in papal elections.

It also tried increasingly (with variable results) to interfere in the dioceses of Italy. Clement VIII forbade the alienation of properties of the church and required the examination in Rome of Italian bishops-elect. The pope conferred the title of Grand Duke of Tuscany on Cosimo de Medici in 1569 for his alleged services to the church, a gesture with large implications for papal authority in political matters; he also forbade masses in Florence honoring Savonarola, that old enemy of Rome who was still venerated locally. The papacy dared even to contest claims of Spain over churches in Milan and Naples, now Spanish territories.

But the papacy was especially concerned about the church in France, which had traditionally claimed substantial autonomy and supported general councils. The pope excommunicated Henri III for his alliance with Protestants against the Catholic League, and declared Henri IV deposed as a lapsed heretic. Popes also had visions of leading a new crusade of Catholic powers against the Turks. To preserve such gains, actual and intended, Pope Paul V founded a secret archive. These assertions of papal absolutism paralleled the absolutist claims now being made by secular rulers.

Papal authority was also employed to crush subversive ideas. Paul IV issued the first modern papal Index of prohibited books in 1557, broadening it two years later; this revision condemned the complete works of some 550 authors as well as individual titles, though later editions of the Index were less sweeping. One result was to depress the printing industry in Venice. Sarpi, doubtless with this interest in mind, complained of papal interference with the international book trade and accused the papacy of altering texts subversive of its own claims. Local lists of prohibited books were also prepared by major theological faculties, as at Louvain and the Sorbonne. Many works by major Renaissance writers were eventually prohibited: all the writings of Machiavelli, Boccaccio, and Erasmus (a ban subsequently modified after suitable expurgation); major works of Lorenzo Valla, especially his attack on the authenticity of the donation of Constantine; the New Testament commentaries of Jacques Lefèvre d'Étaples; Castiglione's *Courtier* for its references to fortune (restored to favor after expurgation); writings of Patrizi and Telesio deemed subversive of Aristotle; works by heretics, including Bruno and Campanella; writings by Savonarola, still considered an enemy in Rome; Galileo's *Two Chief World Systems* for attacking Aristotelian orthodoxy; Sarpi's *Council of Trent*; works of the Jesuit Mariana for attacking autocracy; fideist writings, including Charron's *De la sagesse*, for undermining Christian beliefs by scorning arguments and proofs; William of Ockham for his populist ecclesiology; commentaries on the decrees of the Council of Trent for inviting discussion; and even writings of Bellarmine that had taken too limited a view of papal authority over secular governments. Living authors were also subjected to pressure. Lipsius, after his conversion to Catholicism, was called on to reconcile his Stoicism with Catholicism and forced to admit past errors. "I had wanted," he explained somewhat disingenuously, "to reconcile ancient philosophy to Christian truth; and while I was totally absorbed in that intellectual task, some things crept in and slipped out which perhaps have more of the flavor of the former than the latter. I do not justify myself, rather I promise to make a correction." He also protested his orthodoxy in letters to Bellarmine and Baronius, glossing over the Lutheran and Calvinist chapters in his earlier career. The Paduan philosophers who followed Pietro Pomponazzi on the immortality of the soul only avoided prosecution by Venetian protection. Montaigne found it wise to submit his *Essays* to the authorities in Rome, who professed themselves to be fully satisfied, although he subsequently felt it necessary to "clarify" some passages.

But although it is the Roman Church's effort to control ideas that has chiefly attracted attention, governments and churches everywhere aimed to suppress opposition. Sarpi argued for the general right of governments to ban books likely to cause disorder, and the Venetian state kept a close watch over writings deemed subversive of itself. It also refused to permit the publication of Boccalini's commentary on Tacitus for being too Machiavellian. In Palermo a work of Baronius was banned for casting doubt on Spanish sovereignty, and courts there could impose life sentences in the galleys for circulating writings without official approval.

Catholic and non-Catholic states alike kept careful watch over printing. In Bavaria books could not be printed by non-Catholics, and in Lutheran areas of Germany theological faculties censored writings and aided local authorities to take action against printers and booksellers. In France civil and religious authorities collaborated (and sometimes competed) to control the press; indeed, the Parlement of Paris condemned works of Bellarmine and Suarez for defending papal authority too sweepingly. Fear of ecclesiastical censure was also sufficient to distort many works of this period, including Bodin's *Commonwealth*, and must be taken into account in interpreting them. Bodin refrained, probably wisely, from publishing his *Colloquium of the Seven Sages*. Even Hobbes was careful to appear orthodox; this may help to explain his numerous biblical quotations.

As this suggests, the control of printing was not exclusively motivated by religious concerns. In England Hobbes argued for governmental control over all expression of opinion, and a printer lost his right hand for attacking a proposed marriage of Queen Elizabeth. Governments often censored astrological texts if their prophecies seemed likely to incite disorder.

For those who would not submit there were sterner measures, to general public approval; one of Bodin's protagonists emphasized "the fury of the mob in religious matters." Tasso depicted in his *Gerusalemme Liberata* a double crusade: against the infidel outside the church but also the heretic within. Jews too were sometimes discriminated against; anti-Semitic decrees of Paul IV, though repealed by Pius IV, were reinstated by Pius V; and Jews in the Dutch republic were refused permission to establish synagogues as late as 1612. Europeans generally agreed with Bellarmine that liberty of conscience was liberty to err.

The result was outward conformity; dissenters were driven to subterfuges and evasions of a kind that often make writings of the period seem vague, ambiguous, obscure, or contradictory. Calvin had given the name of "nicodemism" to the concealment of beliefs—after Nicodemus, who came to Jesus only in secret—and it was denounced by Catholics and Protestants alike. At the time of Galileo's trial, censorship was defended by a free-thinking Roman noble, who observed that "when free living has been corrupted, free speech must at times be shackled. Whoever does not do this in due time will accelerate, not prevent, tyranny." Galileo often tried to cover his true thought, though this did not save him in the end. Various self-protective stratagems were devised by writers. Bruno, perhaps imitating Rabelais, hid behind jocular paradoxes in the epistle to his *Ash Wednesday Supper*. Sarpi noted the need for caution, though he often failed to observe it, in his foreign correspondence. Grotius maintained, implausibly, in the prolegomena to his *Law of War and Peace*, that the views he expressed were wholly abstract and not directed to any controversies of the time. Spanish writers put dangerous ideas in the mouths of madmen. Another common tactic was "mental reservation," failure to reveal the whole of one's thought, which was defended by a popular handbook for confessors.

The perils of excessive boldness in discussing sensitive subjects were well known. The Roman Inquisition, or Holy Office, established in 1542, was eventually given jurisdiction over the whole of Italy, its powers expanded to include charges of blasphemy and magic as well as heresy. Its activity increased after the Council of Trent had clarified Catholic orthodoxy, reaching a climax in the last decade of the sixteenth century. The powers of the Inquisition were increased by the willingness of some Italian rulers, including the Grand Duke of Tuscany, to hand over accused heretics. Though its proceedings were secret, wide publicity was given to its sentences. Its condemnation of Galileo and the burning of Bruno are the most notorious of its sentences, but it did not ignore lesser offences. Paolo Veronese was summoned before it in 1573 for his alleged trivialization of a sacred subject by introducing into one of his paintings irrelevant detail. But in spite of this publicity, the activities of the Inquisition should not be exaggerated. It was responsible for fewer than a hundred executions of "obstinate" heretics, although it imprisoned many more.

It is hardly surprising that, as a result of the developments reviewed in this chapter, this period has not been much admired by historians of Christianity. There were occasional bright spots, including the mystical flowering in Spain, the Augustinian revival in France, and the generous formulations of Anglicanism by Richard Hooker. But on the whole the time was one of defensiveness and reaction, in which any sign of independence or originality was dangerous. Louis Dupré has interpreted its intolerance and cruelty as "symptoms of a religious tradition under siege." An element in it was doubtless also, in Max Weber's terms, the replacement of the charisma of the earlier Renaissance by routinization and bureaucratization. For Giorgio Spini, focussing on Italy, it was "an age without apocalypse," of religion without hope. Europe was generally reacting against the openness and freedom of the Renaissance, whose novelties were on the wane as a new chapter in the history of European culture was beginning.

CHAPTER SIXTEEN

Order in the Arts

For many in this anxious age, the arts were a particularly disturbing example of what had gone wrong with their culture. This increasingly popular area of experience (and precisely for that reason peculiarly suspect) often seemed to have lost its proper foundation in nature, traditionally the basis of all human art. Indeed, the conception of nature had itself become problematic; some artists seemed to be trying to disguise or replace with human inventions the realities in nature. And without the controls nature imposed on human creativity, instead of teaching order and morality, the arts tended in the opposite direction. They needed regulation by what Johann Huizinga described for an earlier age as a "system of conventional forms" (though "convention" was now, perhaps, too weak a conception) to rein in the "passion and ferocity" that threatened to make "havoc of life."

The chief culprit responsible for this disorder was identified by Burton as the undisciplined imagination, now too often lost in a chaos of unpredictability and absurdity. For Burton, doubtless thinking of the freedom of his own imagination, such liberty represented little more than brutishness.

> In time of sleep this faculty is free, and many times conceives strange, stupend, absurd shapes, as in sick men we commonly observe. His *organ* is the middle cell of the brain; his objects all the species communicated to him by the *common sense*, by comparison of which he feigns infinite others unto himself. In *melancholy* men this faculty is most powerful and strong, and often hurts, producing many monstrous and prodigious things.

Imagination worked with particular force, he believed, in poets and painters, among whom it should always be "subject and governed by reason."[1] Theodore Beza was at once more severe and more precise. He had himself published Latin verses in his youth, but later he rejected all human fictions as products of the fallen self.

Even rhetoric, the art so enthusiastically cultivated in the earlier Renaissance, was increasingly distrusted in favor of a "plain style" that valued above all, sometimes exclusively, precision in the use of words and logical order in sentences. As one of Bodin's protagonists argued in this changing climate, "nothing is more useful than clarity." The shift in emphasis has been described as the triumph of grammar over rhetoric; it was also, perhaps even more, the triumph of dialectic. Bacon's aim as a writer, as he put it, was "to set everything forth, as far as may be, plainly and perspicuously, for nakedness of the mind is still, as nakedness of the body once was, the companion of innocence and simplicity." Puritans in England, Ramists and Jansenists in France, and in general rigorists everywhere pointed as their model to "the simplicity of Scripture," requiring in sermons "plaine delivery of the Word without painted eloquence." The Huguenot poet Guillaume Du Bartas considered Scripture the model given by the Holy Spirit for all literature. The heroic couplet and other regularities were beginning to rule poetry.

The primary basis of the arts was now imitation, whether of timeless nature itself, or of the ancients who were believed to have imitated nature so successfully; following the ancients themselves was seen as imitation of nature at second hand. Imitation became a fundamental technique in education; through imitation of the great writers of the past, a writer still, culturally speaking, a child could move toward adulthood, a consolation especially to those who, like the English, felt backward. Roger Ascham had early recommended the imitation of the classics for a nation whose culture was still crude. "If ye would speak as the best and wisest do," he wrote, "ye must be conversant where the best and wisest are." Although the art of the Greeks was now increasingly appreciated, and Aristotle's *Poetics* was recognized as the supreme authority for theater, the chief guides to ancient practice in the other arts were still Roman: notably Virgil in poetry, Cicero in prose, Vitruvius in architecture. The result of following the ancients has often been described as "Neoclassicism"; the most admired modern artists were those who were thought to have absorbed most perfectly the rules governing the art of the ancients and thus came closest to the imitation of God's art in nature. From the practice and in some cases the explicit principles of these and other masters, rules for the arts were extracted and systematized, pointing to such formal virtues as unity and coherence, balance and symmetry, precision and economy of means, qualities increasingly required of all the arts.

In this context, the Italian critic Giason Denores distinguished good poems from bad "with the measure of art, and not art with the measure of poems; those who observe it are the perfect ones and those who do not observe it are the imperfect ones." The most admired modern artists were those who were thought to have absorbed most perfectly—which did not necessarily mean literally—the rules governing the arts of the ancients. This implied that imitation might operate at various levels. Slavish imitation was not admired; since the time of Petrarch, the greatest art was recognized to depend on the spirit rather than on detailed imitation of the model. Tasso made the point playfully, observing that although all girls may seem "beautiful and pleasing," they need no teacher because "nature teaches Art, though with some help from mothers and nurses."

Thus the arts, purified and controlled, could again be thought to improve morality and deepen faith. Federigo Zuccaro, a painter of international fame, applied this conception, making it even more sublime, to his own art in his *Idea of Painters, Sculptors, and Architects* (1607), which also depended on a traditional cosmic and hierarchical conception of nature. Art began, for Zuccaro, with the transmission, through the angelic hierarchies by God himself, of an idea grasped intellectually by the artist. His task was to imitate the divine creativity underlying all things, a conception of art that also implied that the highest art should not reflect passion, sense, or a will unguided by reason. Other artists attempted to follow similar principles. For Tasso, poetry, his own art, was superior to the other arts; its sublime task was to teach the right "by means of sacred images." For Jonson, the arts, originally a gift from heaven, should depict "the order of God's creatures in themselves"; he believed that artist best who could "apprehend the consequence of things in their truth." A similar inspiration has been attributed to the poets of the French Pléiade. For Scaliger, more daringly and perhaps risking blasphemy, the poet "maketh a new Nature and so maketh himself, as it were, a new God." It was an aspiration of composers, too, to create music reflecting the harmony in the heavens, the music of the spheres. In addition, the uses at least of visual art for describing and celebrating God's creations in nature gave it not only religious significance but a degree of importance for scientific knowledge. Artists of the earlier Renaissance had already aimed, as Vasari put it, at "the intelligent investigation and zealous imitation of the true properties of the natural world." In this way they were sometimes seen as engaging in a form of worship, and the arts of representation were often approached with a kind of awe. Such a conception also reinforced the reluctance of artists to claim originality, which might have suggested some far less sublime source for their art;

to venture beyond the imitation of nature would have seemed akin to blasphemy.

But obedience to these ideal principles was not enough. Art had also to— and properly performed would automatically—promote religion and morality. In his *Apologie for Poetry* Sidney argued that the imagination of the poet should penetrate through the appearances of this world to the real truth of things; by doing so it could inspire virtue. This made poetry superior to history. For Jonson, the essential task of a poet was to expound an "exact knowledge of all vertues, and their Contraries, with the ability to render the one lov'd, the other hated, by his proper embataling [fortifying] them." Similar conceptions were incorporated into the masques of Jonson and Inigo Jones at the court of James I; these depicted the monarch as a quasi-divine being from whom all the goods of nature and reason radiated, and whose influence could inspire heroic virtue in his subjects. From this standpoint it was especially incumbent on a Christian poet, according to one Italian critic, "to see whatever is appropriate to the imitation of each action, passion, character, by means of beautiful language in order to improve life and to live well and happily." Tasso complained of Ariosto's *Orlando Furioso*, the product of an earlier generation, that it lacked moral examples; it had allowed virtue to go unrewarded and vice unpunished. Even Don Quixote advised a father to praise a virtuous son for composing moral satires in verse, since,

> if the poet is decent in his habits, he will be so in his verses too. The pen is the tongue of the soul, and as ideas are there engendered, so will his writings be. And when kings and princes behold the miraculous science of Poetry in some wise virtuous, and grave subject, they honor, esteem, and enrich him, and even crown him with the leaves of that tree which the lightning never strikes, as if to show that men whose temples are honored and adorned by such crowns should be attacked by no one.[2]

But, more realistic than some of his contemporaries, Cervantes also recommended common sense in applying the principle:

> Fictions have to match the minds of their readers, and be written in such a way that, by tempering the impossibilities, moderating excesses, and keeping judgment in balance, they may so astonish, hold, excite, and entertain, that wonder and pleasure go hand in hand. None of this can be achieved by anyone departing from verisimilitude or from

the imitation of nature in which lies the perfection of all that is written.[3]

Religion and morality were generally assumed to teach the same lessons and to cooperate in enforcing the need for order. But in fact the ethic underlying the moralism of this age was more Stoic than Christian, a distinction not always clear to contemporaries. It emphasized the acceptance of conventional principles of social and political order. This moralism also attributed to favorite writers of the age qualities hardly conspicuous in their work: Montaigne, his deeper significance unappreciated, was applauded for a moral wisdom comparable to that of Seneca. This ethic was invoked so regularly that it could sometimes be repeated tongue-in-cheek and applied to politics by the mid-century iconoclast Thomas Hobbes:

> Nature (the Art whereby God hath made and governes the World) is by the *Art* of man, as in many other things, so in this also imitated, that it can make an Artificial Animal. . . . *Art* goes yet further, imitating that Rationall and most excellent worke of Nature, *Man*. For by Art is created that great Leviathan called a Commonwealth, or State (in Latin Civitas) which is but an Artificiall Man; though of greater stature and strength than the Naturall.[4]

But the notion of imitation as the basis of art was changing. As Europeans became more familiar and more comfortable with the classics, the ancients, as Thomas Greene has remarked, no longer mechanically imitated but, with nature increasingly "domesticated," treated the process more flexibly. Jonson had much to say about the larger possibilities of imitation. He recognized the paradox that imitation, understood literally, is impossible, since that which is imitated is an original; his own conception of imitation thus distinguished between taking in what is "crude, raw, or undigested," and having "a Stomache to concoct, divide, and turne all into nourishment." He also recognized degrees in imitation, for there was "never no Imitator ever grew up to his Author; likenesse is always on this side of Truth." Henri Estienne also sensed this problem; he advised writers "to imitate the ancients so skillfully" that their works would seem "not borrowed" but "the artist's own creation." Thus imitation, internalized, allowed in practice a high degree of creativity that helps to account for the quality of the arts in this period.

On the other hand the freedom such principles allowed had limits. Where the arts were at odds with authority in church or state, they invited repression. A number of figures whose names appear in this book were imprisoned for years (as in the case of Campanella) or even put to death (as in the case of Bruno) for heresies that have not been identified to this day. In addition, institutions were developed to enforce order in the arts, among them learned societies, usually initiated by cultivated laymen, who modeled their academies on what they imagined about the Platonic Academy in ancient Athens. These sprang up for the promotion and regulation of literature, science and the arts, and were eventually converted into more or less official agencies of oversight and control. The most important of the Italian academies was the Roman Accademia dei Lincei (or lynxes— associated with sharp eyes), established by a local noble, Federigo Cesi, in 1603. Galileo belonged to it. Its activity limited to scientific matters, it was officially forbidden to engage in "political controversies and every kind of wordy disputes" and required "to avoid every sort of disturbance." The Florentine Academy was given the task of expurgating Boccaccio's *Decameron*, though less for its sexual license than for its subversion of authority; among the changes required was the substitution of "student" for "priest" each time that word appeared in the text.

The French Academy had similar beginnings in 1629. It met at first informally to discuss literature, but a few years later it was taken over and henceforth supervised by Cardinal Richelieu. High moral and religious qualifications were required for membership, and it was assigned the task of "cleansing the language from the impurities it has contracted in the mouths of the common people, from the jargon of the lawyers, from the misusages of ignorant courtiers, and the abuses of the pulpit." Conversely, it was ordered to impose rules on the usages of French, in order "to render it pure, eloquent and capable of treating the arts and sciences." It rejected Rabelais as a model and condemned Corneille's play *Le Cid* for licentiousness. Descartes, Pascal, and Molière became members. It was, in short, directed to maintain the aristocratic character of French culture and to prevent those changes in usage that are typical of a living language. In this respect, as also in its elitism, it reflected the growing conservatism of the age. An analogous academy of science was also established in France, meeting at first informally in the house of Mersenne. Eventually it included Descartes, Gassendi, Pascal, and Hobbes, and its members were pensioned by—and in that way subject to—the French crown. Other French academies with similar responsibilities were eventually established for painting and sculpture, dance, music, and architecture. England had its Royal Society, a similar scientific organization under the auspices of the king, officially established in 1662. The result of such conceptions was a gradual movement toward order in science and the arts like that we have observed in other areas of European life.

All the arts were thought to require direction and control by the authorities of church and state; but, as the most popular and therefore potentially the most dangerous, theater was believed to need them most of all. It is also usually the closest among the arts to real life, which is rarely intrinsically orderly.

Some form of popular theater had probably always existed in the various European countries, consisting mostly in the beginning, as it was increasingly secularized, of homely farces, of which the English *Gammer Gurton's Needle* (1575), still performed today by undergraduates, is probably typical. The proliferation of traveling theater companies from Italy throughout Europe, whose repertoires sometimes displayed classical influence, standardized and gave more form to theater elsewhere. With the proliferation of native playwrights and theater companies, it quickly became the favored entertainment of all classes in most of Europe.

The lower classes were generally thought to prefer comedy, the upper classes tragedy, which usually traced the downfall of a person of high degree. But theater audiences were likely to be mixed; Shakespeare's ability to entertain all classes is well known. Corneille boasted of his ability to provoke laughter without introducing lower-class clowns into his plays. Madame de Scudéry, who maintained one of the most influential salons in Paris, also attended theatrical performances and complained of the quarrelsome, disruptive, and noisy "monster with many heads" that distracted her attention there. This also suggests the continued variety of Paris audiences.

Theater as the most popular of the arts rapidly attracted talented playwrights in most major countries. Among the most distinguished Italian playwrights were Torquato Tasso, best known for his *Aminta* (1573), and Giovan Battista Guarini, author of *The Faithful Shepherd* (1590). Shakespeare and Jonson are, of course, the best known among a large group of talented English dramatists. In France the most popular early playwright was Alexandre Hardy (1569?–1631), who was alleged to have written some eight hundred plays exploiting spectacle and violence, as we know from one of his upper-class admirers. In Spain, the greatest early dramatist was Lope de Vega, author also of a widely circulated prose work, *The New Art of Writing Plays* (1609).

As the popularity of theater grew, the authorities in both state and church felt compelled to take notice of it. As Madame de Scudéry had also remarked, plays are like "an apothecary's shop" that "contains both poisons and cures" and can be "either beneficial or dangerous." The first concern of rulers was the control of the theater-going populace, which required surveillance over plays that might be seditious or immoral. In Catholic countries the Index and Inquisition, though chiefly concerned with heresy, supplemented surveillance by governments. Much early Spanish drama was included on the Index of 1559; and a play by Lope de Vega about the conversion of Augustine was confiscated for indecency by the Inquisition. It also suspended other plays pending cuts. Italian theater, too, had to cope with the Inquisition; performances of classical drama there were attacked for suggesting the inescapability of fate, thereby denying free will.

Secular governments also watched theater closely. In Venice, surveillance over it was a responsibility of the notorious Council of Ten, ever on the watch for subversion. Various agencies in Venice inspected theater buildings, licensed productions, and controlled opening and closing times and even prices of admission. In England the youthful Jonson was briefly imprisoned for an early play deemed subversive. In Spain, the government approved and expurgated plays, forbidding performances during Lent or in convents. Cervantes perhaps approved; his friendly priest observes, though this may be the irony of the author, that many evils would cease

if there were some intelligent and judicious person at court to examine all plays before they are performed. . . . Then no magistrate in any town would allow any play to be performed without this man's approbation, under his hand and seal; and so the comedians would take good care to send their plays to Madrid, and could then act them in safety. The writers, too, would take more pains with their work, out of fear of the rigorous examination they would have to pass at the hands of someone knowing the business. In this way good plays would be produced, and the purpose of such entertainment successfully achieved: which is not only popular amusement, but also the good reputation of Spanish genius, the profit and security of the actors, and the avoidance of the need to punish them.[5]

In this atmosphere schools everywhere used theatricals to inculcate moral values. The playwright George Chapman thought "moral instruction, elegant and sententious excitations to virtue, and deflexion from her contrary" to be "the soul, limbs, and limits of an authentical tragedy," and his contemporary George Gascoigne praised comedy as "a figure of the rewards and punishments of virtues and vices." Thomas Heywood's *Apology for Actors* applauded theater as a stimulus to patriotism.

Theater was thus recognized as a resource for good, however dangerous; it was increasingly accepted, particularly for its value for the moral formation of society: comedy for unmasking vice, tragedy for purging the old Stoic bugbears of pity and fear. It was also appreciated for deeper reasons, though these may not have been often articulated. For, if the arts can be thought generally to "endow the world with meaning," theater may do so best of all and for a wide audience. It has a special ability to strip away distracting and irrelevant detail, to make what is hidden visible, to reveal the feelings underlying human interaction, to demonstrate the power of ideas, to hint at inwardness.

It is clear that, as was widely believed, theater could provide a practical, if sometimes morally ambiguous, schooling in life. Don Quixote commended theater to Sancho Panza as "instrumental in conveying a great benefit on the commonwealth," for plays represent truthfully both "what we are and what we ought to be." Jonson aimed in his plays, he claimed,

> to please . . . attentive auditors,
> Such as will joine their profit with their pleasure,
> And come to feed their understanding parts.

Whether theater should give more profit or more pleasure was sometimes debated, but the great French dramatist Corneille dismissed the argument as pointless since "it is impossible to give pleasure in accordance with the rules without including a great deal that is useful." Even Campanella, recognizing that theater was "both learned and beautiful," sought to incorporate it into his City of the Sun. It was not forgotten, after all, that theater had the sanction of antiquity. As Bacon observed, it had been "carefully watched by the ancients, that it might improve mankind in virtue, and great philosophers have thought it [was] to the mind as the bow to the fiddle."

And the benefits of theater were celebrated along with its evils. Madame de Scudéry said that since plays constitute "the finest branch of human literature," they "should not be rejected but corrected," although "solid judgment must control the impetuosity of genius, so that philosophical enlightenment, presented through stories, may become more readily and agreeably accessible to an audience."

Some plays might seem at first morally or politically dangerous, and they had to be introduced with caution. Plays about heroic pagans were sometimes accompanied by disclaimers, like that attached to Giovanni Della Porta's *Ulysses* (1614):

> The present tragedy is enacted by Gentiles [pagans]; and therefore if there are to be found such terms as fate, destiny, chance, fortune, the power and coercion of the stars, gods, and the like, they have been used to conform to their ancient customs and rites. But according to the Catholic religion, these words are but emptiness, for all consequences and all events are to be attributed to Blessed God, the supreme and universal cause.[6]

Secular theater might also be expected to pay its respects to faith, as at the end of *The Tempest*, when Prospero, having displayed the "magic power" of theater but in despair, his own powers "all o'erthrown," prays for grace.

But virtuous ancients, as well as biblical figures and saints, were often represented on stage as models to be emulated. Pious drama contrasted the blindness of human love with the illumination provided by celestial love. In the words of one Italian playwright:

> Truly the law by which Love rules the world is so just and right that in his kingdom, when one least hopes for reward of his service, the more he then receives. But human nature, which is imperfect, does not discern his celestial arts and manners and the unknown ways by which he places his followers in unhoped-for joy.[7]

But though theater everywhere emphasized the need for order in the self, it tended to take somewhat different forms. In England it focussed on resistance to fortune; in France on the control of passion, especially love; in Spain on the protection of personal honor.

The moralism absorbed and taught by theater in this age was, however, as I have noted, more Stoic than Christian, emphasizing duty to the family and the state and submission to providence. The strengths celebrated were those of reason, products of a proper education, enabling rational beings to triumph over fortune, at least within themselves. Morality thus became a product of a classical education, a "high" thing, largely confined to the upper classes who monopolized the power of control.

Much of this is apparent in the formal regularities based on what was thought to be ancient practice, especially as described in Aristotle's *Poetics*. This development began in France with the later plays of Corneille, especially after the criticism of his *Le Cid* (1636), a work based on his read-ings in Spanish literature; and Corneille's critics were backed by the French Academy. Henceforth the major French dramatists sought to maintain what came to be known as "the three unities" of time, place, and action. The first two were thought to discipline the wantonness of the imagination by requir-ing that the action on stage be as realistic as possible. The unity of time pre-scribed that the action, which actually took a mere two or three hours, should ideally be depicted as taking place in a space of time as close to that period as possible, preferably no more than a single day. Unity of place required the action to be limited to a single location, perhaps at most a single city. These two unities conformed to the principle of probability. Unity of action was a matter of organization. It called for a play to have three dis-tinct parts: a beginning, which introduced the main characters into a prob-lematic situation; a middle section that developed the action and increased suspense; and a conclusion that resolved the problem and provided the satisfactions of closure.

These principles were first propounded in France in 1572 by Jean de La Taille, who, citing Aristotle, argued that tragedy, in contrast to comedy, should be "in no way plebeian," that is, irregular and disorderly. Of the three unities, that of action was considered most important, as Lope de Vega pointed out in his influential *New Art of Writing Plays*:

> The play should contain one action only, seeing to it that the story in no manner be episodic; I mean the introduction of other things which are beside the main purposes; nor that any member be omitted which might ruin the whole of the context. There is no use in advising that it should take place in the period of one sun, though this is the view of Aristotle. . . . Let it take place in as little time as possible, except when the poet is writing history in which some years pass; these he can relegate to the space between the acts, wherein, if necessary he can have a character go on some journey; a thing that greatly offends whoever notices it. But let him who is offended not go to the theater.[8]

It has been suggested that this final unity obscurely reflected both the unity of the newly centralized monarchies and the pressures in this period for unity of belief.

Some of these principles had doubtless been followed instinctively by better playwrights everywhere; they distinguished serious theater from the miscellanies that often constituted popular entertainment. Sidney in England had earlier ridiculed popular theater for ignoring probability.

Jonson was already following the rules before the end of the sixteenth century.

In France they were increasingly explicit after the 1630s, and often, for more rigid minds, prescriptive. One of the more serious advocates of the rules, Jean Mairet, after beginning his discussion with "the rule of time," continued:

> I have enough respect for the ancients never to depart from their opinions and habits unless I am obliged to do so by a clear and pertinent reason. It seems quite apparent that they established this rule for the benefit of the spectator's imagination: experience shows that he derives incomparably more pleasure from a play composed in this manner than from one which is not: he sees the events without difficulty or distraction, as if they were actually happening before him, whereas if the time is extended, as it sometimes is ten or twelve years, the imagination is diverted from the pleasure of the spectacle, must try to understand how the actor who spoke in Rome in the last scene of Act I has reached Athens, or if you like Cairo, by the beginning of Act II.[9]

What was being controlled here, of course, was not only the structure of the play but the imagination of the audience, which, as we have seen, was considered a major source of the dangers lurking in the arts. By the middle decades of the seventeenth century, the chief principles governing serious theater were of this kind.

Not all playwrights, even in France, felt equally bound by the rules. Desmarets de Saint-Sorlin concluded a discussion of the subject by observing that "nothing noble will be achieved by minds worried by such laws. It's variety that delights and surprises us: a hundred fine effects combined in an action, giving rise to a swarm of diverse thoughts and reactions." Corneille himself insisted on flexibility in applying the rules. "It is a good thing," he argued, "for an author to take a chance at times, rather than abiding slavishly by regulations." The protagonists in plays, he insisted, citing the authority of Aristotle himself, "must be treated in accordance with verisimilitude and necessity," and in ways that gave pleasure to the audience. The great French classical playwrights of later decades succeeded in giving satisfaction to their audiences without slavish obedience to rules.

In general, however, it is hardly surprising that the arts in general and theater in particular, shackled by constraints, gradually lost their earlier vitality. The importance of the artist declined along with his individuality;

in Italy, even Bernini, though well rewarded financially, was never as much admired as Michelangelo. The universality of mind that had been common in the earlier Renaissance was declining; Galileo was still a man of a literary as well as a scientific culture, but Paolo Sarpi, so like him in other respects, had no interest in literature, especially poetry. He regarded Homer merely as the historian of a primitive age. Even the interest of Londoners in theater was declining after 1610, long before the closing of the theaters. The numbers of new plays fell, and Jonson himself stopped writing for the popular stage, turning instead to court masques and poetry for a smaller, aristocratic audience. Spanish theater declined as Spanish power ebbed; theater remained vigorous only in France, where it was primarily an expression of the values of the higher levels of society. The golden age of theater, as it has been commonly known, was coming to an end. Not the least among the elements in its decline was the discontent it stimulated in what I have described as the crisis of the self.

Conclusion

The past is often described as "a seamless web." But historians are generally concerned to distinguish one moment in the past from another and to identify, to explain, and to describe change. Sometimes the changes with which they deal seem to point chiefly in a single direction, and when this occurs the historian's task may be relatively simple. But in other cases—and this has been notably true for the period of the present book—change is varied, complex, multi-directional, and even contradictory. This explains the strategy required here. During the later sixteenth and earlier seventeenth centuries processes discernible in the earlier Renaissance continued and even reached a climax, but at the same time other changes moved in quite different and even contrary directions.

It has been the task of this book, therefore, to depict both kinds of change. Although they were occurring simultaneously, I have chosen to divide them into two groups and treat them consecutively. The first section of the book deals with movements that appear largely to continue and even to bring to a climax tendencies that have been conventionally associated with the culture of the Renaissance, a culture often treated as liberation from conventions inherited from the past. The first section of this book is intended to show the truth in this view of the Renaissance. But even as the movements of the Renaissance gathered strength, they were setting off a reaction in the opposite direction. The final section of the book describes this reaction against what were increasingly seen as the frightening excesses of the freedom traditionally associated with Renaissance creativity. A middle group of chapters is concerned to explain why this reaction occurred. But although these three major tendencies are treated successively in this book, and indeed were in some degree successive, all three were also occurring simultaneously and playing off against each other.

The eventual result would be a major alteration in the European cultural landscape, an alteration not so much absolute as still one of balance among opposing human needs operating at a very fundamental level. Balance historically, however, is usually precarious, as one set of changes stimulates a reaction in the opposite direction. The result for the period discussed in this book, as it seems to this historian, was a pattern of alternation; conflicting impulses were often simultaneously at work, without a clear resolution yet, between the creativity and spontaneity of cultural freedom and a growing tendency toward order and restraint. But the general impression this period presents is one of tension between the fundamental needs for both freedom and order. This tension, always precarious and often shifting, gives the period its special interest. During this time we can study both of the fundamental but competing needs met by human culture.

Notes

CHAPTER 1

1. Quoted by William Farr Church, in Orest Ranum, ed., *National Consciousness*.
2. Quoted by John Hale, *The Civilization of the Renaissance in Europe* (New York: Athenaeum, 1994), 284.
3. *Don Quixote*, trans. J.M. Cohen (Harmondsworth: Penguin Classics, 1950), 569. I cite this edition throughout.
4. *Of the Advancement of Learning* (1605), ed. G.W. Kitchin (London: Everyman, 1915), 59. I cite this edition throughout.
5. Quoted by Stephen Greenblatt, *Marvellous Possessions: The Wonder of the New World* (Chicago: University of Chicago Press, 1991), 10.
6. *Don Quixote*, 490.

CHAPTER 2

1. "Of Presumption," *The Complete Works of Montaigne*, trans. Donald M. Frame (Stanford: Stanford University Press, 1948), 484–5. I cite this edition throughout.
2. "Of the Inconsistency of Our Actions," 244, in *ed. cit.*
3. Thomas Hobbes, *Leviathan*, ed. Richard Tuck (Cambridge: Cambridge University Press, 1996), 70. I cite this edition throughout.
4. *The New Organon and Related Writings*, ed. Fulton H. Anderson (Indianapolis: Bobbs Merrill, 1960), 209.
5. *Of the Laws of Ecclesiastical Polity*, ed. Georges Edelen (Cambridge: Harvard University Press, 1977), I, 151. I cite this edition throughout.
6. *Apologie for Poetry*, in G.G. Smith, ed., *Elizabethan Critical Essays* (Oxford: Oxford University Press, 1904), I 156.
7. Quoted by Erwin Panofsky, *Idea* (Columbia: University of South Carolina Press, 1968), 87–8.
8. *Of the Laws of Ecclesiastical Polity*, V, 306–7.

CHAPTER 3

1. *Dialogue Concerning the Two Chief World Systems*, trans. Stillman Drake (Berkeley: University of California Press, 1953), 18, cf. 320; "Letters on Sunspots", in *Dialogues and Opinions*, 126–7.

2.   *Of the Advancement of Learning*, 25–7.
3.   Quoted by John Headley, *Tommaso Campanella and the Transformation of the World* (Princeton: Princeton University Press, 1997), 324.
4.   Quoted from "Pleasure Reconciled to Virtue" by Smuts, *Court Culture*, 89.
5.   Quoted by R. Hooykaas, *Humanisme, science et réforme: Pierre de la Ramée (1515–1573)* (Leiden: Brill, 1978), 15.

CHAPTER 4

1.   Jean Bodin, *Six Books of the Commonwealth* (1576), trans. M.J. Toohey (Oxford: Blackwell, n.d.), 109–10.
2.   Quoted by Thomas M. Greene, *The Light in Troy: Imitation and Discovery in Renaissance Poetry* (New Haven and London: Yale University Press, 1982), 265.
3.   Quoted by Katherine Duncan-Jones, *Sir Philip Sidney, Courtier Poet* (New Haven and London: Yale University Press, 1991), 170.
4.   Quoted by David Riggs, *Ben Jonson: A Life* (Cambridge: Harvard University Press, 1989), 197.
5.   Quoted by Nanerl O. Keohane, *Philosophy and the State in France: The Renaissance to the Enlightenment* (Princeton: Princeton University Press, 1980).
6.   *Anatomy of Melancholy*, 35–6.
7.   "Of the power of the imagination," 76.
8.   Quoted by Greene, *Light in Troy*, 34.
9.   *Anatomy of Melancholy*, 454.
10. Quoted by Hale, *The Civilisation of the Renaissance in Europe*, 560–1.

CHAPTER 5

1.   *The Ash Wednesday Supper*, trans. Edward A. Gosselin and Lawrence S. Lerner (Hamden: Archon Books, 1977), 88–90.
2.   Jean de Lery, *History of a Voyage to the Land of Brazil, Otherwise Called America*, trans. Janet Whatley (Berkeley: University of California Press, 1990), 67.
3.   *Two Bookes of Constancie*, trans. Sir John Stradling (London, 1594). I quote in the edition of Rudolf Kirk (New Brunswick: Rutgers University Press, 1939), 110.
4.   Jean Bodin, *Colloquium of the Seven about Secrets of the Sublime*, trans. Marion Leathers Daniels Kuntz, (Princeton: Princeton University Press, 1975), 154.
5.   "Of Coaches," *Essays*, 692–3.
6.   *Letters on Sunspots*, included in *Discoveries and Opinions of Galileo*, trans. Stillman Drake (Garden City: Doubleday, 1957), 34.
7.   Quoted by John Headley, "Campanella and the End of the Renaissance," *Journal of Medieval and Renaissance Studies*, 20 (1990), 164.
8.   Quoted by Arthur O. Lovejoy, *The Great Chain of Being: A Study of the History of an Idea* (Cambridge: Harvard University Press, 1948), 187.
9.   Quoted by Charles Webster, *The Great Instauration: Science, Medicine and Reform 1626–1660* (London: Duckworth, 1975), 17.
10. *Pensées*, no. 72; from the Modern Library edition (New York: Random House, 1941).
11. *Hamlet*, II.ii. 116–18.

CHAPTER 6

1. "Of Vanity," 758–9.
2. "Maxims of Prudence," in Giovanni Botero, *The Reason of State*, trans. P.J. and D.P. Waley (New Haven: Yale University Press, 1956), 46.
3. Quoted by Bouwsma, *Venice and the Defence of Renaissance Liberty* (Berkeley: University of California Press, 1965), 410–11. This debate is printed in Enrico Cornet, ed., *Paolo V e la Republica Veneta* (Vienna, 1859).
4. "Of Delays," *Essays*, 98–9.
5. *Methodus*, 158.
6. *Laws*, III, 32.
7. *Opere politici*, 128. For Paruta in general, see Bouwsma, *Venice and the Defence of Renaissance Liberty*, esp. Ch. V.
8. Bernard de Girard du Haillan, in his *Histoire de France* (1576), quoted by William Farr Church, *Constitutional Thought in Sixteenth Century France* (Cambridge: Harvard University Press, 1941), 80.
9. *Laws*, III, 334, 434–5.

CHAPTER 7

1. Most accounts of its religious history are shaped by denominational interests; but cf. the distinction between "religious" and "ecclesiastical" history in the fundamental article of Lucien Febvre, "Une question mal posée: Les origines de la Réforme Française et le problème des causes de la réforme," *Revue historique* CLXI (1929), reprinted in his *Au coeur religieux du XVIe siècle* (Paris, 1957), 3–70, and translated in *A New Kind of History from the Writings of Lucien Febvre*, ed., Peter Burke (London: Routledge, 1973), 44–107. Febvre's position is accepted, with reservations, by H. Outram Evennett, *The Spirit of the Counter-Reformation* (Cambridge: Cambridge University Press, 1968), 3.
2. Quoted by Tuck, *Philosophy and Government*, 63, from a seventeenth-century English translation, which I have slightly revised. Cf. the characterization of the movement by the Dutch theologian Hadrian Saravia, writing to the Archbishop of Canterbury in 1608, quoted by Tuck, 64: "Whatever is written about Christ in the New Testament is [for them] an allegory, which destroys its historical truth." Plantin, he continued, "verbally agreed with us in everything except the use of ceremonies and the outward worship of God. While admitting the latter to be necessary for the common people, he claimed it to be superfluous for the perfect. But the perfect should not despise it, lest they be a stumbling block to the weaker brethren."
3. *Laws*, I, 59.
4. "Apology for Raymond Sebond," *Essays*, 375.
5. Quoted by Greenblatt, *Ralegh*, 143.
6. *Laws*, II, 345–6.

CHAPTER 8

1. Quoted by Morford, *Stoics and Neostoics*, 109.
2. *Colloquium*, 37. Curtis the Calvinist is speaking.

3. Quoted by Delumeau, *Sin and Fear*, 131.
4. Quoted by Leah S. Marcus, *Puzzling Shakespeare: Local Reading and Its Discontents* (Berkeley: University of California Press, 1988), 65–6.
5. "Of Giving the Lie," *Essays*, 505.
6. *Anatomy of Melancholy*, 54.
7. *Ibid.*, 515–16.
8. Quoted by Greenblatt, *Ralegh*, 153.
9. Described by F. Gonzalez-Crussi, *The Day of the Dead and Other Mortal Reflections* (New York: Harcourt Brace, 1993), 79.
10. Quoted by Nancy Roelker, *The Paris of Henry of Navarre as seen by Pierre de l'Estoile*, (Cambridge: Harvard University Press, 1958), 24–5.
11. *Anatomy of Melancholy*, 80–1.

CHAPTER 9

1. An epigram of Sir John Davis, quoted by Andrew Gurr, *Playgoing in Shakespeare's London* (Cambridge: Cambridge University Press, 1987), 209.
2. Vaclav Havel, *Letters to Olga* (New York: Henry Holt, 1982), 250, 275.
3. The Duke of Gloucester, later Richard III, in *Richard III*, III.ii. 182–94.
4. *Macbeth*, I.5. 62–5.
5. Quoted in Duncan-Jones, *Sidney*, 21.
6. Quoted by Mullaney, *Place of the Stage*, 8.
7. From Stephen Gosson, *Plays Confuted in Five Actions* (1582), quoted by Gurr, *Playgoing*, 206–7.
8. Quoted by Barish, *Anti-Theatrical Prejudice*, 112.
9. Quoted in *ibid.*, 91–2.
10. *Anatomy of Melancholy*, 53.

CHAPTER 10

1. *Laws*, I, 65–6.
2. Quoted by Gary Tomlinson, *Monteverdi and the End of the Renaissance* (Berkeley: University of California Press, 1987), 23.
3. *Don Quixote*, 505.
4. "Of Repentance," 618–19.
5. Du Vair, quoted by J.B. Schneewind, ed., *Moral Philosophy from Montaigne to Kant* (Cambridge: Cambridge University Press, 1990), 211–12.
6. "Of Constancy," 137.
7. *Two Chief World Systems*, 56.
8. "Magic and Festivity," 637.

CHAPTER 11

1. *Two Books of Constancie*, trans. Sir John Stradling (1594), Rudolph Kirk, ed. (New Brunswick: Rutgers University Press, 1939), 80.
2. *Methodus*, 29–30. In this youthful work, however, perhaps fearing censorship, he admitted that such a view could not "satisfy a man of lofty soul."

3. *Moral Philosophy of the Stoics*, in Schneewind, 210.
4. Quoted by Ronald Levao, *Renaissance Minds and their Fictions*, 125.
5. "Of Three Kinds of Association," 622.
6. *Don Quixote*, 518.
7. *Leviathan*, 236–7.

CHAPTER 12

1. Domenico Morosini, in a letter to Casaubon, quoted by Cozzi, "I tra Canaye e Casaubon," 88.
2. *Anatomy of Melancholy*, 262–5.
3. *Two World Systems*, 53–4, using Sagredo as his mouthpiece.
4. Cf. Redondi, *Galileo Heretic*, 37; for Bacon, see Hooykaas, *Religion and Science*, 105.
5. Letter to the Duchess of Tuscany, in *Discoveries and Opinions*, 183, 196–7.
6. Quoted by Drake, *Discoveries of Galileo*, 223.
7. Cf. Blumenberg, *Copernican World*, 138–9.
8. *Two World Systems*, 129; but cf. 276–7, which seems less empathic. There is also a hint (pp. 397) that the new science, seen as a reflection of Platonism because of its mathematical foundations, suffered from the rivalry between the partisans of the two most famous philosophers of antiquity. Redondi, *Galileo Heretic*, 40, suggests that hostility on the part of the Aristotelians to Augustine, "father of heresies," was also at work. Cf. the introduction by John Patrick Donnelly to Robert Bellarmine, *Spiritual Writings* (New York: Paulist Press, 1989), 29, 39.
9. *The New Organon*, 28–9.
10. *Leviathan*, 33–5.
11. *Ibid.*, 463.

CHAPTER 13

1. *Methodus*, 300.
2. *Ibid.*, 300–2.
3. Quoted by Frances A. Yates, *Giordano Bruno and the Hermetic Tradition* (London: Routledge and Kegan Paul, 1964), 279, 308.
4. "Of Vicissitude of Things," *The Essays of Francis Bacon*, 270–1.
5. In J.I. Packer, ed., *The Works of Thomas Cranmer* (Appleford: Sutton Courtenay, 1964), 13–14, 230–1.
6. *Don Quixote*, 85–6.
7. "Epistle to the Reader," *The Annals of Baronius*, III (Cologne, 1609).

CHAPTER 14

1. *Don Quixote*, 471.
2. Quoted by Mark Morford, *Stoics and Neostoics: Rubens and the Circle of Lipsius* (Princeton: Princeton University Press, 1991), 124–5.
3. *Methodus*, 2–3, 335–6.
4. Quoted by Frederick J. McGuiness, *Right Thinking and Sacred Oratory in Counter-Reformation Rome* (Princeton: Princeton University Press, 1995), 145.

5. Logan P. Smith, ed. *The Life and Letters of Sir Henry Wotton* (Oxford: Oxford University Press, 1907), I, 66–7.
6. Quoted by Christopher Hill, *Intellectual Origins*, 256.
7. "Sermon on Pride," in *Works*, V, 335–6.
8. *Commonwealth*, 10–12, 199.
9. *Laws*, III, 397.
10. From his address to Parliament in 1609, in *Political Works*, 307–8.
11. Quoted by Yates, *Bruno and the Hermetic Tradition*, 314–25.

CHAPTER 15

1. "Apology for Raymond Sebond," 419.
2. Quoted by George Huppert, *Bourgeois Gentilshommes*, 157, from various passages in Pasquier's letters.
3. *Laws*, II, 252.
4. Laurent Joubert, *Popular Errors*, trans. Gregory David de Rocher (Tuscaloosa: University of Alabama Press, 1989), 33–4. First published in 1578.
5. Quoted by McGuiness, *Right Thinking and Sacred Oratory*, 30.
6. Quoted by Martimort, *Gallicanisme de Bossuet*, 46.

CHAPTER 16

1. *Anatomy of Melancholy*, 139–40.
2. *Don Quixote*, 570.
3. *Ibid.*, 425–6; this is the canon's case against books of chivalry, but it seems to me to clearly reflect the author's view.
4. These are the opening lines of *Leviathan*, 9.
5. *Don Quixote*, 430–1.
6. Quoted by Louise Clubb, *Italian Drama in the Age of Shakespeare*, 231.
7. From Pietro Cresci, *Tirena, favola pastorale* (1584), quoted in *ibid.*, 110–11.
8. Quoted and discussed by Melveena McKendrick, *Theatre in Spain, 1490–1700* (Cambridge: Cambridge University Press, 1989), 109–17.
9. From the preface to Mairet's *Silvanire*, included in William D. Howarth, ed., *French Theatre in the Neo-Classical Era, 1590–1789* (Cambridge: Cambridge University Press, 1997), 253.

Bibliographical Note

This book is based substantially on a reading of the leading authors and major texts of the Renaissance, and the principal primary sources underlying it have been cited in the text. This bibliographic note is intended to offer suggestions of secondary works to the interested reader. It has been restricted to works available in English. Where a work is cited more than once I give full bibliographic details upon the first mention, and subsequently the shortened form of author and title only.

The central point of reference, useful as a source or target for almost every section of the argument, is of course J. Burckhardt, *The Civilization of the Renaissance in Italy*, first published in 1858, and now conveniently available in a translation by S.G.C. Middlemore (Harmondsworth, 1990); and see the introduction to that edition by P. Burke. Peter Burke is also the author of *Culture and Society in Renaissance Italy: 1420–1540* (London, 1972) and *The European Renaissance: Centres and Peripheries* (Oxford, 1998), both broad and important books. The literature on the Renaissance is limitless, and differing interpretations can usefully be obtained from W. Kerrigan and G. Braden, *The Idea of the Renaissance* (Baltimore and London, 1989). S.J. Greenblatt, has written a consistently stimulating sequence of books, including *Renaissance Self-fashioning: From More to Shakespeare* (Chicago, 1980), and *Marvellous Possessions: The Wonder of the New World* (Chicago, 1991). See also T. Helton (ed.), *The Renaissance: A Reconsideration of the Theories and Interpretations of the Age* (Madison, Wis., 1964), and A. Brown (ed.), *Language and Images of Renaissance Italy* (Oxford, 1995), and the work of J. Hale, the author of a number of fine books in the field including *The Civilization of Europe in the Renaissance* (New York, 1994). Some earlier thoughts of my own on the historiography of the Renaissance are collected in William J. Bouwsma, *A Usable Past: Essays in European Cultural History* (Berkeley, California, 1990). For an independent perspective see also Randolph Starn, "William Bouwsma and the Paradoxes of History", *Culture, Society and Religion in Early Modern Europe: Essays by the Students and Colleagues of William J. Bouwsma*, a special issue of *Historical Reflections*, 15 (Spring 1988), 1–11. The classic works of F. Braudel, *Civilization and Capitalism, 15th–18th Century* (3 vols., London, 1981–4), and E. Cassirer, *The Individual and the Cosmos in Renaissance Philosophy* (Oxford, 1963), remain rich sources for thought. An interesting critique of Braudel's work is found in J.H. Hexter, "Fernand Braudel and the Monde Braudellien", *Journal of Modern History*, 44 (1972), 480–539.

A recent series of volumes produced by The Open University under the general title "The Renaissance in Europe: A Cultural Enquiry", provides a thorough and up-to-date overview in three well-illustrated volumes of text and two source books: Lucille Kekewich (ed.), *The Impact of Humanism*, David Mateer (ed.), *Courts, Patrons and Poets*, and Peter Elmer (ed.), *The Age of Reform*, accompanied by, for the important primary and secondary writings, Peter Elmer, Nick Webb and Roberta Wood (eds.), *The Renaissance in Europe: An Anthology*, and Keith Whitlock (ed.), *The Renaissance in Europe: A Reader* (all New Haven and London, 2000).

For the book which opened a new way of thinking about every part of the past, and which has long influenced my own work, see J. Huizinga, *The Waning of the Middle Ages: A Study of the Forms of Life, Thought and Art in France and the Netherlands in the XIVth and XVth Centuries* (Mineola, N.Y., 1999, and other editions), first published in London in 1924. Huizinga's innovation has stimulated considerable response: see Heiko Oberman, *The Harvest of Medieval Theology: Gabriel Biel and Late Medieval Nominalism* (Cambridge, Mass., 1963), Rosalie Colie, "Johan Huizinga and the Task of Cultural History", *American Historical Review*, 59 (1964), 607–30, and my own essay, "*The Waning of the Middle Ages* Revisited", *Daedalus, Journal of the American Academy of Arts and Sciences*, "Twentieth-Century Classics Revisited", 103, no. 1 (Winter, 1974), 35–43. For a related view, see Lynn White Jr., "Death and the Devil" in Robert S. Kinsman (ed.), *The Darker Vision of the Renaissance: Beyond the Fields of Reason* (Berkeley and Los Angeles, 1974) and, for an overview of the early medieval period, the classic R.W. Southern work, *The Making of the Middle Ages* (New Haven, 1953). On cultural systems, I have learned from Mary Douglas, especially *Purity and Danger: An Analysis of Concepts of Pollution and Taboo* (London, 1966) and *Natural Symbols* (London, 1972), from Clifford Geertz, *The Interpretation of Cultures* (New York, 1973), and from Marshall Sahlins, *Culture and Practical Reason* (Chicago, 1976).

For the wider geographical horizons of later Renaissance culture, see Burckhardt, *The Civilization of the Renaissance in Italy*, Burke, *The European Renaissance*, Hans Baron, *The Crisis of the Early Italian Renaissance* (Princeton, 1966), H.J. Hillerbrand, *The Reformation in its Own Words* (London, 1964), A. Goodman and A. MacKay (eds.), *The Impact of Humanism on Western Europe* (London and New York, 1990), C.H. Nauert, *Humanism and the Culture of Renaissance Europe* (Cambridge, 1995), H.A. Oberman, *Luther: Man Between God and the Devil* (New Haven and London, 1989), J. Overfield, *Humanism and Scholasticism in Late Medieval Germany* (Princeton, 1984), R. Porter and M. Teich (eds.), *The Renaissance in National Context* (Cambridge, 1992), and L.W. Spitz, *The Northern Renaissance* (Englewood Cliffs, N.J., 1972).

The chapters on the liberation of thought, the self, scholarship, space, and time build on a very wide corpus of writing, much of it taken from primary sources. Useful studies in a general context include M. Colish, *The Stoic Tradition from Antiquity to the Early Middle Ages* (Leiden, 1985), Carl J. Friedrich, *The Age of the*

Baroque, 1610–1660 (New York, 1952), the essays in Trevor Aston (ed.), *Crisis in Europe, 1540–1660* (London, 1965), Burckhardt, *The Civilization of the Renaissance in Italy*, Burke, *The European Renaissance*, W.J. Bouwsma, *Venice and the Defense of Republican Liberty: Renaissance Values in the Age of the Counter-Reformation* (Berkeley, 1968), John Dunn, *The Political Thought of John Locke* (Cambridge, 1969), Christopher Hill, *The Intellectual Origins of the English Revolution* (Oxford, 1965). J.G.A. Pocock, *The Machiavellian Moment: Florentine Political Thought and the Atlantic Republican Tradition* (Princeton, 1975) provides interesting reflection on the anxiety of Renaissance rulers. For the writings of Montaigne, see J.M. Cohen (ed./trans.), *Montaigne: Essays* (Harmondsworth, 1958) and M. Screech (ed./trans.), *Michel de Montaigne: The Complete Essays* (Harmondsworth, 1991). On cosmology, skepticism and scientific thought, see P. Burke, *The Italian Renaissance: Culture and Society in Italy* (Cambridge, 1987), N.L. Clulee, *John Dee's Natural Philosophy: Between Science and Religion* (London, 1990), S. Clark, *Thinking with Demons: The Idea of Witchcraft in Early Modern Europe* (Oxford, 1997), F. Yates, *Giordano Bruno and the Hermetic Tradition* (Chicago, 1964), A. Cunningham, *The Anatomical Renaissance: The Resurrection of the Anatomical Projects of the Ancients* (Aldershot, 1997), S. Pumfrey, P.L. Rossi and M. Slawinski (eds.), *Science, Culture and Popular Belief in Renaissance Europe* (Manchester, 1991), C.B. Schmitt, *Aristotle and the Renaissance* (Cambridge, Mass., 1983).

On Renaissance theater and drama, Burckhardt, *The Civilization of the Renaissance in Italy*, Burke, *The European Renaissance*, L.G. Clubb, *Italian Drama in Shakespeare's Time* (New Haven and London, 1989), S. Greenblatt, *Renaissance Self-fashioning*, M.T. Herrick, *Comic Theory in the Sixteenth Century* (Urbana, Ill., 1964), and D. Norbrook (ed.), *The Penguin Book of Renaissance Verse: 1509–1659* (Harmondsworth, 1993).

On the arts more generally see E.H. Gombrich, *Ideals and Idols: Essays on Value in History and Art* (Oxford, 1979), Sydney Anglo, *The Martial Arts of Renaissance Europe* (New Haven and London, 2000), Burckhardt, *The Civilization of the Renaissance in Italy*, M. Hollingsworth, *Patronage in Renaissance Italy: from 1400 to the Early Sixteenth Century* (London, 1994), M. Kemp, *Leonardo da Vinci: the Marvellous Works of Nature and Man* (London, 1981), E.S. Welch, *Art and Authority in Renaissance Milan* (New Haven and London, 1995), and E. Welch, *Art and Society in Italy, 1350–1500* (Oxford, 1997). A work that has particularly influenced my own understanding of these matters is Michael Baxandall, *Giotto and the Orators: Humanist Observers of Painting in Italy and the Discovery of Pictorial Composition, 1350–1450* (Oxford, 1971).

On religion, see J. Bossy, *Christianity and the West, 1400–1700* (Oxford, 1985), W.J. Bouwsma, *John Calvin: A Sixteenth-Century Portrait* (Oxford, 1988), E. Duffy, *The Stripping of the Altars: Traditional Religion in England, 1400–1580* (New Haven and London, 1992), Oberman, *Luther*, H. Kamen, *The Spanish Inquisition: An Historical Revision* (London and New Haven, 1997), Diarmaid MacCulloch, *Thomas Cranmer* (London and New Haven, 1996) (and see also J. I. Packer, *The Works of Thomas Cranmer* (Appleford: Sutton Courtenay, 1964)), S.E. Ozment, *Mysticism and Dissent: Religious Ideology and Social Protest in the Sixteenth Century* (New Haven and London, 1973), S.E. Ozment, *Protestants: The Birth of a Revolution* (London, 1993), and K. Thomas, *Religion and the Decline of Magic: Studies in Popular Beliefs in Sixteenth and Seventeenth Century England* (London, 1971).

On historical consciousness and historical writing, see many of the books mentioned above, and P. Burke, *The Renaissance Sense of the Past* (London, 1969), Roger Chartier, *The Cultural Uses of Print in Early Modern France* (Princeton, 1987), E. Cochrane, *Historians and Historiography in the Italian Renaissance* (Chicago, 1981), and E.L. Eisenstein, *The Printing Revolution in Early Modern Europe* (Cambridge, 1993). Wallace K. Ferguson, *The Renaissance* (New York, 1940) and *The Renaissance in Historical Thought* (Boston, 1948), are books which influenced me at an earlier time. Also useful are E.B. Fryde, *Humanism and Renaissance Historiography* (London, 1983), John Hale, *Renaissance Europe: The Individual and Society, 1480–1520* (London, 1971); A. Grafton and L. Jardine, *From Humanism to the Humanities: Education and the Liberal Arts in Fifteenth and Sixteenth Century Europe* (London, 1986), L. Jardine, *Worldly Goods* (London and Basingstoke, 1996), D.R. Kelley, *Foundations of Modern Historical Scholarship: Language, Law and History in the French Renaissance* (New York and London, 1970), J. Stephens, *The Italian Renaissance: The Origins of Intellectual and Artistic Change before the Reformation* (Harlow, 1990), and J.B. Trapp, *Erasmus, Colet and More: The Early Tudor Humanists* (London, 1990).

Index